FICTION AND FICTIONALISM

Are fictional characters such as Sherlock Holmes real? What can fiction tell us about the nature of truth and reality? In this excellent introduction to the problem of fictionalism R. M. Sainsbury covers the following key topics:

- what is fiction?
- realism about fictional objects, including the arguments that fictional objects are real but nonexistent; real but nonactual; real but nonconcrete
- the relationship between fictional characters and nonactual worlds
- fictional entities as abstract artifacts
- fiction and intentionality and the problem of irrealism
- fictionalism about possible worlds
- moral fictionalism.

R. M. Sainsbury makes extensive use of examples from fiction, such as Sherlock Holmes, Anna Karenina, and Madame Bovary and examines the work of philosophers who have made significant contributions to the topic, including Meinong, David Lewis, and Bas van Fraassen. Additional features include chapter summaries, annotated further reading, and a glossary of technical terms, making Fiction and Fictionalism ideal for those coming to the problem for the first time.

R. M. Sainsbury is Professor of Philosophy at the University of Texas at Austin. He is a past editor of the journal Mind.

New Problems of Philosophy
Series Editor: José Luis Bermúdez

The New Problems of Philosophy series provides accessible and engaging surveys of the most important problems in contemporary philosophy. Each book examines either a topic or theme that has emerged on the philosophical landscape in recent years, or a longstanding problem refreshed in light of recent work in philosophy and related disciplines. Clearly explaining the nature of the problem at hand and assessing attempts to answer it, books in the series are excellent starting points for undergraduate and graduate students wishing to study a single topic in depth. They will also be essential reading for professional philosophers. Additional features include chapter summaries, further reading, and a glossary of technical terms.

Also available:

Analyticity
Cory Juhl and Eric Loomis

Forthcoming:

Physicalism
Daniel Stoljar

Noncognitivism in Ethics
Mark Schroeder

Consequentialism
Julia Driver

Perceptual Consciousness
Adam Pautz

Moral Epistemology
Aaron Zimmerman

Folk Psychology
Ian Ravenscroft

Embodied Cognition
Lawrence Shapiro

Game Theory
Don Ross and Tadeusz Zawidzki

Semantic Externalism
Jesper Kallestrup

Self Knowledge
Brie Gertler

FICTION AND FICTIONALISM

R. M. Sainsbury

Routledge
Taylor & Francis Group

LONDON AND NEW YORK

This edition published 2010
by Routledge
2 Park Square, Milton Park, Abingdon, Oxon OX14 4RN

Simultaneously published in the USA and Canada
by Routledge
270 Madison Ave, New York, NY 10016

Routledge is an imprint of the Taylor & Francis Group, an informa business
© 2010 R. M. Sainsbury

Typeset in Joanna and Scala Sans by
Bookcraft Ltd, Stroud, Gloucestershire
Printed and bound in Great Britain by
MPG Books, Bodmin

All rights reserved. No part of this book may be reprinted or reproduced or utilised in any form or by any electronic, mechanical, or other means, now known or hereafter invented, including photocopying and recording, or in any information storage or retrieval system, without permission in writing from the publishers.

British Library Cataloguing in Publication Data
A catalogue record for this book is available from the British Library

Library of Congress Cataloging in Publication Data
Sainsbury, R. M. (Richard Mark)
Fiction and fictionalism / by R. M. Sainsbury.
  p. cm. – (New problems of philosophy)
Includes bibliographical references and index.
  1. Literature—Philosophy. 2. Material culture in literature. I. Title.
  PN45.S2145 2009
  809.3–dc22   2009006641

ISBN10: 0-415-77434-9 (hbk)
ISBN10: 0-415-77435-7 (pbk)
ISBN10: 0-203-87256-8 (ebk)

ISBN13: 978-0-415-77434-5 (hbk)
ISBN13: 978-0-415-77435-2 (pbk)
ISBN13: 978-0-203-87256-7 (ebk)

CONTENTS

Chapter summaries		vi
Preface and acknowledgements		xvii
	Introduction	1
1	What is fiction?	4
2	Realism about fictional objects	22
3	Fictional objects are nonexistents	44
4	Worlds and truth: fictional worlds, possible worlds, impossible worlds	68
5	Fictional entities are abstract artifacts	91
6	Irrealism: fiction and intentionality	115
7	Some fictionalists	152
8	Fictionalism about possible worlds	175
9	Moral fictionalism	193
10	Retrospect	205
Glossary		209
Notes		216
Bibliography		231
Index		238

CHAPTER SUMMARIES

1 What is fiction?

1.1 Fictive intentions
Producers of fiction have distinctive intentions: getting an audience to make-believe what they write. Largely following Currie, I take this to be the characteristic feature of fiction.

1.2 Pretending to assert
Many writers have suggested that what is distinctive of authors of fiction is that they pretend to assert. This is neither necessary nor sufficient for the production of a work of fiction.

1.3 Pretending, imagining, and making believe
How are these attitudes related? They are distinct, though connected. Make-believe involves imagining, and may also involve pretending, but it can't be reduced to either.

1.4 Make-believe and emotional response
We seem to respond to fiction emotionally, with fear or grief or joy. How is this possible? Walton's view is that our responses depend upon our using pretense to imaginatively extend the fiction, so as to include ourselves and our reactions.

Rejecting this view on the grounds that our reactions are largely involuntary, whereas we can pretend what we like, I suggest instead that the vivid presentation of states of affairs can naturally arouse emotional responses.

1.5 Varieties of fiction

What feature, if any, do novels, plays, paintings have in common that makes them all count as species of fiction? Fictive intentions can be present in artistic activities other than writing novels. However, they are absent in the case of myth. In order to make room for myth, I suggest a disjunctive condition: a fiction is either the product of fictive intentions, or, though it starts life as serious narrative, it rightly comes to be treated as a work to which make-belief, not belief, is the appropriate response.

2 Realism about fictional objects

2.1 Where do we start?

Realism about fictional objects is the view that these objects, things like Sherlock Holmes and the planet Tralfamadore, belong to our reality. This view will be refined and discussed in this chapter and the four chapters that follow. Determining the right thing to think on this question involves explaining common-sense opinions and also the opinions of the experts – literary critics.

2.2 Literalism: fidelity and truth

Literalism is the view that a sentence like "Holmes lived on Baker Street" is literally true. Some theorists think that this is both correct and accepted by common sense. Literalism entails realism about fictional objects, for "Holmes is a detective" could only be literally true were there such an object as Holmes. I think literalism is incorrect, and is not believed by common sense. Contrary opinions can be explained away by our mistaking truth on a presupposition for absolute truth. Since literalists think the truths in question are made true by what is said in the stories, it's plain they can't be thinking of the sentences as *really* true. In any case, such a view would lead to contradictions: fictional truth is demonstrably not a species of truth.

2.3 "Of course there are fictional characters"

It just seems obvious that there are fictional characters. But realism requires that the fictional characters belong to our reality, not just to the world of the fiction. It's indeed uncontentious that, in fiction, there are characters; but not uncontentious that, in reality, there are such people as Sherlock Holmes. The contentious view I express by the phrase: there are *robust* fictional characters.

2.4 A theoretical reason for realism: the semantics of names
Can a name be meaningful even if it does not have a bearer? If the answer is No, then we have a simple argument for robust fictional characters. But I say that the answer is Yes. The full justification for the answer is not given here, but there is a simple motivation: on the face of it, fictional names like "Sherlock Holmes" are meaningful but have no bearer.

Appendix: reference without referents
This sketches the framework (called RWR) that justifies the claim that there can be meaningful names without bearers. RWR undermines a motivation for realism about fictional names. The main idea is that a name purports to refer, but may not succeed in doing so. If it does not, a simple sentence containing it is false. This leaves many arguments for realism in place, for realists typically look for *true* sentences containing fictional names.

2.5 Evidence for realism
This section lists a series of apparently true sentences, like "Anna Karenina is more intelligent than Emma Bovary", whose truth seems to require robust fictional characters. These constitute the main case for realism.

3 Fictional objects are nonexistents

This is the first of three chapters in which specific versions of realism about fictional objects (the view that there are *robust* fictional characters) are set out and discussed. The three versions are that fictional objects are real but nonexistent (this chapter), that they are real but nonactual (chapter 4) and that they are real but nonconcrete (chapter 5).

3.1 Formulating Meinongianism
The view that there are nonexistent objects is usually attributed to Alexius Meinong, so, though not wishing to enter into exegesis, I call this view Meinongianism. In this section it is made more precise and applied to fictional entities.

3.2 Motivating Meinongianism

I offer four possible motivations for Meinongianism. (1) As a form of realism about fictional objects, it can help us understand how some problematic fiction-related sentences can be true. (2) Some hold it's a commonsensical view: of course there are things that don't exist, dragons, witches, etc. (3) Meinongianism solves the "puzzle of existence", explaining how we can truly say of, e.g. dragons or Vulcan, that they do not exist. (4) Meinongianism gives the best account of thinking about things (intentionality): it seems we can think about things that don't exist, so there are nonexistent things we think about. I suggest that none of these motivations is very compelling, save possibly the first, which at this point is *sub judice*.

3.3 Contradictions within Meinongianism?

If Meinongians are committed to round squares, or impossible objects in fiction, are they not committed to contradictions? And so can we not simply reject the view? I present some ways in which Meinongians have rebutted this charge. They may distinguish nuclear from extranuclear properties. Alternatively, nonliteralist Meinongians may say that the only properties nonexistent objects possess are representational ones, and something that in itself is perfectly consistent may represent something inconsistent.

3.4 Creativity and nonexistent objects

Meinongians cannot regard creating fictional characters as bringing them into existence, for on their view they don't exist. This makes pressing what I call the selection problem: how does an author pick out, from among the cloud of nonexistents, the right one to be the fictional character he wants to create? This question simply does not arise for irrealists (those who don't accept any form of realism about fictional characters). For them, making up a character is just making up a story.

3.5 Other problems for nonexistents

A variety of problems for nonexistents are canvassed. Here are two: Meinongians cannot assign any different metaphysical status to fictional characters like Hamlet, and to characters who are only fictionally fictional (like Gonzago). Both come out simply as nonexistent, yet intuitively there is a significant difference. The other problem I'll mention here is that if an author says there are several sisters, but is never more specific, it seems that a Meinongian must hold that there are several nonexistent sisters but deny that there is any nonexistent sister; this is hard to understand.

3.6 Retrospect on Meinongian views
We cannot reject Meinongianism out of hand. But a properly developed Meinongianism has to steer through some very treacherous metaphysical waters.

4 Worlds and truth: fictional worlds, possible worlds, impossible worlds

The aim of the chapter is to consider whether we can take seriously the idea that fictional characters are nonactual inhabitants of nonactual worlds. I call this view nonactualism about fictional characters.

4.1 Possible worlds in modal logic
This section gives a brief introduction to the use logicians have made of possible worlds. Those who have encountered this before should skip this section.

4.2 Realism about possible worlds (and their occupants)
Lewis's modal realism (realism about possible worlds) is, I argue, required for a view of fictional characters according to which they are real but nonactual objects. Superficial objections are rejected.

4.3 Fiction operators as quantifiers over worlds
In a famous paper ("Truth in Fiction", 1978) David Lewis argues that we can understand operators like "According to such-and-such fiction ..." in terms of quantification over possible worlds. This position is not required by the view that fictional characters are nonactual objects, but it may seem to entail that view. In any case, I argue (for familiar reasons) that Lewis's account does not work.

4.4 Which possible object is Sherlock Holmes?
The problem is that in the nonactualist's picture, there will be many different candidates for being the one and only Holmes, hence no one of them is Holmes (this argument goes back to Kripke). I endorse this argument, pointing out that even if a certain supervaluational semantic theory assigns truth to "There is just one Holmes", the associated metaphysical picture does not accord with that assignment.

4.5 Strange worlds and objects: incomplete and impossible
Can we do better for nonactualists by adding to our worlds ones which classical logicians do not countenance, worlds that are impossible or

incomplete? I argue for a negative answer. The incompleteness of fictional characters requires all of them, even those who are lucky enough to inhabit perfectly consistent stories, to belong to impossible worlds.

5 Fictional entities are abstract artifacts

The form of realism about fictional entities with the largest current following is that they are abstract things. A specific (and less popular) version of this view, but in my opinion the best version, is that they are abstract artifacts: abstract things produced by human agency.

5.1 Abstract artifact theory

Abstract artifacts are things like marriages and contracts: man-made (so artifacts) but lacking spatial extent (so abstract, or as I prefer to say nonconcrete). The abstract artifact theory of fictional objects, following Thomasson's view, assigns them to this category: they are man-made but nonconcrete. This involves something like the distinction between exemplifying and encoding properties. If Sherlock Holmes is nonspatial, he does not smoke a pipe. The abstract artifact theorist (in the version I develop) says that Holmes *encodes* this property but does not *exemplify* it.

5.2 Applying abstract artifact theory

Although it might seem that abstract artifact theory has an easy time with authorial creation, some versions of the theory make very implausible claims about what creation involves. There are other versions which are much more plausible.

5.3 Motivating abstract artifact theory

The main motivation comes from doing justice to sentences that apparently need a realistic interpretation. This motivation has been explored at length by Peter van Inwagen, whose views are examined in detail in this section.

5.4 Problems for abstract artifact theory

One difficulty is doing justice to existential sentences. If Holmes is an existent abstract artifact, then "Holmes exists" ought to be true. Some ways of fixing this are discussed. A more general problem is identified. Encoding is really just representing. Everyone agrees that there are real representations. But fictional characters were supposed to be something more than representations.

6 Irrealism: fiction and intentionality

6.1 Options for irrealists

This is the hardest chapter in the book. It's also one I care about a lot, as it's where I fix the outstanding problems for RWR. An irrealist about fictional objects says that there are no robust fictional objects. There wouldn't be much point struggling to develop a coherent irrealist theory of fiction unless one could also supply an irrealist theory of intentionality. Irrealists need to explain how the mind can think about things that don't exist without there being such things. In this section, various strategies are spelled out, many of them involving paraphrase, or related notions.

6.2 A first irrealist look at a problematic case

Interfictional comparisons (e.g. "Anna Karenina was more intelligent than Emma Bovary") are often used to ground realist views. This section shows that we can adopt an extension of a familiar irrealist response: to the extent that such sentences are true, they are governed by a fiction operator. (It's a bit tricky to see what the operator might be in this case: that's the point of the section.) However, I voice a preference for a different approach: such sentences are not true absolutely, but only under a presupposition, perhaps the presupposition that there really are such people as Anna and Emma.

6.3 Marks of intensionality

We have to broaden our enquiry to consider intensionality in general, and not merely fiction. This section aims to identify the phenomenon. I argue that realism has little or nothing to contribute to the more general project.

6.4 Operator and predicate intensionality: reduction

Operator intensionality is induced by sentence operators (expressions that take a sentence to make a sentence), for example "John believes that p" or "According to the fiction, p." Predicate intensionality is induced by an intensional verb, like "seeks": Ponce de León seeks the fountain of youth. This section considers attempts to reduce the latter kind of intensionality to the former. The point of the reduction in this context is that operator intensionality is entirely conformable with, and explainable by, RWR. Although I argue that there is no general reduction, I highlight reductions for two important cases: "John thought about Pegasus" and "Holmes is famous."

6.5 Operator and predicate intensionality: entailment

Even if there's no reduction of the kind envisaged in the previous section, it's plausible that there's entailment: every sentence dominated by an intensional predicate is entailed by some sentences that either lack intensionality or are dominated by intensional operators. If that's right, the ontology of the sentences dominated by intensional predicates cannot exceed that of the sentences dominated by intensional operators. By RWR, we know that an irrealist ontology will work for operator-dominated sentences. Hence irrealism will work across the board. This is a crucial section.

6.6 Presupposition and relative truth

It remains to explain intuitive evaluations of some sentences that motivate realists. I argue that in many cases our treatment of a sentence as true is really treating it as true upon a presupposition. I think it's very interesting how easily one can slip in and out of presuppositions, and how they can be embedded and iterated. I give some examples drawn from fiction itself.

6.7 A final review

This section lists the responses I think irrealists should make to various examples used to support realism.

7 Some fictionalists

This chapter introduces the work of various authors who have been or might be called fictionalist. The main aim of the chapter is to distinguish fictionalism from other metaphysical views.

7.1 Early history

The earliest clearly fictionalist author I have discovered is the sixteenth-century figure Osiander, who presented his words as if they were those of Copernicus. Other candidates for being fictionalists (Berkeley, Hume, Bentham, Russell) turn out on closer inspection not to qualify.

7.2 Van Fraassen's constructive empiricism

1980 was a major year for modern fictionalism, with the publication of Bas van Fraassen's *The Scientific Image* and Hartry Field's *Science without Numbers*; towering works, and indisputably fictionalist. This section gives a brief survey of van Fraassen's position and of some of the problems it has to address.

7.3 Field's mathematical fictionalism
A brief survey of Field's position and an indication of some difficulties.

7.4 Some features of fictionalism
This section harvests the fruit of the labors of the previous sections in the chapter. Fictionalism is distinguished from reduction and eliminativism; its relation to the attribution of error is set out; and I indicate some typical motivations.

8 Fictionalism about possible worlds

Whereas the previous chapter was primarily motivated by an attempt to describe the essential features of fictionalist approaches, this chapter and the next look in close detail at specific fictionalisms.

8.1 A partial taxonomy of fictionalisms
The main fictionalist idea is that, in some region, thoughts don't have to be true to be good. There are then various options, relating to whether the normal thinkers of these thoughts appreciate this fact about them, or whether the thoughts as they stand need to be modified. What norms are being invoked by the "don't have to be"? Don't have to be true, given what aims or purposes?

8.2 Fictionalist values
What does the "good" amount to in "doesn't have to be true to be good"? This may vary from case to case, but one important answer is that fictionalist sentences can serve as inference bridges. A mickey mouse example of how this might work is offered.

8.3 Fictionalism about possible worlds
This fictionalist claims that talk of possible worlds cannot be taken fully seriously, for there are no worlds other than our world. A fictionalist hopes to preserve talk of other worlds as a useful fiction. In particular, Lewis's theory of possible worlds, abbreviated PW, is taken as the canonical "fiction".

8.4 Comparisons with other forms of irrealism
By contrast, an eliminativist would say we should just junk all talk of nonactual worlds, and a reductionist would say we should reduce worlds

to ontologically respectable things, for example, maximal sets of consistent sentences.

8.5 Problems for fictionalism about possible worlds
There's a quick alleged refutation of fictionalism about possible worlds. However, as is now well recognized, the refutation doesn't work, through failure to pay close attention to the details of Lewis's possible worlds story. But there is a useful lesson: much depends on very fine details of translating modal idioms into PW.

8.6 Motivations for fictionalism about possible worlds
It's unclear what the benefits are of retaining possible worlds talk, if one thinks there are no such things as worlds. PW makes very definite pronouncements about disputed features of modal logic; why should we think it is right?

8.7 Whence modal knowledge?
This leads to a general problem for the fictionalist about possible worlds. There are various possible "fictions", variants of PW. How can a fictionalist ground a choice between them? If it's all done by a prior conviction about modal facts, expressed just by modal operators, it becomes quite unclear what role PW is playing. But it hardly seems right to let PW call the tune (as Lewis does). After all, it's meant to be just a story.

9 Moral fictionalism

Moral fictionalism can be motivated by the view that there's no room for moral properties in the natural order. That's not the version I mostly discuss. Rather, I look at a quite intricate argument by Mark Kalderon, designed to establish, on very different grounds, that fictionalism is the only tenable view to take about morality.

9.1 Noncognitivism
The first stage in Kalderon's argument for fictionalism is to argue for noncognitivism. This is the view that moral commitments are not best explained as beliefs, attitudes to truth evaluable propositions. Kalderon uses an original argument to the conclusion that morality is noncognitivist, based on the view that, in a moral dispute, we can properly be "intransigent": we don't have even a lax obligation to reconsider in the light of the disagreement. I

argue that Kalderon is mistaken: our obligations to reconsider don't differ as between moral and nonmoral cases.

9.2 Fictionalism and semantics
Kalderon claims to be able to offer a plausible semantics for moral discourse. The semantics involves referring to properties, like being evil, but is not committed to these being instantiated. It seems to me that moral fictionalism would be better off not requiring there to be distinctively moral properties; many semantic theories, including RWR, impose no such requirement. Indeed, RWR allows that singular terms, as "courage" and "evil" seem to be, can have an acceptable semantics without commitment to any distinctively moral entities.

9.3 The value of morality from a fictionalist point of view
How can a mere fiction guide our lives? Reading ordinary fiction may, of course, be morally uplifting, making us see the destructive consequences of idleness or cowardice, making us feel the excellence of noble conduct, and so on. But how can a fiction according to which some course of action is right get us to perform that action? Kalderon pays little attention to this problem, but it is the focus of an article by Richard Joyce, who suggests that fiction can help stiffen resolve towards prudent actions when prudential considerations on their own risk being overwhelmed. I argue that this falls well short of doing justice to the role that morality plays in our lives.

10 Retrospect

This chapter looks back at the various connections between the metaphysics of fictional discourse and the metaphysical approach embodied by fictionalism.

PREFACE AND ACKNOWLEDGEMENTS

The origin of this book relates to the semantics of names. Historically, two views have been dominant: one traces back to Frege and Russell and says that proper names have descriptive meaning; the other traces back to Mill and says that the meaning of a proper name is simply its bearer. There are familiar problems with both views. For example, Millian theories have to say that a name without a bearer is a name without a meaning, from which it should follow that it cannot be part of a meaningful sentence, a consequence that seems plainly at variance with the facts. Fregean views were sharply attacked by Kripke (1972), who pointed out (among other things) that people belonging to a single practice of using a name, and so people for whom the name should have the same meaning, nonetheless may not have in common any descriptive information to associate with the name.

Some time ago, it seemed to me that the arguments against both these theories were successful, but that there were other theoretical positions to choose from. I outlined one of these in an earlier book, *Reference without Referents* (Sainsbury 2005), calling it RWR. That book acknowledged a problem that it did not fully resolve. RWR allows that proper names can be intelligible even if they have no bearer, but does not allow for simple sentences containing such a name to be true: it counts "Pegasus was a flying horse", "Holmes was created by Conan Doyle" and "The Greeks worshipped Zeus" as false. That unqualified ruling is unsatisfactory.

The first inspiration for the present book was that I now know (I think!) how to fix this problem. The essence of RWR survives intact, but there are various additions to deal with problem cases. In thinking about these issues, fictional names tend to be salient. At one point I thought that it was clear that they could be used as examples of names without bearers, and so as counterexamples to Mill: they have no bearer, so on Mill's theory they have no meaning; but they are plainly meaningful, so Mill's theory must be abandoned.

This argument now seems naïve. Many theorists hold that fictional proper names do have bearers, in which case these names can happily fall within the scope of Mill's theory. Some theorists hold that fictional names are not really meaningful (we merely pretend that they are), and so again pose no threat to Mill's theory. These proposals raise a number of semantic and metaphysical questions, and these form the subject of the early chapters of this book.

If fictional names like "Sherlock Holmes" have bearers, these entities cannot be ordinary objects: ones that actually exist and fill space. If they were that kind of object, we would have found them long ago. Taking fictional entities seriously requires one to explore unfamiliar realms – realms of nonexistent things, or nonactual things, or nonconcrete things. This leads one to many taxing metaphysical questions. And once metaphysics becomes a dominant theme, it's natural to consider a form of metaphysical project that is nowadays gaining increasing momentum: fictionalism. Fictionalists about some region of thought say that these thoughts are, or should be regarded as, like the thoughts we have when we engage in fiction. They may have value, but their value does not require them to be true. It follows that the value of these thoughts can be detached from the commitment they appear to have to the entities that would need to exist for them to be true. For example, suppose one is a fictionalist about the theories of elementary physics. The theories claim that there is a whole panoply of unobservable particles, hadrons, quarks, fermions, and these are used to explain observable phenomena. A fictionalist will say that the theory does not need to be true to be good. All we need *believe* is the predictions concerning observable phenomena. We can treat the unobservable entities just like fictional entities: they have their uses in calculating the predictions, but are not to be taken metaphysically seriously. To accept the theory is to believe its observational consequences, but does not require believing the fantasies about subatomic particles.

There's clearly an interaction between the metaphysics of fiction and the metaphysical picture proposed by fictionalists. Suppose that it turns out that, perhaps because fictional names do have bearers, there really are fictional characters, and these are nonexistent entities. This places limits on the lightness of metaphysical being the fictionalist can aspire to. For example, perhaps treating talk of subatomic particles as fiction frees us from belief in existent subatomic particles, but only at the cost of requiring us to believe in nonexistent subatomic particles. Or perhaps fictionalism about mathematics, according to which math is just a useful myth, to which we can help ourselves without believing in numbers, nonetheless requires us to believe in nonexistent entities as the referents of numerals. This upshot could obviously derail certain kinds of motivation for fictionalism about mathematics.

In keeping with the aims of this series, I've written the book in such a way that most of the chapters are self-standing. If you want to read less than the whole, I suggest looking at the chapter summaries above. This should enable you to devise a path that suits your interests.

Each chapter is followed by some suggested reading. Here's an entirely general suggestion: nowadays there is a huge amount of material on the web, accessible with the usual search engines. (Try the search string "mathematical fictionalism".) The best single site is the superb Stanford Encyclopedia of Philosophy (plato.standford.edu): very high quality and up-to-date contributions with good bibliographies.

I've had more help with this book than with anything else I've written. Both at the time of the proposal, and after submitting the manuscript, Routledge found excellent referees, whose comments have been very valuable. In addition, the following people responded to draft versions of all or parts of the book with extremely helpful suggestions: José Luis Bermúdez, Tim Button, Emily Caddick, Tim Crane, Maite Ezcurdia, Markus Glodek, Victoria Goodman, Alex Grzankowski, Daniel Hill, Robin Jeshion, Barry Lee, Aidan McGlynn, Alex Oliver, David Papineau, Bryan Pickel, Gabriel Segal, and Amie Thomasson. Working through these comments led to a large number of improvements. I am also grateful to the students in my graduate seminar at the University of Texas at Austin, Spring Semester 2008, who gave valuable feedback on an early draft. Parts of the book were tried out on various audiences, whom I thank for comments and questions: at King's College London, Oxford's Jowett Society, the Logos group in Barcelona, and the Arche group at St Andrews. My thanks also to the University of Texas for the award of sabbatical leave (Faculty Research Assignment) in the Fall Semester 2007, during which period I wrote most of the first draft.

INTRODUCTION

> I fear that Mr Sherlock Holmes may become like one of those popular tenors who, having outlived their time, are still tempted to make repeat farewell bows to their indulgent audiences. This must cease, and he must go the way of all flesh, material or imaginary.
>
> Doyle 1930: Preface

Life begins in play, and play involves pretense, making things up, fiction. Predatory mammals engage in pretend chase-and-kill routines from almost as soon as they can move.[1] From at least as early as about 18 months, when their use of language is still pretty primitive, human children engage in spontaneous pretense, as fun (that is, with no ulterior motive, like the intention to deceive): they pretend that a banana is a telephone and that they are talking on it; that there is a dragon under the bed when there is nothing; that a doll's face is dirty when it is clean (cf. Leslie 1987). This behavior seems likely to be the primitive precursor of the highly sophisticated fictions that the word "fiction" naturally evokes: literary fictions are most salient, followed by plays and movies, arguably followed by painting and sculpture.[2]

In central cases, fiction involves representation. In telling a tale, a novelist represents a course of events; some paintings and sculptures are intended to represent. One main question in this book is what we should say about representation in order to make room for a correct account of representation in fiction. One thing we need to say is that attaining truth is not an essential aim of fictional representation. We value fictions for other properties. This connects fiction with the philosophical notion of fictionalism.

Fictionalism has, in recent years, been understood in a very broad way. Typically, the starting point for fictionalism is some kind of ontological scruple: one cannot bring oneself to believe in moral values, nonactual things, unobservable things, or abstract things. But one has somehow to do justice to the fact that one cannot simply throw away the related regions of discourse: morality, modality, elementary physics, or mathematics. Fictionalism to the rescue. To be a fictionalist about some region of thought is to say that the things thought are of value (are in some sense to be accepted, esteemed, or commended), but this value does not consist in their being true. Our evaluation accordingly is not in terms of truth and falsehood, and is not governed by norms appropriate to these properties. Two standard examples: Bas van Fraassen (1980) proposed that scientific theories which speak of unobservable entities like quarks should not be evaluated for truth, but rather for "empirical adequacy", that is, their capacity to give correct predictions of observable fact. Hartry Field (1980) proposed that we should think of mathematics in a similar way: its value consists not in its being a true report of how things are with abstract things like numbers, but in its usefulness in guiding us to facts not essentially involving numbers, like how thick to make the girders of a bridge. For both philosophers, the analogy with fiction is that something does not have to be true to be good. Our attitudes to discourse for which fictionalism is correct should reflect this: we should not believe, but should "accept": appreciate their merits (empirical adequacy, or concrete utility). In this way we can reap the rewards of elementary physics and of mathematics, without committing ourselves to the entities our ontological scruples require us to abjure: unobservables or abstracta.

Fictionalism also can be, and has been, understood in a narrower way. There are real facts about what is said to happen in a story, even if the story is just a story and recounts nothing real. We can make the contrast by using what I shall call fiction operators. According to the Sherlock Holmes stories, Holmes played the violin. That is true; but it is not true that Holmes played the violin. Another way of understanding fictionalism is as the view that we implicitly prefix the sentences of some region of discourse by a fiction operator, or at least we could do so without losing any beliefs we really value. These operators can make truth out of what is not true, and so perhaps reveal in terms of truth what is of value about the relevant discourse.

A well-known application of this implementation of fictionalism has been to modality: statements which, taken at face value, commit to nonactual things like nonactual possible worlds should be understood as prefixed by a fiction operator on the lines "According to the possible worlds story …" (Rosen 1990).

Fictionalists have tended not to say a great deal about the nature and semantics of fiction. On the other hand, those topics have been hotly debated in their own right. The main idea for this book is to bring the two debates together. The first six chapters attempt to give an account, part survey, part proposal, of what fiction is and how its semantics work. The subsequent three chapters address fictionalism, with the optimistic idea that we will better understand it if we already have to hand an account of the nature and semantics of fiction. A final chapter brings together the main themes of the book.

Here is one simple example of the value of the joint treatment. One option within the semantics of fiction is to view fictional names as referring to abstract things, "fictional characters". If all fictions are like this, fictionalism about arithmetic would not be well motivated by a desire to avoid commitment to abstracta. Even if arithmetic is a fiction, the "fictional characters" which it introduces – the numbers – are abstracta, according to the semantic proposal in question; so we might as well have left things as they were, regarding arithmetical statements as about abstract numbers.

Another example. Fiction operators like "According to the Sherlock Holmes stories …" typically involve apparent reference to stories, or, more generally, fictional discourses. These seem not to be concrete things: they are to be distinguished from acts of storytelling (for the same story may be told in different acts) and from the texts which record them (for the same story may be told in different languages, and so using different texts). If they are abstract things, then ontological scruples about abstracta would not be well served by a fictionalism which relies upon fiction operators.

1
WHAT IS FICTION?

1.1 Fictive intentions

Fiction is both artifice and verisimilitude.

Wood 2008: xiii

We contrast fact and fiction, but we cannot say what fiction is just by saying it's not fact, or that it is not represented as fact, or that it is represented as not being fact. An out-of-date timetable may misinform you of something, so is not fact, but it is not fiction either. Many fictions contain straightforward truths, which the reader is supposed to take as true. In such cases, the author provides "local color" by telling us things which not only are true, but which the reader is intended to realize he is supposed to treat as true. In more complex ways, many fictions are supposed to reveal truths about love, honor, the human condition, or whatever, even if the truths are not explicitly stated. Proust probably wants us to believe some of the "psychological laws" he hints at, including his cynical view that love is projection, even though they are illustrated by fictional events. The purely fictional and the things the author is trying to get us really to believe may be closely related, both thematically and in presentation. For example:

> Even the sight of Gilberte, which would have been so exquisite a pleasure only yesterday, would no longer have sufficed me. For I should have been

anxious all the time I was not actually with her. That is how a woman, by every fresh torture that she inflicts on us, often quite unwittingly, increases her power over us and at the same time our demands upon her. (*The Guermantes Way*)

The last sentence smoothly moves out of narrative, which we are not supposed to take as a report of fact, into a statement of an element in Proust's theory of love, which we are supposed to take factually seriously. In this example, the fictional and the factual separate neatly into sentences, but this is not always so: a single sentence may contain elements of both. Tiresias was asked by Zeus and Juno to compare the pleasure of men and women in the sexual act. According to one rendering, he replied:

If one be the measure of the pleasure of men
The pleasure of women is counted as ten.

According to the story, this is what Tiresias said; so it's fiction. But Ovid, one famous recounter of the mythical episode, could well have intended his audience to believe as factual truth the claim the lines make. Somewhat similarly, Eco no doubt intended his audience to believe some of the details of the workings of Foucault's pendulum, to get them in the mood to swallow some of the nonsense in the book with that title.

In seeking to understand what fiction is, we can look either to the producer or the consumer or to some combination. Consumers can be mistaken: the public might treat a novel as if it were factual narrative, or a factual narrative as if it were a novel. A documentary might be mistaken for an ordinary drama-movie, or vice versa. An interesting feature of these mistakes is that they are consistent with the consumers grasping the content of the work. The movie shows a scene of rioters in Chechnya; that is made plain (they are certainly rioting, and the street signs and buildings are distinctive of Chechnya). This does not tell us whether we are in the realm of fact or fiction, documentary or drama. We can know the content without yet knowing whether the work is fact or fiction. This shows that there is no distinctive species of meaning, "fictional meaning", distinct from everyday meaning, and it shows that what it is to be fictional cannot be an intrinsic property of the content of a text or film.

Given that consumers are fallible, we should look to something distinctive about the production of fiction.[1] Whether something is fiction is determined by how it came into existence, and in particular by the aims and intentions of the producer. This already suggests a feature of how fictions are to be individuated. If two authors, by some extraordinary accident, produce fictions which are word-for-word the same we should say that two works of fiction have been produced, because they originated in different acts. By contrast, if the second author was not really an author, but was simply transcribing the first work, then there is only one fiction. Even if the second author is acting with some of the aims and intentions characteristic of a producer of fiction (for example, he is trying to get the work treated as a fiction by audiences), he also has aims which prevent it from being a fiction: he is not making the story up, but relying on an already extant text.

Currie (1990: 35) suggests (provisionally) that "a work is fictional if and only if it is the product of a fictive utterance". This seems a promising suggestion, so long as we can give a good account of what a fictive utterance is, that is, an utterance intended as part of the original recounting of a fiction. Not just any recounting of a fiction is an event partly constitutive of the creation of that work. When I read a bedtime story, I recount a fiction, and I have fictive intentions (I intend the children to treat what I say as fiction). But I am not creating the fiction. Currie deals with the point by stressing that in this case the work is not the product of my utterance, so we do not have a counterexample to his proposal.

If we think of an utterance as the utterance of just one sentence, one fictive utterance does not a fiction make – or, at least, this would be a very untypical case. Not only are most written fictions created using many sentences, there are typically many different episodes of fiction-making activity, taking place over weeks, months, or years, the author pausing for meal breaks, vacations, or other projects in between. We need to recognize that when a work of fiction is created, there are a whole series of utterances, possibly spread over wide stretches of time, connected by complicated relations, and typically not all having the same status. At one moment, our author is describing the purely fictional events of purely fictional characters; we are not supposed to mistake this for a historical record. At another, she is seeking to convey a realistic sense of place by describing the statues on Prague's Charles Bridge.[2] Then our author should get things right, and critics will point out errors as defects. Even if some fictive utterances are not beholden to reality, others are. At another moment, our author is making lofty pronouncements about the nature of honor, which we are supposed to regard as literally true, not just fictionally so, though this is not a contribution to local color, and the demand of "getting things right" does not play out in a straightforward way. At yet another moment, the author is making an ironical utterance within the fiction: we are not supposed to take this even as literally true in the fiction, but only as pointing us to some fictive truth not directly expressed. Jane Austen's famous first sentence ("It is a truth universally acknowledged …") is not to be treated either as something Austen is trying to get us to believe absolutely, or as something she is trying to get us to believe is so in the story. (The most important characters in the story are counterexamples.) Rather, Austen is using the sentence to sketch a milieu to which some of her characters belong, one in which it would be universally acknowledged that …, and also agreed that this truth is universally acknowledged. And there are many other kinds of intentions involved in the production of fiction. What we may nonetheless hope to find is something distinctive of fiction: a distinctive intention would ensure that a given utterance is a contribution to a work of fiction, even if the total work is woven with threads of a very different composition as well; and a distinctive intention would be required of some utterances in a series if the series is to constitute the production of a work of fiction.

We can make a modest improvement to Currie's definition: a work is fictional if and only if it results from some interconnected utterances, a reasonable number of which count as "fictive", that is, produced with distinctively fictive intentions. This works most straightforwardly for novels, but perhaps we can think of utterances very broadly, to include what playwrights, movie-makers, and some painters and sculptors do. (What it will not extend to is myth, which I think should be regarded as fiction, though it is not necessarily produced with fictive intentions.) Completing the account needs a description of fictive intentions.

Currie suggests two conditions to make an utterance-intention fictive. Assume the content of the uttered sentence, s, is that p. The intention must be that a potential audience should, on encountering s in its context, make-believe that p.[3] That is the first condition. The second is that p should not be true, or, if true, true only by accident. The second condition is to eliminate cases like this: the first condition is satisfied by an author mistakenly thinking he is producing something purely fictional, whereas he is actually producing factual truths concerning his own life which he has repressed, and so he does not recognize them as memories. In these cases, we say that it's not really a work of fiction but an autobiography. This is because of the systematic and reliable link between what the work says and the early life of the author.

The first condition is the crucial one. What is it to intend that a potential audience should make-believe that p? We fail to make-believe that p if our response is simply "That's false". We have in some sense to "suspend disbelief", in Coleridge's telling phrase. We have to open ourselves to immersion in the story, so that we care about how it unfolds, and are ready to speculate about the characters' motivations. We do not have to believe that the events really happened or that the characters portrayed really exist. But in make-believe we can combine the real and the fictional just as the author does. We can argue that if the purely fictional character crossed the Charles Bridge in daylight, she must have seen the statues, even if she paid them no heed. We'll see in the next section whether we can add more detail to an account of make-believe by considering Walton's reflections on games of make-believe.

This is the simplified structure of the proposed account. A fictive intention is one in which the utterer intends a potential audience to make-believe something. When a work results from a systematically connected series of utterances some reasonable proportion of which are issued with fictive intentions, and whose truth is at best accidental, it is a work of fiction; otherwise it is not.[4]

1.2 Pretending to assert

Pretending seems a fairly well-understood notion. Can we use it to analyze make-believe? Or can we use it to replace the notion of make-believe?

John Searle has suggested that "an author of fiction pretends to perform illocutionary acts which he is not in fact performing" (Searle 1975: 326). Illocutionary acts "include making statements, asking questions, giving orders, making promises, apologizing, thanking, and so on" (1975: 319). Searle's main point is that story-tellers are not necessarily engaged in the illocutionary act of assertion, which seems right: to concoct or retell a fiction is not as such to assert anything. One case which Searle offers as an example seems quite convincing: some of the Holmes stories are written in the first person, with Watson as narrator. For these cases, it seems right to say that "in first-person narratives, the author often pretends to be someone else making assertions" (Searle 1975: 328). However, it's not obvious that this pretense entails pretending to assert. I can pretend to be someone else singing without pretending to sing (but instead really singing); likewise I could pretend to be someone else making assertions by making assertions while pretending to be someone else.

Authors of fiction are typically not primarily engaged in assertion. It does not follow that they are pretending to assert anything, and it seems unnecessary that they should do that. Certainly we found no need for the idea that a creator of fiction pretends to assert; the main idea was that a creator of fiction is (really) trying to get the audience to engage in make-believe.

This reflection does not provide a counterexample to the claim that an author of fiction pretends to assert, but Kendall Walton thinks we can find clear counterexamples when we recall that some paintings and sculptures need to be included among works of fiction. He writes:

> Pierre-Auguste Renoir's painting *Bathers* and Jacques Lipchitz's sculpture *Guitar Player* surely belong to the fiction category. But I very much doubt that in creating them Renoir and Lipchitz were pretending to make assertions. (Walton 1990: 82)

The example does not seem decisive. Perhaps some paintings are "factual", that is, they aim to represent how things were on a certain occasion (like David's painting of Napoleon's coronation), and the audience is intended to treat them as a factual record. This is painterly "assertion". It may contain falsehood, or an analog thereof, as David's painting did (it portrays Madame Mère as present, though in fact her dislike of Josephine kept her away). Perhaps other paintings in some way trade on this convention, so that Renoir is pretending to represent how things were; that is, he is pretending to assert. Although Walton does not agree, the example would do little to persuade an opponent.

Currie offers a counterexample to the sufficiency of pretending to assert for the production of fiction: a case of someone who puts on "a verbal performance to illustrate an idiotic line of reasoning". The performer pretends to assert the elements of the reasoning, but his words "don't thereby count as a work of fiction, however truncated or impoverished" (Currie 1990: 17). This seems convincing, assuming we put some emphasis on *work*, though it leaves open the possibility that pretending to assert is a necessary condition for the production of fiction. Currie deals with this by showing that his account (in terms of intending to get a potential audience to make-believe) is sufficient, so that no other attitude on the part of the author is necessary. Pretending to assert is not as such well adapted to getting someone to make-believe. If we think someone is pretending to assert because they are practicing a speech, we may have no disposition to make-believe that what is said is true. (Imagine that what is being practiced is what you know to be an entirely deceptive speech to the shareholders' meeting.)

A doubt remains. Isn't a story-teller in some ways like someone who is recounting known truths? He will normally take care not to give rise to the impression he is really doing that; but is he not in some way mimicking doing that, acting rather as if he were recounting known truths? He invites similar questions from the audience in both cases: what happened next? why did she say that? what did he hope to gain by going to see her? Mightn't this similarity be what Searle has in mind by the claim that an author of a fiction is pretending to assert? This is how the suggestion (or a similar one) works out in the hands of David Lewis:

> The storytellers pretend to pass on historical information to their audience; the audience pretends to learn from their words, and to respond accordingly. (Lewis 1978: 276)

Since the standard way of passing on historical information is by assertion, Lewis's view seems not so far removed from Searle's.[5] Both Searle and Lewis would need to accept the insufficiency of the description (a liar can pretend to pass on historical information without thereby creating fiction – in the literal sense). Lewis, in the context, is stressing the interactive nature of the activity, the fact that story-teller and audience share a "game of make-believe". This suggests that this is what the story-teller should be intending to bring about; it should not be an accidental or unintended result of the storytelling. So once spelled out in more detail, the crucial feature of Lewis's idea seems close to Currie's: a story-teller is trying to get the audience to make-believe the things he says,[6] whereas a recounter of fact is trying to get the audience to believe the things he says.

Even if pretending to assert supplies neither a necessary nor sufficient condition for the production of fiction, it is clear that related activities like imagining play some important role in the production and reception of fiction. The next section (section 1.3) offers some preliminary remarks about make-believe, and the following one (section 1.44) discusses Walton's account.

1.3 Pretending, imagining, and making believe

Pretending, imagining, and making believe are similar but distinct activities. The corresponding verbs have slightly different formation profiles. I can pretend to be an elephant or to clean the windows, but cannot imagine or make-believe to be an elephant or to clean the windows (though I can imagine or make-believe that I am an elephant or that I am cleaning the windows). We can imagine an elephant, but cannot pretend or make-believe one. Are these differences mere grammatical oddities?

We don't have to do any pretending to produce or engage with fiction. The author need not pretend he is doing anything other than what he is doing, telling a story; and telling a story is simply not the same as pretending to recount facts, for the latter is something liars do and story-tellers may not be liars. The reader need not pretend she is doing anything other than reading the story, entering into it, and, with luck, enjoying it. So pretending seems to lack a special role in a discussion of fiction. But that's not so for imagining and making believe. Readers, as well as authors, have to imagine, and have to be imaginative. However, this can be so in the production and consumption of nonfiction. So if we are looking for an attitude distinctive of fiction, make-believe seems the most promising.

Suppose an atheist wishes to marry a theist, and foresees that religious differences could lead to problems. If he is of a flexible disposition, he could pretend to believe in god. The most natural way to proceed would involve deception.[7] "You do believe in God, don't you dear?" "Yes, of course. How could one not?" It would be very different to make-believe that there is a god, or make-believe in god (if that makes sense). One could make-believe that there is a god by refraining from making atheist observations, making no objection in principle to engaging in religious observances, and being willing to couch the appropriateness of actions in terms of whether or not they would meet with god's approval. It could be common knowledge between the atheist and the believer that the atheist was indeed an atheist, and was humoring the believer: there need be no deception, and nothing happily called pretense. To be good at it, the atheist would need to set his atheism aside, "suspend disbelief", and roll with the religious outlook. This does not involve self- or other-deception. It's not that "setting aside" the atheism is abandoning it; though it does involve somehow according it a less salient cognitive position.

When consuming a fiction, the consumer typically makes-believe that the story is true, though she does not believe it is. There need be no deception or self-deception, and no false belief. The fact that it is just a story need not be relinquished or even forgotten, though it is "set aside" in not being allowed to become too salient. Concerning the fictional scenes, one can appropriately ask oneself questions about motivation, unrecorded activities, and so on, just as if one were dealing with a factual narration. These responsive activities are constrained by the norm: make-believe that p only if, according to the story, p. This mirrors the norm of truth for belief: believe that p only if p. These principles prevent one making believe or believing things one should not. One shouldn't make-believe just anything that's so according to the story (not even anything that's so according to the story up to that point), for perhaps boring and uninteresting things are so according to the story. The right rule for make-believing is something like this: if the question whether to make-believe that p arises, do so if, according to the story, p. Analogously, one should not aim to believe every truth, as so many are boring, and the result would be informational overload. Rather, the rule is something like: if the question whether to believe that p arises, do so if p. By contrast, there is no right rule for pretending, and that's why we can't give an adequate account of fiction by drawing only upon that attitude.

Like belief, but unlike pretense, make-believe is often involuntary. To open a novel with a normally receptive mind is to start make-believing. Likewise, to engage in conversation with a normally receptive mind is to start believing. It may turn out that one should not have made-believe or believed what one did: unreliable narrators are to be found in fiction as well as fact.

One can resist the temptation to make-believe by an effort of will, saying to oneself that one is reading mindless drivel which one should not engage with. This deliberately destructive attitude is one of the few ways to avoid the involuntary surge of emotion that one otherwise feels when affecting fictional scenes are vividly described.

It would be good to be able to say more about the nature of make-believe. We should turn to Walton's account; an account that is supposed to do proper justice to our emotional response to fiction.

1.4 Make-believe and emotional response

What, frighted with false fire?

Hamlet, III.ii.263

Every movement of the theatre, by a skillful poet, is communicated, as it were by magic, to the spectators, who weep, tremble, resent, rejoice, and are inflamed with all the variety of passions which actuate the several personages of the drama.

Hume, Enquiry Concerning the Principles of Morals, 5.2

> *Imitations produce pain or pleasure, not because they are mistaken for realities, but because they bring realities to mind.*
>
> Johnson 1765

> [T]erribleness ... is written large on terrible things.
>
> Findlay 1935: 112

Walton encourages us to improve our understanding of fiction by thinking of "games of make-believe":

> Appreciating paintings and novels is largely a matter of playing games of make-believe with them of the sort it is their function to be props in. (1990: 53)

The passage addresses what it is to appreciate a work of fiction, rather than what it is to be a work of fiction. We can expect a close connection: normally, to be a work of fiction is to be produced with the intention that it be appreciated as such by a potential audience. So we could expect games of make-believe, and the notion of a "prop" (a technical term for Walton), to help us say what a fiction is. Following Walton, let's see if we can use the notion of a *game* of make-believe to throw light on the nature of make-believe; and following Currie we'll make use of the notion of make-believe in specifying the intentions distinctive of fictive utterances.[8]

Walton asks us to consider a children's game in which the participants pretend that tree stumps are bears. Such a game can arise very easily, with only minimal stage setting. For example, walking in the woods with friends, one child might point at a stump and say "That bear looks mean". The game may catch on: another child, pointing to a different stump, says "Watch out, there's another bear over there". It imposes certain norms: to the extent that you are a participant, you are supposed to treat stumps as bears. Likewise, reading fiction imposes certain thoughts and activities. There can be things that are true in the game, even if they are not appreciated by the participants. For example, a stump none of them has noticed counts as a bear in the game, regardless of whether any of them will ever appreciate this. Likewise, there can be things true in the fiction that no one has yet appreciated. Maybe Hamlet suffers from an Oedipus complex. This claim, true or false, is not undermined by the undoubted fact that no one believed it for several hundred years after the play was written.

The game is a game of make-believe, making believe that stumps are bears. Such games bring with them a notion of fictional truth, of what is so according to the game (that this stump is a bear), and conform to various principles. For example, some properties of the stumps are to be projected onto bears: a large stump is a large bear, a distant stump is a distant bear, and a stump surrounded by poison ivy may well need to be treated as a bear surrounded by poison ivy. By contrast a rotten stump is probably not a rotten bear, a stump struck by lightning not a bear struck by lightning, and a stump we recently sat on probably not a bear we recently sat on.

In general, real objects that figure as the stumps do in a game, generating fictional truths, are what Walton calls props ("Props are generators of fictional truths", 1990: 37). His theory is that a text or picture that is fiction is a prop in a game of make-believe. An audience should make use of it in the way the children make use of stumps.

Walton is surely right to stress the importance of active imagining on the part of consumers of fiction: that's what the children do in the game, and that's how to get the best out of fiction. We do well to make vivid to ourselves what it would be like to be in a certain situation, or to be a certain kind of person, to reflect on what options are open to a character, how other characters are likely to respond, and so on. An author will typically hope an audience will respond with such active imaginings. But active imagining does not add up to make-believe, and is not proprietary to fiction. It can properly accompany various nonfictional texts like travel brochures and histories (Martinich and Stroll 2007: 54). And although it may be sensible for me to actively imagine being in the Bahamas, as an aid to packing appropriately for my forthcoming trip there, I don't, while shivering in London, have to make-believe I'm already there. So it seems that even if make-believing involves actively imagining, it is not exhausted by it.

Let's suppose, though, that examples like the stump game help us see what make-believe is. Can we use this to say what fiction is? Here's a dissimilarity (noted by Carroll 1991): in typical children's games, the quality of the props is of minor concern. The joy of make-believe is precisely that it can make a sword from a dead stick, a bear from a stump, and an airplane from a child with outstretched arms. Typically, a more sword-like stick wouldn't improve the game, and a real airplane in the backyard would bring the game to an end. By contrast, the quality of a fictional text is very important: to our interest in continuing to read, to how vividly the scenes come before our eyes, and to how worthwhile we regard the experience of reading. Text quality is typically critical to enjoyment in a way that prop quality in children's games is often not.⁹ Walton's analogy does not help us understand the difference.

In playing a game, we are adding to the game, "extending" it. We spot a very small stump and say that there's a cub; this may be the first introduction of the concept *cub* into the concepts exploited in playing the game. This incident of extension is partly constitutive of what takes place in the game. One might think that things are different in fiction: we read, but we don't extend the fiction: that's not our business. We are just the audience, we are not participants in the story. Walton rejects this view, thus conserving the analogy between fiction and games. He thinks that much of what happens in a reader's response to a fiction constitutes an extension of that fiction, a way of making things to be so according to an extended version of the story.

This idea plays a quite particular positive role in Walton's account: he uses it to explain away a supposed puzzle about our emotional responses to fiction. The puzzle can be set out as an inconsistent triad of appealing claims.[10]

1   At least some emotions require corresponding beliefs. For example, we can only fear something if we believe it to be dangerous. Moreover the corresponding belief plays a role in determining what emotion the state of arousal actually constitutes: it's fear rather than excitement or curiosity because of its link with the belief in danger, rather than a link to other beliefs.

2   In reading fiction, we have genuine emotions of fear, sadness, anger, and so on.

3   We do not have the corresponding beliefs (for example, Charles does not believe that the green slime in the horror movie is dangerous, for he knows that in reality there is no such thing).

Walton's solution is to deny that the states we refer to as, for example, "being frightened by the green slime" are really the emotional states they seem to be; in short, he denies (2). If, in the green slime example, Charles were really afraid of the slime, then he would indeed have to believe it to be dangerous, and he does not. The truth is that Charles makes it so, according to an extension of the movie, that he is afraid, and also that, according to this same fiction, he believes the slime is dangerous. Within the fiction, emotion and belief go together as usual; but outside the fiction, neither the emotion nor the belief exists. The within-the-fiction state is all we can properly refer to when we say that the subject is afraid of the slime. It is an emotional state, and may even count as fear, but it is not *fear of the slime*.

Walton supports this denial of (2) by another consideration. Fear is a behavior-affecting state: people who are afraid run away, or call the police. But Charles has no disposition to do such things. The natural explanation is that he is not afraid: "Fear emasculated by subtracting its distinctive motivational force is not fear at all" (Walton 1990: 202).[11]

There is a further consideration that might be adduced. If "afraid of" works in a normal (i.e. extensional) way, like "to the left of", then it seems that "Charles is afraid of the slime" cannot be true if there is no slime, any more than "Charles is to the left of the slime" could be true. It's not certain that Walton is influenced by this consideration. He stresses at one point that "grief, as well as pity and admiration, would seem to require at the very least awareness of the existence of their objects" (204), which is a very different thesis from the claim that some emotions require corresponding beliefs: beliefs may be false, but one cannot be aware of the existence of something that does not exist. The natural response is to accept that "afraid of" is a special sort of verb phrase, a sort which, unlike "to the left of", can form truths even when the noun phrase in the second place has no referent. This raises a slew of issues that will be set on one side for the time being (see chapter 6 below), though the note attached to this sentence gives a brief introduction.[12]

One who says that Charles is not afraid of the slime needs to provide an account of his disturbed mental state. According to Walton, this arises through his participation in the game of make-believe which uses the movie as a prop, and essentially involves Charles making believe, in an extension of the movie, that he is afraid. The explanation leaves at least two unanswered questions: (1) why should Charles choose to make it true in the extended fiction that he is afraid? Presumably an alternative extended fiction has it that he is too brave to fear even the hideous slime; might that not be an appealing alternative scenario for Charles to make-believe? (2) why should its being fictionally true that he is afraid raise Charles's heart rate? Being fictionally rich does not help with everyday expenses, and being fictionally a 4-minute miler does not get the body to move.

Attending to the first question brings out a dissimilarity between games like the bear game and the consumption of fiction. In the bear game, participants have choices. Perhaps there are some constitutive rules (stumps are bears, etc.), but there is a wide range of freedom ("That bear looks harmless: let's go close and see"). By contrast, typical emotional responses to fiction present themselves as unchosen, as forced on us whether we want to feel the response or not. We can drop out of the bear game easily enough ("I'm tired; I'm dropping out"), but once our eyes have scanned the page, there is no resisting the emotion that arises; typically, we cannot simply drop out. Imagining that we are terribly brave in the extended story is not likely to make us any less perturbed now; and this imagining cannot be regarded as an alternative way of "playing the game". Our emotional responses are typically beyond our control.

Walton would prefer to see our question turned around. He writes:

> It is partly the fact that he experiences quasi fear, the fact that he feels his heart pounding, his muscles tensed, and so on, that makes it fictional that he is afraid. (1990: 243)

He suggests more specifically that changes in the sensations which constitute what he calls quasi-fear (e.g. changes in their intensity) correlate with changes in what is so according to the extended fiction (e.g. how intensely Charles is afraid). It still seems appropriate to ask question (2), how Charles's muscles and pulse came to be in that condition. A natural answer is that it was because he was afraid, but that answer of course is not available to Walton. He has something else to say:

> Why does the realization that fictionally one is in danger produce quasi fear [the relevant sensations, changes in heart rate and muscle tone, etc.] when it does? Why does it bring about a state similar to one of real fear, even if the person knows he is not really in danger? The answer does not matter for our purposes, but a Darwinian explanation may be available. Psychological participation in games of make-believe is of great value to us. Probably it has survival value. So evolutionary pressures may be responsible for our being organisms of a kind susceptible to quasi emotions in situations in which they might enrich our psychological participation in games of make-believe. (1990: 245 n.)

The explanation is hard to follow. Does "enriching" our participation mean we do it more often, or with greater pleasure? It's hard to see how unpleasant sensations could contribute to that. Maybe the relevant enrichment is in the lessons we are supposed to learn: this sort of fictional thing gives rise to unpleasant experiences, so now you know how you may or should react if you encounter something like it in reality. This lesson is opaque: in engaging with the fiction, Charles stayed in his seat, and that's not likely to be a survival-promoting strategy for genuine dangers. By contrast, a theory which allows that Charles is afraid has no difficulty. He is afraid because he is presented with something frightening, and his body reacts in the way it does because that is a standard amygdala-initiated bodily response which partially constitutes fear.

Let's return to Walton's motivation for his view. If fearing the slime requires believing that it is dangerous (and so believing that it exists), then Charles does not fear the slime. Walton avoids commitment to the general truth of the antecedent of this conditional: "Fear may not *require* a belief that one is in danger" (245). He is moved by the possibility of pathological fears. There are also more ordinary cases in which a fear is highly unspecific: "ghosts are frightening, and I'm afraid of them, though I am convinced they do no harm. They're just *eerie* and *unsettling*." This suggests an alternative way of dealing with the inconsistent triad: just deny (1), the claim that fear requires belief in danger. Since Walton is not certain that the claim is true, it seems that he ought to tell us why we cannot deny it. Perhaps it's normally true; but Walton seems willing to allow that pathological fears (and he might add unspecific fears) are exceptions, so why not fiction-generated fears as well?

This would be my own preferred approach, and it's motivated by some general considerations about the nature of emotions, rather than about fiction specifically. I see many emotions as rather like perceptions, though with a special coloration or valence: in the positive emotions, like joy and admiration, something is presented as good or beneficial in specific ways, and in the negative emotions, like fear and anger, something is presented as bad or detrimental in specific ways. Just as in perception, how things are presented typically leads to belief that they are so. That's what gives rise to the view that, for example, fear requires belief in danger. But that's an overshoot, treating the normal case as the only case.

In the Müller–Lyer illusion, one line looks shorter than the other, even though one knows they are the same length. The lines are presented as having different lengths, and no amount of knowledge of the real sameness of length can make that presentation go away. What one knows on independent grounds does not always affect how perception presents things as being. Likewise in pathological fear, say of spiders, one knows they are harmless but they are presented to one as dangerous. Knowing they are harmless does not block the illusory presentation. Likewise fiction offers often very vivid presentations of emotionally charged scenes, scenes which naturally elicit fear, joy, sorrow, or whatever. It should be no surprise that these vivid presentations elicit their standard emotions.[13]

This discussion of emotions started in an attempt to see whether games of make-believe could help us attain a better understanding of the nature of fiction. We considered Walton's extreme view, that to respond appropriately to fiction is to use it as a prop in a game of make-believe. This approach delivered particular views about the emotions generated by fictions. Because Walton thinks that we typically do not have real emotions in response to fictions, he needs another account of what is going on. His highly active picture of consuming fiction, involving creating extensions of the fiction that is presented, helps him find a place for states that resemble emotional states. But if there is no need to do this, if we can accept that the emotional states are real, the picture crumbles. We cannot choose our responses to vividly presented emotional scenes. We are not as in control as Walton's picture suggests. So make-believe, understood as Walton understands it, as the active extension of a fiction to one in which the reader is herself a character, cannot constitute an essential ingredient in an account of the nature of fiction.

Breaking the link between emotions and belief does not involve abandoning the view that emotions are in some sense cognitive. In an emotional state, a situation is presented in a certain light. When all goes well, an emotional state is like a perceptual state: the subject believes that the state of affairs presented has the features it is presented as having; and, all being well, it does. There are times in which, for one reason or another, the natural route from presentation to belief is blocked. Defeating collateral knowledge functions as one block; knowledge of the fictional nature of the presentation another.

The headline in the morning's paper is that nearly a million people died last night in a flood in Bangladesh. We pour more maple syrup on our pancake, take another sip of coffee, and turn to the sports pages. A great tragedy leaves us largely unaffected. By contrast, the relatively minor tragedy told by the sound of the axes bringing down the cherry orchard in Chekhov's play can be highly affecting. Fiction affects because of the vivid way in which it presents; a dry recital of something much worse may be less affecting.

On this view, we don't have to see it as only fictionally true that Charles is afraid. That's a good thing, because it's consistent with his being entirely unafraid that it is fictionally true that he's afraid, or that he's imagining a development in a story according to which he is afraid. He's really and not just fictionally afraid, just as the person with a pathological fear of snakes is really afraid. Unlike Walton, we need engage in no fancy reconstrual in order to regard what Charles says after the movie as literally true: "Boy, was I scared!" (Walton 1990: 249).

1.5 Varieties of fiction

It's easy to think mostly of novels when thinking of fiction, and doing so is not inappropriate to our overall project of using a discussion of fiction to evaluate various forms of fictionalism. But in saying what fiction is, we ought also to leave room for other genres. Plays are fairly easy to add in, though we have to find room for an additional element, the performance. Plays are fiction because a significant number of the utterances involved in their production are ones whose content their authors intend a potential audience to make-believe, whether as a reader of the play or as a member of an audience at a performance. More exactly, what we are to make-believe is not that the things the characters say are true, but that it's true that they said them (and likewise that they moved and gestured as presented). Similar remarks could bring movies within the fold of fiction.

One of the interests of Walton's book is the way he offers an integrated account of literature, drama, and the plastic arts. Paintings, photographs, and sculptures, he says, can "prescribe imaginings", and thus meet his criterion for being works of fiction. Some do so more obviously than others. A staid painted record of an actual event (earlier we mentioned David's *Coronation of Napoleon*) may call for imagination or make-believe to no greater extent than an equally staid historical narrative. No doubt we have to appreciate (or imagine?) that the columns of the cathedral are really three-dimensional and have surfaces that are not shown, and so on. But likewise when we are told in narrative prose that the Te Deum was sung, no doubt we would normally be expected to appreciate (or imagine?) that the word "laudamus" was also sung. Other paintings (Walton mentions Renoir's *Bathers*) have no such narrative function, and so exemplify painting used as fiction. We don't have to suppose that Renoir wanted us to believe that at a certain moment bodies and trees were once disposed in just the way the painting presents, and he would rightly treat the comment that they never were as irrelevant. Furthermore, some problems, like the metaphysical status of fictional characters, arise as much in the plastic arts as in novels: what is the metaphysical status of the unicorn in the Unicorn Tapestries?

Fictionalism, however, will have little concern for nonverbal fictions, so we can confine our attention to verbal ones. There is one category which we need to include, but which our Currie-style account excludes: myth. Myths are typically not propounded as myths, but start life propounded and accepted as truths. Should we regard them as fiction at that early stage? Presumably not. They are taken too seriously. Recountings of them are intended to secure or reinforce belief rather than make-belief. They start to count as myths when they cease to be believed, even though they are still in some sense accepted. They are counterexamples to the claim that fictionality depends upon being produced with fictive intentions. As Walton puts it, there is "continuity across enlightenment" (1990: 96). It's the same work, transformed from misguided factual narrative to resonant fiction. The work is not produced by fictive intentions.

So we'll need a disjunction: a fiction is either the product of fictive intentions, or, though it starts life as serious narrative, it rightly comes to be treated as a work to which make-belief, not belief, is the appropriate response. Fictionalists are going to need to say that certain regions of discourse are riddled with myths.

Suggested reading

Three classics on the nature of fiction: Currie (1990), Wolterstorff (1980), and Walton (1990). The question of our emotional engagement with fiction is of independent interest. Radford (1975) is a source for the current debate, nicely elucidated by Kim (2005b).

2

REALISM ABOUT FICTIONAL OBJECTS

[P]ure logic is powerless to tackle the problems of existence.
                                                                     Marcel Proust, The Guermantes Way

[F]ictional characters [are] intrinsically superior – sharper, clearer and more cohesive than their counterparts, with the added advantage that all there is to know about them can be confined within the pages of a book.
        Hilary Spurling attributes this opinion to Julian Barnes, Observer, March 2, 2008

Most fictions speak of real places and times (like nineteenth-century London in many novels by Dickens), and often of real people as well (like Napoleon in *War and Peace*). Most fictions also contain purely fictional characters, ones which are entirely "made up" like Kilgore Trout; some fictions similarly contain purely fictional places, like the planet Tralfamadore, or purely fictional weapons, clothing, and beasts. How should we think about these made-up people, places, and things? Should we think of them all in the same way? Should we include ideal gases and spatial points of zero size in a homogeneous category with Kilgore and Tralfamadore? Fictional objects don't occupy space in our world, so we can never encounter them or visit them. Should we say that they are things that don't exist? Or that they are merely possible things? Or that they are existent but abstract (and so non-space-occupying) things? Or should we simply deny that there are any such things? The first three options, according to which there really are fictional characters but they are nonexistent, or merely possible, or abstract, correspond to three ways to be a *realist* about fictional characters; the fourth option (there are no such things) I count as *irrealism* on this question. The realisms are so called because they say that there really are such things as fictional objects and they belong to our reality, though the objects are "exotic": they are nonexistent, or nonactual or nonconcrete, unlike ordinary objects, tables and mountains, which exist, are actual, and are concrete. The exotic nature of a realist's objects is demanded by the agreed datum that we can never literally encounter purely fictional characters or places, not in the way we could encounter George W. Bush or Timbuktu; as Peter Strawson said, you can't spill your coffee on them. Realist approaches are considered in the three chapters that follow this. These are followed by a chapter describing and arguing for a form of irrealism. The present chapter aims to get clearer about the nature of the debate between realists and irrealists about fiction.

2.1 Where do we start?

Is there a god or not? Standardly there are three possible answers: theistic, atheistic, and agnostic. Theists say that the answer to the question is yes, atheists that it is no, and agnostics that they do not know how to answer the question. With respect to god, theists are realists, atheists are irrealists, and agnostics are – well, let's say agnostics. (In practice, philosophers tend to be opinionated, so agnosticism is rare. But see Rosenkranz 2007.)

Theists believe something about the nature of reality: it contains a god (and they generally have further beliefs about god's nature). Realists about fictional characters believe that our reality contains such things. In philosophical debates between realists and irrealists, both in general and in our special case of fictional characters, it is common to appeal to "intuitions" or "folk beliefs". Does this mean that we relinquish the task of finding out what is true in favor of the less interesting task of finding out what people commonly believe is true?

On the face of it, we can distinguish two questions. (1) Are we (or the folk, or those with common sense) realists or irrealists? This has the overall form of a descriptive sociological question (with of course psychological and linguistic aspects). (2) Is realism true? Or irrealism? Or is there no truth in either? This has the overall form of a metaphysical question. The questions are at least superficially independent, in that it is theoretically possible that we, or the folk, or common sense are mistaken, and so are in thrall to a false metaphysical view. In the history of philosophy it has not been uncommon for philosophers to attribute realism to the folk – "the vulgar" – while holding that some form of irrealism is the right view, the view fit for "the learned". (A famous example is Berkeley, briefly discussed in chapter 7.)

Applying this apparent distinction to fiction would suggest that there are two questions: *are* ordinary people realists about fictional characters? And, regardless of the answer, is realism about fictional characters *correct*? In practice, some philosophers have not allowed these questions to remain sharply separated. In answering the metaphysical question, arguments based on common sense, or folk intuitions, are quite common. As an example, here's a criterion of the adequacy of a theory of fiction: "a good theory will be consonant with ordinary pretheoretical talk about fiction" (Martinich and Stroll 2007: 10–11: the consonance the authors have in mind is that pretheoretical beliefs should be vindicated by the theory). Moreover, in making claims of a more sociological kind, philosophers are reassured if they can find, within common sense, views which they regard as metaphysically correct; and a conflict between a philosophical theory and common sense is often regarded as a "cost", one that may or may not be outweighed by benefits in other respects.

Other philosophers, by contrast, at least affect to despise common sense, implicitly laying claim to have better ways to find out how things are in reality. Thus Russell:

> I regret to say that all too many professors of philosophy consider it their duty to be sycophants of common sense, and thus, doubtless unintentionally, to bow down in homage before the savage superstitions of cannibals. (1925: 143)

In practice, there is typically no starting point except the common-sense opinions that come to us naturally. Even Russell, so keen to debunk the cannibalistic superstitions, thought that his superior replacement views could be recommended by their recapitulating at least the structure of the superseded primitive views. There are certainly cases in which philosophical theory clashes with common sense. Philosophers have argued against the reality of time, against the possibility of anything surviving change, against the truth of arithmetic, against the reality of mountains, and against the possibility of knowing anything. But the uncommonsensical philosophical theories are typically supposed to have some grounding either in common sense itself, or in science. For example, evil genius skeptical arguments appeal to common sense, despite their outrageous conclusions. In such a case, the clash does not feature common sense on the one side and theory on the other, but common sense divided against itself. What else could recommend, for example, the view that nothing could survive change, other than some basically commonsensical considerations (say about the nature of properties like being bent)? The problem is that though we may start out with common-sense positions and try to reason commonsensically from them, we may end up somewhere weird. As Russell said, jokingly, "the point of philosophy is to start with something so simple as not to seem worth stating, and end with something so paradoxical that no one will believe it" (1918: 193). Even if that's not the point of philosophy, it happens. But it doesn't represent two sources of philosophical knowledge, one based on common sense and another on theory.

Common sense divided against itself is one tension that philosophers try to resolve. Another tension is between common sense and science. According to standard scientific theories of matter, material bodies are mostly empty space, and aren't "solid" as we would most naturally understand the term. Is this a genuine collision of views, in which case one of them must be abandoned, or can they be reconciled? The more we learn about humans, and especially about brain science, the harder it is to find a place for agency in the scientific picture. A similar question arises: does science show that agency is a kind of illusion? Or can we reconcile agency with what we know from science? The closest we come to a similar tension in our debate is this: perhaps theorists, literary critics for example, have one view about fictional characters and common sense another. In practice, there seems to be no such tension. All philosophers agree that a good answer to the debate between realist and irrealist approaches must do justice both to common sense and to the perspectives adopted by literary critics.

I'll first single out significant common-sense beliefs about fiction, adopting a critical attitude: not necessarily accepting them (at least not at face value) if there seem to be reasons not to. Then I'll provide a preliminary listing of what I take to be the best arguments in favor of realist metaphysics.

2.2 Literalism: fidelity and truth

Nonphilosophers say and think that Sherlock Holmes lived on Baker Street in London, and that this city and street are the same ones they can visit.

Martinich and Stroll 2007: 11[1]

If you say that Holmes lived in Baker Street I may wager that you are mistaken. ... Even if I were careful to hedge my bet, by counterclaiming only that Holmes did not live in Baker Street, what you say wins: what I say loses.

Woods 1974: 13

[I]t is our intuition that ["Hamlet was prince of Denmark"] can be used to make a true assertion.

Martin and Schotch 1974: 377

We can truly say that Holmes lived in Baker Street.

Lewis 1978: 261

What we call truth in a fictional world is not a kind of truth.

Walton 1990: 41

Some philosophers think that what I'll call the Holmes sentence

> Holmes lived on Baker Street

is generally believed to be true, and indeed is strictly, literally, and without qualification true. I call these theorists literalists (following the usage of Fine 1982). The first part of their claim is sociological: it concerns what "people" believe. The second part of the claim is an endorsement of this belief as literally correct. Literalism, in the presence of modest further assumptions, entails realism. The Holmes sentence can only be true if something is Holmes. Hence literalists have to be realists. If the sentence is generally believed to be true, the folk are committed to something being Holmes, and so the folk are committed to realism. Holmes is not an existent, or actual, or concrete object. Realists are committed to the opinion that Holmes is an exotic entity (nonexistent, nonactual, or nonconcrete). For realists, Holmes is real, but exotic.

I think the literalist position needs qualification on both counts: people don't think that "Holmes lived on Baker Street" is *really* true, and contrary appearances are easily explained away; and people would be right not to think that these sentences are genuinely true.

An initial point against the literalist's sociological claim is that we certainly don't hold that all fictional sentences are true. A fantasy in which Germany won the Second World War might contain the sentence "As the crowds cheered on the pavements, Nazi tanks rolled down Broadway", and we don't think this is true. Even for those sentences which, according to literalists, we do think are true, like the Holmes sentence, we behave oddly, having much less inclination to accept the equivalent "Baker Street numbers Holmes among its inhabitants". The effect is stronger with other examples. If the story says that Holmes had tea with Gladstone, literalists claim that we treat the sentence "Holmes had tea with Gladstone" as true. But we certainly would not without qualification (in, say, writing a life of Gladstone) treat the equivalent sentence "Gladstone had tea with Holmes" as true (Woods 1974: 41–2).

We need to recognize, in addition to a conception of absolute truth, a conception of truth relative to a presupposition or a pretense. An atheist anthropologist has been working on Aztec and Mayan civilizations, paying special attention to their pantheons. He explains to a no less atheistical colleague: "The difference between the fisher gods Atlaua and Chac Uayeb Xoc is that the latter was more concerned with the fate of the fish themselves, whereas Atlaua was responsible for the fate of fishermen." He has made an assertion and (let's suppose) got things right. What he said is true, relative to the presupposition in question: that we are concerned with Aztec and Maya belief systems. Has the anthropologist abandoned his atheism? Of course not. His colleague may dispute the assertion: "No. You've got it all wrong." This response is not made true, as truth is naturally understood in this context, by there being no gods.

Suppose you are in the driving inspector's office, undergoing a viva voce exam as part of a driving test. The examiner asks: "You are approaching a railroad crossing. The bell is ringing and the lights are flashing but the barrier is still vertical. As a driver, what are you doing now?" You might answer: "I'm applying the brakes and coming to a complete halt before the crossing." To say this is to get things right (in the context)[2] even though you may never have driven anywhere near a railroad crossing in your life, and you're certainly not applying any brakes at the time you are speaking. Your sentence is not true (absolutely),[3] but it's assertible and it gets things right.

This notion of truth on a presupposition, along with the correlative notion of assertibility on a presupposition, explains the curious asymmetry noted a couple of paragraphs back: we're more disposed to accept that "Holmes had tea with Gladstone" is true than that "Gladstone had tea with Holmes" is true. The explanation is that the first word of a sentence tends to set the relevant presuppositions. Holmes is well known to be a fictional character; this makes salient, as a dimension of assessment, truth relative to the presupposed Holmes fiction. Gladstone is well known to be a real person; this makes real truth, absolute truth, the salient dimension of assessment. It's not that we are giving conflicting verdicts. Rather, the "true" verdict in the first case pronounces on how things are in the stories (the story says – or so we are pretending – that Holmes had tea with Gladstone), whereas the "false" verdict in the second case pronounces on how things are in reality.

We can also explain why we are not at all disposed to regard as true the (supposedly fictional) sentence: "As the crowds cheered on the pavements, Nazi tanks rolled down Broadway". We don't know any fiction in which this is said, so we can't readily slip into the mode of assessing the sentence relative to a fiction. The natural assessment is as genuinely true or false, in which case there is only one thing to think. Or let's suppose there is a fictional work containing the sentence, but one which is very obscure. Only in a very special situation would the relevant presupposition be set, so only in such situations would we have any inclination to regard the sentence as true. The Holmes sentence, by contrast, is not only tiresomely familiar: we know that, for better or worse, it's part of our cultural heritage, so we know that (almost) all the people we meet are familiar with it, and we know that they know that (almost) all the people they meet are familiar with it, and so on.

Literalism isn't literally true. The Holmes sentence does not affirm a genuine truth. In the right contexts, it's assertible, and indeed true relative to some presupposition made salient in the context. But drop the presupposition, and we no longer have truth. In this perspective, we can see where a certain argument for literalism goes wrong:

1   We know where Holmes lived, viz. in Baker Street.

2   What is known is true.

3   So it is true that Holmes lived in Baker Street. (cf. Woods 1974: 24)

The first premise invokes the presupposition of the Holmes stories. If we hold that in place, the conclusion delivers merely truth on that presupposition.

If we let go of the presupposition, either the first premise is false, or the argument equivocates, illegitimately moving from a presupposition-relative conception of truth to verify the first premise to an absolute conception in the conclusion.

The claim that some uses of "true" are presupposition-relative can be understood in more than one way. It could be the claim that an optimal representation of the semantics of the word "true", as used on that occasion, treats it as a kind of fiction operator governing everything else: it's true in such-and-such a story or culture that .... This requires us to treat the speaker as having in mind (albeit implicitly) a specification of the relevant qualification. An alternative view invites us to see us, the audience, as supplying the context and viewing the remark as falling within it. The following distinct reports of what the first anthropologist said illustrate the options:

> The anthropologist said that, according to Mayan/Aztec cultures, the difference between the fisher gods Atlaua and Chac Uayeb Xoc is ....

> Comparing Aztec and Mayan cultures, the anthropologist said that the difference between the fisher gods Atlaua and Chac Uayeb Xoc is ....

The second report does not specify how the speaker thinks of his presuppositions, his frame of reference. For example, he might have a (false) theory according to which the very notion of *Aztec* is confused, as there were two totally different cultures which happened to overlap at some places and times, and which people wrongly refer to as a single culture. Then the first report would be incorrect, whereas the second would not. In the second, it is up to us, who hear the report, to bring to bear our concepts of Aztec and Mayan cultures in understanding the framework which restricts the anthropologist's remarks.

This phenomenon of framework or presupposition relativity is quite widespread. We readily enter into a game, an opponent's position, or a world view, and are then equipped to make sincere assertions which we don't take to be true absolutely. When we do this, it's not right to say that we must suspend or bracket our own position, or that, in one sense of this slippery notion, we need to presuppose the *correctness* of the perspective we adopt. The following makes perfect sense: "You and I both know that there are no gods (and perhaps we can agree on how to explain the human frailty which leads people to believe such nonsense). Let us never forget, suspend, or bracket this atheism. But here's an interesting result of my recent research: the difference between the fisher gods Atlaua and Chac Uayeb Xoc is that the latter was more concerned with the fate of the fish themselves, whereas Atlaua was responsible for the fate of fishermen." Here the first remarks ought to defeat any pantheistic presuppositions, yet the last is in no tension with the atheism: it does not involve the speaker in any deistic commitment.

To return to literalists: they agree with their opponents that the truth they claim to find in fictional sentences like the Holmes sentence is made so by how things are in the stories (and not by how things are in London). We all know that writing a story according to which p does not make it the case that p, and does not make it true that p. The Holmes sentence, according to literalists, has the property of *being true*. If this property arises just from how things are said to be in the stories, then it can't be real-world truth, but rather fidelity to how things are said to be in the stories.

That might seem to dispose of literalism, but there is a remaining move open: is not truth relative to a fiction a species of truth, as scarlet is a species of red? If so, it must be in some sense correct to ascribe truth to the Holmes sentence.

Here's an argument that a literalist who takes this idea seriously might advance:

1 We all agree that the Holmes sentence is true-in-the-fiction.

2 Truth in fiction is a species of truth: it's a way of being true, like being necessarily true.[4]

3 So the Holmes sentence is true.

Truth in fiction, I claim, is not a species of truth. If it were, then all fictional truths would be true (as the argument above assumes). On standard views, which I share, if something, A, is true, then its negation, not-A, is not. But it may be true according to a fiction that A, and also true according to the same or a different fiction that not-A. The interesting cases in which this arises within a single fiction are not those attributable to authorial oversight, but those which are essential to the story. In some science fiction, the hero, many years after his birth, goes back in time and kills his own grandmother and so was never born.[5] So it's true-in-the-fiction that the hero was born, and true-in-the-fiction that the hero was not born. No species of truth, however restricted, could share this feature. It could not be true that our hero was born and was not born. So here's a compelling reason not to be a literalist: being one would commit one to regarding some sentences and their negations as both true. (Woods 1974: 48 recognizes this challenge.)

Truth in fiction can clash with truth in fact. We've already mentioned the unpleasant fantasy in which Nazi troops marched down Broadway to roars of applause in 1944. It's true in that fiction that they did; and so, for literalists, it's true. But it's also not true, as we all know. In sum, literalists (taken literally) are committed to contradictions in three possible ways.

1. There may be a single fiction according to which *p*, and according to which not-*p*.

2. There may be a fiction according to which *p* and another according to which not-*p*.

3. There may be a fiction according to which *p* when, in reality, not-*p*.

In all these cases, the literalist is committed to believing both p and not-p.

Even the most ardent literalists accept something like the following:

> What establishes the truth of my statement that Holmes lives in Baker Street is an appeal to Doyle's stories. (Woods 1974: 25)

It's not that Conan Doyle functions as a witness. The "establishing" is not the provision of evidence: it is what makes it so. The world makes it so that Baker Street is in London; the story makes it so that Holmes lived in Baker Street. The cat is out of the bag: since the Holmes sentence is made true just by there being a certain story, it's true only in the story, not in reality. It's not literally true.

Whereas the truth of the Holmes sentence certainly seems to require "Holmes" to refer to something, it's far from obvious that its fidelity does. What's needed in being faithful to a story is reproducing a content to which the story is committed. Unless the very notion of content leads us to realism (to be discussed in section 2.4 below), fidelity will not; nor will merely presupposition-relative truth. However, as we'll see in section 2.5 below, there are other sources of realism, including beliefs which are in one way or another *about* fiction, and which call for assessment as genuinely true rather than as faithful.

2.3 "Of course there are fictional characters"

> QUEEN: *This is the very coinage of your brain*
> *This bodiless creation ecstasy*
> *Is very cunning in.*
>
> Hamlet, III.iv

We all agree that *in some sense* there are fictional characters. So isn't realism just plain common sense? Why suppose we need an argument for it?

Here's one sense: "there are fictional characters" just means that there are stories in which characters are portrayed, though reality contains no such people. It's like "There are mythological unicorns." This does not say that there are unicorns of a special mythological kind. It simply says that there are myths according to which there are unicorns. If we understand "there are fictional characters" on this model, it means something that's consistent with irrealism: there are stories in which characters are portrayed. This is indeed platitudinous, and needs no argument.[6]

Realism about fictional characters is not platitudinous; it is, and is intended to be, a controversial claim. It says that reality (our reality) contains such things as Kilgore Trout and Sherlock Holmes. It argues for what I call *robust* fictional characters, by which I mean that it claims that fictional characters belong to our reality, and not just to some fictional world. We all agree that, in fictional worlds, there are all sorts of things, events, people, and so on, which deserve to be called fictional. That's the platitude. The controversial claim, distinctive of realism, is that fictional characters are not confined to fictional worlds: they are also part of our world, the one and only real and actual world.

Robust fictional characters cannot be occupiers of space (for there is nowhere they are and they have a zero carbon footprint). They must be *exotic* objects: *nonexistent* or *nonactual* or *nonconcrete* things. These are the three forms of realism to be discussed in the next three chapters.

Philosophers, of course, try to have things both ways: a substantive and controversial claim that is at the same time obviously true, or in need of none but the most modest argument. Here is an example of an argument designed to show not only that there are robust fictional characters, but also that this is easily established:

> Given such a work of literature [one containing purely fictional names], nothing more is required, no extra ingredients are needed, to "get" a

fictional character, just as *nothing more is required* for there to be a pair of gloves than for there to be a matching left glove and right glove, and nothing more is required for there to be marriages than that certain legal principles be accepted and their criteria fulfilled. In each case, the existence of the former entities (according to our ordinary understanding of terms like "pair", "marriage", and "fictional character") is guaranteed by the existence of the latter entities. (Thomasson 2003: 221–2)[7]

Fictional characters exist thanks to the existence of stories; it's uncontroversial that stories exist; so it's uncontroversial that fictional characters exist. As we saw, in a sense this conclusion is correct. But Thomasson intends the claim in a more controversial way: on her view, fictional characters are as much part of our reality as are pairs of gloves and marriages. They are fully real, albeit abstract, entities. Do her considerations show, as they are supposed to, that there are such *robust* fictional characters?

Let's see what we can extract from the analogy with pairs. A pair of gloves is constituted by two matching gloves, and nothing more. That's why nothing more is needed to have a pair than to have two matching gloves. Let's agree that stories, novels, movies, and so on form part of our reality. They are abstract things, for they are independent of their concrete manifestations in pages, texts, screenings, or narrations: a story can survive the destruction of any concrete text, can be told in different languages, etc. Using the analogy of pairs, perhaps we should think of characters as *constituents* of stories, as we think of individual matched gloves as constituents of the pair. We would then have a strong case for saying that fictional characters belong to our reality:

1   Stories belong to our reality.

2   Fictional characters are constituents of stories.

3   Fictional characters belong to our reality.

The argument seems to me valid, and the first premise seems to me beyond challenge. Irrealists will worry about premise (2). It seems uncontroversial to say that stories represent people, places, events, and so on. But it's hard to combine the view that X represents Y with the view that Y is a constituent of X. Words or thoughts represent objects or states of affairs; but the represented objects or states of affairs are not literally constituents of the words or thoughts that represent them: Fido is not a constituent of "Fido", and the state of affairs of Fido barking is not a constituent of the thought that Fido barks (consider in particular the case in which the thought is false). Thomasson would need to complete this argument (if indeed it's the one she intends) by special reasons for believing (2).

Thomasson may be accused of simply insisting that there is a primitively correct inference from "According to the story, there are characters who ..." to "There are characters who, according to the story ...." We know that inferences like this, *exportation inferences* as I shall call them, are in many cases demonstrably incorrect. We cannot infer that there are pigs that, according to John, fly, from the fact that, according to John, there are pigs that fly. In saying that there are pigs that fly, John may have had no specific pigs in mind, in which case there are no pigs of which he said that they fly.

This contrast points to a special problem for realism. We distinguish, among people who feature in a work of fiction, those who are also real from those that are purely fictional. The standard example of the former is Napoleon, who features in *War and Peace*. The novel is in part about a real person. Quite generally, a character in a novel may be a real person around whom some fantasy is woven. A purely fictional character, by contrast, is one who does not exist in reality, like Levin or Kitty. The contrast can be marked as follows:

> X features as a real character in a fiction iff inferences of the following pattern are valid:
> if, according to the fiction, X is thus-and-so, then X is such that, according to the fiction, (s)he is thus-and-so.

As one might put it: real characters in fictional contexts support exportation inferences; that's what distinguishes them from the purely fictional characters.

A realist cannot avail herself of this way of expressing the distinction. On her view, Levin and Kitty are as much part of reality as Napoleon. The realist is required to accept a range of exportation inferences like this one:

> Given that, according to *Anna Karenina*, Levin marries Kitty, Levin and Kitty are such that, according to *Anna Karenina*, they marry.

The realist will then have to make out the distinction between spinning a tale around a real character and making up a character from scratch in some other way; perhaps as the difference between spinning a tale around a non-exotic object (one that is existent, actual, and concrete) and spinning a tale around an exotic object (one that is nonexistent, nonactual, or nonconcrete). The fact remains that, intuitively, this is not how we see the contrast. We see it as a contrast between a real object that is introduced into a fiction, and an object which exists only within the fiction. Our intuitive view on this point is irrealist. Intuitive views cannot be counted upon to be correct; but they cannot lightly be dismissed.

Everyone must admit that "fictional" is not a regular intersective adjective: maybe a square box is something both square and a box (so "square" is intersective), but many realists, including Thomasson herself,[8] deny that a fictional detective is something both fictional and a detective. So how does "fictional" work? Irrealists will say that it serves to locate things in the realm of fiction rather than reality. But robust fictional characters are supposed to belong to reality, not just to fiction. We cannot in good conscience conclude from "There are fictional characters" that there are *robust* fictional characters without offering a detailed account of how "fictional" works. Such an account needs to defeat the irrealist view that "fictional" serves to qualify a whole phrase or sentence. This, the irrealist will say, explains the consistency of "There are fictional circle-squarers but no real ones." It amounts to something like: in fictions, there are circle-squarers, but in reality, there are none. The realist who wishes to make a big deal of our intuitive acceptance of "There are fictional characters" owes an alternative account, and I don't know where to begin to look for one.

The salient relation between story and character is representational: the story tells us about, or describes, the character. This seems uncontroversial. But in the project of determining whether fictional characters belong to extra-fictional reality, we are back at the beginning. On some views, intentionality, or aboutness, or representation always requires an object, regarded as an element of reality; these are the realist views. Applied to fiction, these views say that a fiction can be about or represent something only if there is something (in our reality) which the fiction is about, or represents. On opposing irrealist views, this does not hold. The irrealist will claim that just as there can be a picture of a unicorn without there being any unicorns, or even any abstract ersatz unicorns, so there can be stories about a unicorn, or stories about Sherlock Holmes, without there being any unicorn or Holmes.

To summarize: realists and irrealists alike can accept that *in some sense* there are fictional characters. Realists interpret this claim as entailing that there are robust fictional characters, ones that belong to our reality. Irrealists will see the claim as amounting to no more than that there are stories in which characters are portrayed, and will go on to claim that just as none of us believes that all the *events* that are portrayed in fiction have any kind of being or existence in reality, we should think the same about the *characters* that are portrayed. Irrealists, in short, deny that there are robust fictional characters. We'll see (in section 2.65, below) that they have to contend with a range of arguments from realists other than the claim that it's just obvious that there are fictional characters.

2.4 A theoretical reason for realism: the semantics of names

> *[A] simple English sentence containing a proper name that fails to denote is not even meaningful.*
>
> Zalta 1988: 123

A tempting view of proper names like "London" and "Winston Churchill" is that they simply stand for their bearers, and it is to this that they owe their meaning. This suggests the widely held view that every meaningful proper name needs a bearer; an example is the fairly popular "direct reference" or "Millian" view of the semantics of names.[9] Confronted with fiction, there are two options for direct reference theorists. First, retaining the natural opinion that fictional names like "Tralfamadore" and "Kilgore Trout" are meaningful, one can cast around for suitable bearers. These will be the robust fictional characters. Since we know that they cannot be found in actual space, they need to be exotic objects.

A second option is to hold that fictional names are not meaningful. This seemingly heroic position has had its defenders. It can be made more palatable by saying that part of what we do when we engage in fiction is *pretend* that the names are meaningful (see Evans 1982; Walton 1990); or by saying that even though the names are not meaningful they can be used to invoke information (see Adams et al. 1997). On this option, the theorist has no need to invoke fictional entities, so Millian theories of this ilk can combine happily with irrealism.

These are options for those who believe that meaningful proper names need bearers. Whether or not this is the right view of names has been debated at great length. Frege (1892) is perhaps the most distinguished example of someone who holds that a proper name without a bearer can be meaningful. Frege argued that proper names with the same bearer can differ in their semantic properties. "Hesperus" was introduced to name the first star to appear in the evening, "Phosphorus" to name the last star to disappear in the morning. It turned out that Hesperus is Phosphorus; this is a different piece of knowledge from the triviality that Hesperus is Hesperus. By hypothesis, the difference cannot be explained in terms of any difference in the bearers of the names, for they have the same bearer. Frege accordingly posited another semantic dimension, that of sense. Sense is what we come to grasp when we understand a name, and it determines the name's bearer, if any. Names with the same bearer may differ in sense, like "Hesperus" and "Phosphorus". Some names have sense without reference; Frege cites the fictional name "Odysseus" as an example.

I will assume that we cannot appeal to Millian views to establish realism about fictional characters. Even if we accept such views, we still might refuse to be realists about fictional characters, for we might be what I called heroic Millians. More interestingly (in my view) we can reject the Millian picture altogether, adopting an approach that is Fregean, at least in spirit. That's what I'll do in this book. As an appendix to this section, I'll set out some more detail concerning the kind of Fregeanism I favor (originally defended by Sainsbury 2005), and which I refer to as RWR (for reference without referents). The appendix can be skipped by those familiar with the view.

Adopting a Fregean position, more specifically RWR, means that we cannot move from the premise that fictional names are intelligible to the conclusion that they have bearers. This does not entail that we can do justice to the truth of sentences containing these names without bearers. The general presumption must be that when a name without a bearer occurs in a simple sentence like the Holmes sentence, the sentence is not true; and according to RWR such a sentence is false.[10] The reason is very general: intuitively, what's necessary and sufficient for the sentence "Holmes lived on Baker Street" to be true is that there are entities x and y and a relation R such that: "Holmes" refers to x, "Baker Street" refers to y, "lived on" refers to R, and x is R-related to y. Since, on the irrealist view, there is nothing to which "Holmes" refers, the sentence is not true. This in itself poses no problem. Why should the sentence be true, absolutely? It is indeed assertible in many contexts, but we've already seen that this does not require absolute truth. However, in the next section we'll see that even those who reject literalism are under pressure to accept that there are simple truths involving fictional names; these argue for the realist conclusion that fictional names have bearers, albeit exotic bearers.

If we embed the Holmes sentence in a suitable operator, we can generate a real-world truth: according to *A Study in Scarlet*, Holmes lived on Baker Street. This is because the embedded sentence does not have to be true for the whole sentence to be true, so the failure of the Holmes sentence to be true does not prevent it contributing to a truth when embedded. This is an example of what philosophers call "nonextensional" embeddings.[11] Other examples are propositional attitude ascriptions. In believing something, a believer is related to a content: *that London is a city* or *that the earth is flat* or *that Holmes roomed with Watson*. It can be true that one believes something, even if what one believes is not true. Once we have the intelligibility of fictional proper names, we pave the way for the truth of a range of sentences which use them, sentences in which the names occur only within a nonextensional embedding.

Realists should not try to advance their cause by appealing to truths in which fictional names are embedded within nonextensional operators. That's because although their opponents may agree that these sentences are true, they don't have to agree that the fictional names need a bearer for this to be so. Nor should realists try to advance their cause by offering sentences like the Holmes sentence. That's because their opponents will not agree that these sentences are literally and absolutely true, and so will not grant this reason for thinking that the names have bearers. In the next section, I offer examples of sentences that are genuinely problematic for irrealists. These are the ones on which defenders of realism should focus.

Appendix: *reference without referents*

The most important feature of the version of Fregeanism that I have defended is that it allows for intelligible empty names, and so allows us to classify purely fictional names as empty but intelligible. This is an initially highly appealing view, but it has received a somewhat wary press, if not a positively bad one, thanks to its association with the view that the meaning of a proper name is the meaning of a definite description. The association goes like this: if a name is empty, you can't give its meaning by saying what it refers to. So the only way you can give its meaning is by revealing it as, implicitly, some sort of description. Descriptivist views have been denounced by Kripke (1972) and many others, and are now largely out of favor. A reader might suppose that if one rejects descriptivism one must embrace Millianism, and doing so would give a very different character to this book.

By contrast, the theory developed in *Reference without Referents* (Sainsbury 2005), which I call RWR, is neither Millian nor descriptivist. It is not

Millian, for it allows that there are intelligible empty names, but it is also not descriptivist in that it denies that any names have a meaning that is properly captured by a definite description. How is this middle way achieved?

The first general point is that we can't expect to give a reductive account of the semantic contribution of all the words in our language, at least not if we think of a word's semantic contribution as what it helps us to say when we use language. No doubt for some purposes it is useful to say of the word "snow" that it refers to atmospheric water vapor frozen into ice crystals and falling in light white flakes or lying on the ground as a white layer. But one who says "Snow is white" does not say that atmospheric water vapor frozen into ice crystals and falling in light white flakes or lying on the ground as a white layer is white; she says that snow is white. So the only correct account of the semantic contribution of "snow" is on the lines: it refers to or introduces snow. Color words provide a range of examples of semantically irreducible expressions: "red" stands for red, or is true just of red things. That's the only kind of thing we can correctly say from a semantic point of view. "Red" also stands for the color of fire engines, but someone who asks "Are fire engines red?" is not asking whether fire engines are the color of fire engines, so we can tell that this fact about the word "red" is not part of its semantic contribution.

Many people would accept the general idea of irreducibility, but would claim that what confers meaning on words is their link to something in the world. In saying that "snow" stands for snow we are indicating a link between a word and the world. Sometimes we will have to re-use the very word in question, in order to pick out the right thing in the world, or the right aspect: it's *snow* that "snow" stands for. That's the sign of irreducibility. But, this line of thought continues, you can't give this kind of semantic account without there being a worldly thing to attach the word to. If there were proper names lacking bearers, this would be something you could not do: there would be no worldly thing to attach the name to, so there would be no coherent account of the name's semantic contribution, which would show that it makes no semantic contribution at all: it's not intelligible.

The second main idea of RWR is that this line of reasoning is incorrect. We can do justice to irreducibility without requiring word–world links in every case. Here's how. Standard semantics does indeed link a name with a bearer, saying, for example, that "Hesperus" stands for Hesperus. Now let's consider a variant: "Hesperus" stands for something just in case that thing is Hesperus. This gives a slightly different edge: we might say that in this version "Hesperus" is being linked to the property of *being Hesperus*, rather than to Hesperus directly. Now let's apply the idea to an empty name: "Sherlock Holmes stands for something just in case that thing is Sherlock Holmes." In my view, nothing is Sherlock Holmes, so this delivers the correct result that there is nothing for which "Sherlock Holmes" stands.

There's a wrinkle. In classical logic, the logical system that for many people holds pride of place as the authority on what logic is, even a claim like *"Sherlock Holmes" stands for something iff that thing is Sherlock Holmes* entails the existence of Sherlock Holmes. The remedy, in my view, is to change the logic. Let's use a version of so-called "free" logic (logic free of existence assumptions), in particular the "negative" version. Free logic allows for names without bearers and blocks the inference from a sentence in which a name is attached to a predicate to a corresponding sentence saying that the predicate is true of something. Negative free logic says that simple sentences containing empty names, for example "Pegasus flies", are false. This leads to a very natural treatment of existential claims. "Pegasus exists" is false, just like "Pegasus flies", since the name is empty. So its negation is true. We typically express this as "Pegasus does not exist." In negative free logic, we cannot infer that there is something that does not exist.

The essence of the RWR approach is that a referring expression can make a perfectly good semantic contribution even if it fails to refer. We are familiar with this general idea with definite descriptions, which intuitively count as referring expressions (though of course there is a famous tradition, stemming from Russell (1905a), in which this natural view is denied). "The best seller I'll write next year" is a perfectly intelligible referring expression, but my guess is that it has no referent. Extend that idea to names, and you have RWR. As Frege said, "Odysseus" is perfectly intelligible, even though Odysseus did not exist. Frege's approach differs from RWR in that whereas Frege thought a simple sentence with a bearerless name is neither true nor false, according to RWR such a sentence is false.

RWR as such by no means delivers simple solutions to the problematic sentences realists will offer (as in section 2.5 below). All RWR ensures is the intelligibility of sentences containing empty names. It does not ensure their truth. The realist will press examples of sentences which intuitively seem true, despite containing purely fictional names. The RWR theorist treats these names as empty, and so it looks as if he must deny the intuition that the sentences which contain them are true.

I doubt that this book relies essentially upon RWR as opposed to other versions of anti-Millianism. But I thought the reader should know the specific kind of anti-Millian view I bring to bear on the issues.

2.5 Evidence for realism

> *The motivation [for realism] should come ... from a host of particular propositions which we believe and which seem to commit us to ... objects.*
>
> Parsons 1980: 32[12]

In this section we'll look at some sentences which pose problems for irrealists, sentences which seem to require that we accept the exotic objects that realists posit. The idea is that the sentences are genuinely and absolutely (not merely fictionally) true; yet admitting this requires us to recognize robust fictional characters.

1   Anna Karenina is more intelligent than Emma Bovary.

2   Ulysses is Odysseus.

Intuitively, these are genuinely true. It's hard to see how we can explain this away in terms of fidelity, for there is no fiction which mentions both these characters; for example, no fiction according to which Anna Karenina is more intelligent than Emma Bovary. For similar reasons, it is hard to see how these occurrences of fictional names could be, implicitly, within the scope of some nonextensional operator. Hence it is tempting to conclude that the fictional names have bearers, in other words, it is tempting to look for a realist solution.

3   Sherlock Holmes is a fictional character/detective.

This seems to be true, but according to the Holmes stories, Holmes was a real person, and not a fictional character. Accordingly (3) cannot be regarded as faithful to the stories. It is tempting to think that, in this sentence, "Sherlock Holmes" refers to something which is a fictional character, indeed a fictional detective. This object will not occupy space, so it needs to be thought of as merely abstract, or nonexistent, or merely possible.

4   "A good proportion of the characters listed [in the *Classical Dictionary*] are mythical, of course; but *most* of them *existed*." (Strawson 1967: 195)

Strawson, drawing our attention to "the pleasant fluidities of thinking"

(1967: 197), shows how natural it is to group mythical and real characters together in a "heterogeneous class". It would seem that we can do this only if there are such things as mythical beings, so the suggestion commits to some kind of realism.

5   Tony Blair admires Phaeton.

We can readily suppose that (5) is true (absolutely). Yet the claim seems to be of the form: a is related to b by relation R (R(ab), for short); and it seems that such a relation can hold only if there are such things as a and b.

6   The Greeks worshipped Zeus.

Many people judge this to be literally true. It raises the same question as (5): worship can only take place, it would seem, if something is worshipped, but there is no existent, actual, concrete Zeus. The realist concludes that there is such a god as Zeus, albeit a nonexistent, or nonactual, or nonconcrete god.

7   There are characters in some nineteenth-century novels who are presented with a greater wealth of physical detail than is any character in any eighteenth-century novel (van Inwagen 1977: 302).

Van Inwagen uses examples of this kind to argue for an abstractist form of realism. The argument runs: Sentences like (7) are true, and apparently require for their truth that there really are such things as fictional characters. This appearance cannot be shown to be illusory by, for example, paraphrasing these sentences so as to embed the quantification within a fiction operator: all adequate paraphrases commit to there really being fictional characters. Hence it must be taken at face value: it's true, really true, and requires for its truth that there really be such characters, i.e. that there are robust fictional characters.

8   I thought about Pegasus all morning.

This looks like a relational sentence, in which case its truth requires that I stand in some relation to Pegasus, in which case there must be such a thing as Pegasus. This is a classic example of so-called "intentionality": the mind's capacity to think about things, even when the "things" in question don't exist. Although fiction provides examples, the phenomenon is more widespread. Suppose there is no cure for cancer. Even so it could be true that someone dreamed of a cure for cancer. I shall suggest that we need to frame some problems relating to fiction within this wider context.

9   Holmes is famous.

There are two ways to understand this sentence. On one understanding, it is to be taken as an attempt to be faithful to the Holmes stories. In this it fails, for Holmes is personally retiring, and is content to let Lestrade and Scotland Yard take the credit for his work.[13] On another understanding, (9) is a contribution to literary sociology. It tells us that Holmes is a famous fictional character, famous to the reading (and listening) public. On this understanding, (9) is indisputably true, and seems to support a realist approach: it seems that (9) is a simple subject–predicate sentence, and it is hard to see how it could be true unless the subject-expression refers to something. At the same time, the example places a constraint on realist approaches: they need to do justice to the ambiguity.

These examples show that there is a significant case to be made for realist approaches to fiction, though it's a case I argue (in chapter 6) should be rejected. The chapters that follow consider the three versions of realism we have mentioned. In chapter 3, Meinongian views are discussed, according to which fictional characters are actual and concrete, but nonexistent. In chapter 4 I discuss the role of possible (and impossible) worlds in accounts of fiction, and the view that fictional characters are nonactual inhabitants of nonactual worlds. In chapter 5, I turn to what is probably the most popular form of realism, the view that fictional characters are abstract things.

Suggested reading

Three advocates of realism: van Inwagen (1977), Thomasson (1999), Voltolini (2006). Critics will emerge in subsequent chapters. Evans (1982) provides an interesting defense of the view that we pretend that fictional names have bearers, and so pretend that they are fully meaningful (when in fact they are not). Walton (1990) adopts a version of this view. For RWR, the source is Sainsbury (2005).

3

FICTIONAL OBJECTS ARE NONEXISTENTS

> The American Museum of Natural History is putting on a big new show of creatures that don't actually exist, "Mythic Creatures: Dragons, Unicorns and Mermaids."
>
> New Yorker, June 4, 2007: 38

> [P]hilosophy cannot concern itself exclusively with things that exist.
>
> Russell 1905b: 531

3.1 Formulating Meinongianism

> There is a perfectly ordinary sense of the word "exists" in which Sherlock Holmes does not exist, and that is the sense that I intend when I call Holmes a nonexistent object.
>
> Parsons 1980: 11

> [T]here are no nonexistent objects; surely that is a truism if anything is.
>
> Stanley 2001: 39

The basic idea of the Meinongian views discussed in this chapter is that fictional characters (and other purely fictional things) are real, actual, perhaps in some sense concrete, but nonexistent. Their nonexistence explains why we don't bump into them, and why they don't contribute to global warming. Their reality means that we can refer to them, and say things about them that are genuinely true. Some nonexistent objects are concrete in that any existent object that duplicates one of them (to the extent that this is possible) has a place in space and time (or whatever you think is enough for being concrete). The nonexistent things belong to our reality, not just to the world of the fiction.

We all think that, for example, unicorns don't exist. We might express ourselves by saying that *unicorns are nonexistent*. If this is regarded as saying no more than that unicorns don't exist, it is uncontentious. If it is taken to predicate a property of unicorns, the property of being nonexistent, then it is a genuinely Meinongian claim, and belongs to our present topic. In this respect, the quotation from Parsons at the beginning of the section is misleading. If he meant no more by "Holmes is a nonexistent object" than "Holmes does not exist", there really would be nothing contentious about his view. But it's plain in the rest of his work that he does mean more than this; for example, he means that one can truly ascribe properties (other than nonexistence) to Holmes.

A *Meinongian* (as I will use the term) holds the following ontological thesis:

MO   Some things do not exist.

Some Meinongians are happy to formulate this view as "*There are* things that do not exist".[1] Others think that we cannot consistently distinguish between "there is" and "there exists", so that the alternative formulation risks degenerating into the inconsistent view that there exist things that do not exist (Priest 2005: 13). Caution commends keeping to the formulation of MO.

In addition, Meinongians (in my stipulated sense) hold the following semantic theses:

MN   Some proper names refer to things which do not exist, and can be used to state truths about such things.

MQ   Some quantifications range over things that do not exist, and can be used to state truths about such things.

Finally, Meinongians apply these views to fiction:

MF   Fictional characters, places and other things, are among the things that do not exist (and so vindicate MO), and discourse within and about fiction exemplifies MN and MQ.

MF can be confused with claims that are much more widely accepted. Many non-Meinongians agree that purely fictional names don't refer to things that exist. That's not the same as saying that they do refer to things that don't exist. Likewise for MO: we all agree that unicorns don't exist. That's not the same as saying that some or all unicorns are nonexistent things. We might think it best to formulate MO as "Some things are nonexistent", and I do think this is a useful formulation. But there is no guarantee that it will be interpreted as the Meinongian intends, that is, as involving the ascription of the property of nonexistence. I do not have to be a Meinongian to believe that President Bush's contribution to stemming global warming was nonexistent; I probably mean only that he has made no contribution, not that some nonexistent contribution is one he has made.

Meinong expressed his view by saying that *Sosein* (being thus-and-so) is independent of *Sein* (being). Things can be thus-and-so without existing. Many people hold something that has a similar structure, one in which objects which in some sense do not exist nonetheless have properties. Socrates does not *exist now* (and in this sense does not exist); but he does have the property of *being dead now*. His Sosein-now is independent of his Sein-now. Meinongianism could be thought of as an extension of this view, dropping the tense. This should make it seem less extraordinary; though I do not mean to suggest that Meinongianism is no more controversial than the analogous view about tensed existence.

3.2 Motivating Meinongianism

> [W]e are all prepared to cite examples of nonexistent objects: Pegasus, Sherlock Holmes, unicorns, centaurs .... Those are all possible objects, but we can find examples of impossible ones too; Quine's example of the round square cupola on Berkeley College will do .... With so many examples at hand, what is more natural than to conclude that there are nonexistent objects — lots of them!
>
> Parsons 1980: 2

Here are four reasons that might be given for accepting some or all of the Meinongian theses, focusing on MO.

First, Meinongianism is a form of realism, and so may help us understand how certain intuitive beliefs can be true. We believe that Holmes was a fictional detective. On some Meinongian views, this is strictly and literally correct. "Holmes" refers to a nonexistent thing, namely, Sherlock Holmes, and this thing really does have the property of being fictional (that is, written about in fiction, but not an existing or factual thing) and also a detective. We believe that some fictional characters are more interesting than others. For example, the Duchesse de Guermantes is more interesting than her husband, the duke. On some Meinongian views, this can be strictly and literally true. Of two nonexistents, one can genuinely possess the property of being more interesting than the other.

The *second* reason is that, perhaps surprisingly, MO is just ordinary common sense. Common sense says that very many things don't exist: dragons, unicorns, Pegasus, and so on. We all agree that there are negative existential truths, truths which state that certain things do not exist: dragons don't exist; unicorns don't exist; Pegasus doesn't exist. The tempting conclusion is that very many things don't exist, from which MO follows immediately.

This is quite a seductive line of reasoning, and there's no doubt that it draws attention to something important. But we can't simply accept it as it stands, for the belief that dragons don't exist can simply be reformulated as the belief that there are no dragons, or that nothing is a dragon, and this belief seems to be inconsistent with the application of MO to dragons (some dragons don't exist). It's certainly true that if, as we all pretheoretically believe, nothing is a dragon, then nothing is a special kind of dragon, viz. a nonexistent one.[2]

Although it's wrong to say that Meinongianism is simply common sense, the phenomenon to which this argument draws attention needs to be addressed; this will be done under the heading of the third reason.

The *third* reason supposedly favoring the nonexistence of some things is based on the solution it provides to the problem of negative existential truths, the "puzzle of existence", as it has sometimes been called. The problem is that intuitively there are such truths (dragons don't exist, Pegasus doesn't exist) yet it seems that they involve referring to the very things they say do not exist: dragons, or Pegasus. If we take this appearance at face value, then dragons and Pegasus need to be counted among the nonexistents: they can be referred to, but they don't exist, and this is just what negative existential truths say about them.

We find this view in an early book by Russell (*The Principles of Mathematics*):

"A is not" must always be false or meaningless. For if A were nothing, it could not be said to be; "A is not" implies that there is a term A whose being is denied, and hence that A is. ... Numbers, the Homeric gods, relations, chimeras and four-dimensional spaces all have being, for if they were not entities of a kind, we could make no proposition about them [not even the proposition that they do not exist]. (Russell 1903: 449)

Here Russell is a Meinongian, attributing being to things that don't exist, like the Homeric gods and chimeras. It's not obvious that he adheres consistently to the view even in the *Principles*, and it's certain that, only a couple of years later (1905a), he repudiated it. Most theorists today accept that repudiation. It's widely held that there is a straightforward alternative way of solving the puzzle of existence in the case of plural or general terms. Although "Dragons" is the grammatical subject of "Dragons don't exist", in this context the word is not used to refer to dragons (existent or nonexistent). Rather, its role is better appreciated when we see that the sentence could be rephrased simply as "There are no dragons." If we see existence or nonexistence as properties to be predicated of things, then it seems that there need to be nonexistent things for the property of not existing, that is, of being nonexistent, to be true of. The contrasting view, nowadays fairly standard, is that "Dragons" introduces a property, and the sentence says that nothing has it. To say that nothing is a dragon is not to ascribe any kind of property to dragons; rather, it's to say that nothing has the property of being a dragon.

This alternative standard view, the "quantificational" view, is sometimes summarized by saying that "exists" should be seen as a quantifier rather than a predicate. Quantifiers are expressions like "all", "some", and "none", that, very roughly, say how many things have a certain property. To say (falsely) that dragons exist is to say that there are dragons, a claim which does not look as if it needs to *refer* to dragons; to say (truly) that dragons don't exist is to say there are no dragons, which again does not require reference to dragons. Rather, it supplies the answer "None" to the question "How many dragons are there?" The most commonly held view is that, even if there are nonexistent things, one cannot argue for them from the puzzle of existence as it applies to plural or general cases, because the quantificational alternative is right.

By contrast, the singular cases are more challenging for the quantificational view. "Pegasus doesn't exist" is true (imagine the context to be one in which you are disabusing someone who has not realized that what he heard about a winged horse was just myth). Perhaps on the quantificational view this is equivalent to "Nothing is Pegasus." Even if the equivalence holds, it may be hard to shake the grip of the idea that "Pegasus" must refer for either sentence, even the quantificational one ("Nothing is Pegasus"), to be true.

Historically, defenders of the quantificational view have held that proper names (at least those that feature in negative existential truths) are "really" definite descriptions, expressions of the form "the so-and-so". (It's not easy to say what underpins the "really" in this sentence!) So "Pegasus" is supposed to be equivalent to something like "the winged horse who served the muses". The sentence "The winged horse who served the muses does not exist" is said to be equivalent to "Nothing was uniquely a winged horse who served the muses"; so this is what "Pegasus does not exist" amounts to. "A winged horse" does not look like an expression which needs a referent, so the puzzle of existence is solved without appealing to nonexistents. In effect, the problem of singular negative existential truth is reduced, on this approach, to the problem of general negative existential truth.

This application of the quantificational approach is controversial because of the controversial view it takes about names. There certainly seems to be no one definite description which every user of a name must know; and this casts doubt on the notion of equivalence used in applying the quantificational story. By contrast, the Meinongian has a straightforward account: "Pegasus" refers to a nonexistent winged horse, and to say of this that it does not exist is to say something straightforwardly true. At this stage in the dialectic, it may be that the Meinongian approach has the advantage.

However, there are a number of alternative ways of explaining singular negative existential truths without appealing to nonexistents. The account I prefer starts from the position that a name like "Pegasus" has no bearer, neither an existent nor a nonexistent one. In general, when a name without a bearer combines with a predicate to make a sentence, the result is false, so "Pegasus flies" is (strictly and literally) false. (That's consistent with it being true according to the myth.) So "Pegasus exists" is false for the same reason. If you negate a falsehood, the result is a truth, so "It is not the case that Pegasus exists" is true. We usually speak and write this as "Pegasus doesn't exist."[3]

In the present context, I can't review other alternatives, nor can I try to establish that one of them is correct. But the existence of these alternatives makes it unwise for a Meinongian to rely heavily on the puzzle of existence in arguing for nonexistent things.

Before leaving this topic, we need to return to the seductive line of argument mentioned as the second reason for believing in nonexistents. This was simply that it's common sense, since according to common sense very many things don't exist: dragons, Pegasus, and so on. Let's suppose we are happy with some non-Meinongian account of the puzzle of existence. This means that we can accept claims like the following without supposing that there are nonexistent things:

> Dragons don't exist.
> Pegasus doesn't exist.

Suppose now we wish to generalize. It's natural to say that the displayed sentences give *examples* of things that don't exist, that is, of nonexistent things, and there are countless more examples; hence, very many things don't exist. But if, as we are assuming, we didn't need nonexistents for the displayed truths, we can't need them just to say there are many such truths. However many truths like the displayed ones there may be, if no one of them requires nonexistents, the totality does not either. This ensures that there's something wrong with the appeal to common sense. Common sense can accept particular cases of true negative existentials without accepting nonexistents. Generalizing from the particular cases, assumed to be free of nonexistents, cannot get us to nonexistents. "There are very many things that don't exist" will be understood by the anti-Meinongian as a loose way of speaking, one we must retract if we are in an ontologically serious mood. In such a mood, the thing to say is just that there are very many truths like the two just displayed.

No one should accept the general inference from "There are examples of Fs" to "There are Fs." Meinongians don't think that there's something answering to just any old collection of properties. They will agree that, for example, there's no existent round square on my desk right now, and there couldn't possibly be one. So there's an example of something that there could not possibly be, an existent round square on my desk right now, but there's no existent round square on my desk right now. This is a counterexample to the inference from examples of Fs to Fs.

The fourth reason one might give for believing in nonexistents is that we can use them to do justice to various beliefs we hold, and especially to those concerning "aboutness" or intentionality. It is a striking feature of mental states (among other things) that they can be targeted on or directed at things. Sitting here in Austin, I can turn my mind to London, and how my friends there are doing. Even more striking, I can think about things that don't exist, like dragons and Pegasus. I seem to have admitted that these thoughts are about nonexistents; hence there are nonexistents my thoughts are about.

This last inference is definitely incorrect. (We saw this in the previous chapter: not all exportation inferences are valid.) Suppose I'm thinking about a sloop in the following way: I wonder what a sloop is, I think maybe one could have fun in a sloop, perhaps I could ask for a sloop for Christmas. No specific sloop is involved in these thoughts; that is, there's no sloop these thoughts are about. Hence one cannot move from "I'm thinking about a sloop" to "There's a sloop I'm thinking about." Hence one should distrust the move from "I'm thinking about things that don't exist" to "There are things that don't exist that I'm thinking about." This consequence does not follow by logic alone; one would require some further principles, presumably ones specific to nonexistent objects, to secure it.

The quick argument for MO or MQ, based on the indisputable premise that people can think about things that don't exist, fails. But perhaps something similar can be constructed in a more piecemeal way. We have already seen that there are various arguments for realism based on the need to explain how certain beliefs we take to be true can be true. I'll recall some of these now, presenting the cases explicitly as arguments for a Meinongian version of realism.

> "Anna Karenina is more intelligent than Emma Bovary." This is a true relational sentence, and so it states a relational fact. A relational fact involves a relation, *R*, and objects *x* and *y* related by *R*. Since no existent objects enter into the relational fact our sentence states, the objects must be nonexistent.

> "A good proportion of the characters listed [in the *Classical Dictionary*] are mythical, of course; but most of them existed" (Strawson 1967: 195). This is true, but, as Strawson says, its truth presupposes a heterogeneous class of objects, some existent, some merely mythical, and so nonexistent.

> "The Greeks worshipped Zeus." This states a relational fact, involving the Greeks, as subject, and Zeus, as object. Zeus doesn't exist. So something, at least one thing, doesn't exist. [One may still be puzzled

about how the Greeks managed to get into such an intimate relation to a nonexistent object.]

"There are characters in some 19th-century novels who are presented with a greater wealth of physical detail than is any character in any 18th-century novel" (van Inwagen 1977: 302).⁴ This truth requires that we can quantify over fictional characters, and hence that there are such things. Since these things that there are don't exist, they are nonexistent.

"Holmes is famous." Understood as true, this ascribes the property of being genuinely famous to a nonexistent object.⁵

It can't be denied that there is something seductive about these arguments, and I'm going to let them stand for the moment. (I'll look at them more closely in chapter 6.) So let's say we have at least a prima facie case for accepting MO. The examples also motivate MN (some proper names refer to nonexistents, and are used to state truths concerning them) and MF (fictional characters are among the things that do not exist).

I now turn to questions that arise only on the supposition that some things don't exist: what are these things like? How many of them are there? What properties do they have?

3.3 Contradictions within Meinongianism?

Meinong's present position appears to me clear and consistent and fruitful of valuable results for philosophy.

Russell 1905b: 538

[W]e have seen reason to reject [Meinong's theory] because it conflicts with the law of contradiction.

Russell 1905a: 491

According to Meinongians, nonexistent objects are in some sense real. True, they do not exist, so if your sense of reality confines you to the existent, the word "real" may seem inappropriate. A Meinongian will evince no such prejudice in favor of the existent. Nonexistents like Sherlock Holmes belong to our reality. On a view which one might call *literalist Meinongianism*, these fictional objects really have the properties that are ascribed to them in the stories. This version of Meinongianism attracts the criticisms already made of any form of literalism. There is also a nonliteralist version:[6] fictional objects are real things, albeit nonexistent ones, and they are represented in stories as having a range of properties they do not in fact have, like being a detective. They do have properties (Holmes has the property of being a fictional character, of being created by Conan Doyle, of being represented to be a detective, and so on), but not the properties they are generally said to have in the stories. This Meinongian, in common with many other theorists (including irrealists), will treat typical fictional sentences involving purely fictional names as false, and none the worse for that.

On either version, nonexistents are actual things, not merely possible ones. They are, or are represented as being, concrete: since it's true that Holmes smokes a pipe, or at least true that Holmes was represented as smoking a pipe, and since you have to fill space to smoke, it's true that Holmes fills space, or at least that he is represented as filling space. Abstract things, by contrast, are held to be nonspatial.[7] To explain why we can't find Holmes, however much we may have scoured the Baker Street area, and why he has left no traces, we appeal to his nonexistence. Nonexistents typically have modest effects on existents, and the effects they have all pass through the medium of thought. Thinking about Holmes and his insufferable smugness may make me angry; but this is the only kind of way a nonexistent can affect an existent.

The strongest motivating idea behind Meinongianism looks to objects of thought as the paradigm nonexistents. They include all purely fictional objects, for they are clearly objects of thought, indeed typically of systematic thoughts, distributed among many different thinkers. Other nonexistents include such old favorites as the golden mountain and the round square. Most Meinongians are likely to be literalists about at least some nonexistents, holding, for example, that the round square is indeed round. As we've seen, some Meinongians may be nonliteralist about fictional objects, holding that Holmes is not a detective (though he is represented as one). To do justice to the range of Meinongian views, we need one answer to the question (what properties do nonexistents have?) for cases to which literalism applies, and another answer for those cases (if any) to which it does not. Here are two proposals:

M_L if S thinks about an F, then something is F.

M_{non-L} if S thinks about an F, then something is represented to be F.

"F" can be replaced by a single word or by a suitable combination of words (e.g. "golden mountain", or "mountain with a circle of seven naturally occurring golden pillars rising 15 feet high at its peak").[8] There would be similar principles for cases in which we have a definite description "the round square" or a proper name like "Pegasus" in place of "an F": the M_L entailments would be that something is the round square, or is Pegasus; the M_{non-L} entailments would be that something is represented to be the round square, or is represented to be Pegasus. In general, any object with the M_L-entailed properties will have the M_{non-L}-entailed ones, but the converse does not hold.

Traditional Meinongians were literalists about the round square, so they were committed, by a suitable version of M_L, to there being a round square, and hence to there being something both round and square. This sounds contradictory. One option open to a Meinongian theorist is to abandon M_L, for example, replacing it by M_{non-L}. There is nothing contradictory about there being something represented as both round and not round. A more usual response is to say that contradictions have a different status in the world of nonexistence, typically coupling this with a restriction on M_L to a proper subset of properties. Let's examine these developments.

Anything that's round is not square, so a round square is square and not square, which classically entails a contradiction.[9] A Meinongian might say that it's only among existent things that anything round is not square; we can't assume that this holds for nonexistent ones, and the round square itself should increase our doubts on this point.

A response on these lines would only defer the problem. We can think about something that's round and not round. By M_L, something is round and not round. Isn't this a contradiction? It's not technically of the form A and not-A, which is how a contradiction is usually defined: a conjunction one of whose conjuncts is the negation of the other. Maybe a Meinongian could say that we'd have something which entailed a contradiction only if we had: something exists and is round and not round. And this is just what we lack. To support this position, the Meinongian would have to make some change in classical quantifier rules, but that would be natural in any case. Whereas classically there's no difference between "There exists something such that …" and "Something is such that …", both being formalized "$\exists x(...)$", from the Meinongian perspective there's a big difference. "Something doesn't exist" is true for the Meinongian, for "something" is neutral on whether what's needed is something existent or something nonexistent. There's no need for the theorist to make the paradoxical claim that there exists something that doesn't exist. So a Meinongian should see "there exists" as an abbreviation of "Something is such that it exists and ...": the classical quantifier is understood as formed by restricting the neutral quantifier to a proper subset of all the things there are, viz. the existents. Our present problem for M_L does not deliver a consequence expressible using the classical quantifier. A Meinongian will deny that the classical rule for quantifiers applies to the neutral quantifier; the argument indicated in note 9 will be blocked (the final existential quantifier elimination step will be invalid for the neutral quantifier), and we will not have a contradiction. Nonexistents are weird. They can verify "Something is both round and not round" without generating contradictions.

This line of defense is unsatisfactory for two reasons. First, if something is round and not round, MN suggests that we could introduce a name for it, say "ρ". Then presumably we should affirm both that ρ is round and that ρ is not round; this is a contradiction, of the form "A and not-A".

The second reason for regarding the attempt to defend M_L as unsatisfactory is that M_L is vulnerable to a contradiction within the theory itself. As Russell pointed out, we can think about an *existent* round square. (For example, we could begin an argument by saying: suppose there exists a round square ... .) By M_L it follows that something *exists* and is round and square. But it was conceded that no *existent* object can be both round and square, on pain of contradiction. In Russell's words (1905a: 183), presenting an abbreviated version of this argument, we arrive at "an intolerable breach" of the law of noncontradiction.[10]

Russell presented this argument as an attack on Meinong. Thus understood, it can be criticized for overlooking Meinong's distinction between existing and being an existent (the distinction is nicely described by Smiley 2004: 104–5, esp. n.13). Meinong accepts that we can think about something which does not exist *as existent*. If we know what we are doing, we can even think in this way without error. (For example, we can begin an argument in much the way envisaged in the previous paragraph: suppose there's an existent round square.) This requires Meinong to deny that there's a sound inference from "An existent round square is existent", which manifests the view that the relevant objects have the properties associated with them in thought, to "An existent round square exists." Being an existent is a property, but not one ascribed by "exists".

Even if a Meinongian could in this way rebut Russell's argument, there are other reasons to think that M_L leads to contradictions. According to Graham

Priest (2005: 83), M_L would enable us to prove anything thinkable, and hence must be rejected. Let A be an arbitrary thinkable proposition (A could be a contradiction). We can think about an object which is self-identical and such that A holds. By M_L, something is self-identical and is such that A holds. From this it follows that A holds.[11]

One way to deal with this problem is to restrict the range of properties of which M_L speaks. Some theorists (for example Parsons 1980) distinguish "nuclear" and "extranuclear" properties. Nuclear properties are supposed to belong to the nature of an object; extranuclear properties relate to, among other things, the object's metaphysical status, including whether or not it exists. A principle like M_L is to hold only for nuclear properties: we can conclude that there is a round square, because *being a round square* is a nuclear property; but we cannot conclude that there is an existent round square, because *being existent* is an extranuclear property. We would have to say that *being self-identical and such that A holds* is extranuclear (at least for many choices of A), in order to block Priest's argument.

One could use this distinction to make sense of the ambiguity in "Holmes is famous." The Meinongian might say that "famous" can introduce either a nuclear or an extranuclear property. As a nuclear property, fame is one Holmes lacks, for a fictional object's nuclear properties are those ascribed to it in the fiction. As an extranuclear property, fame, like nonexistence, is one Holmes possesses.

The distinction between nuclear and extranuclear properties is well known to be troublesome, and much ingenuity has been expended in attempts to make it both clear and intuitively acceptable. Here is a familiar problem: the intuitive idea behind nuclear properties is that they are those that get attributed in the act of thinking. But it is especially plain in the case of fictional characters that existence is typically attributed by authors to their characters. (According to the play *Hamlet*, Hamlet exists; by contrast, according to the play, Gonzago does not, for, within the play, he is just a fictional character.) Yet existence is the paradigm of a property that needs to be extranuclear, on pain of Russell's contradiction. In general, there is nothing to stop us thinking about something having any intelligible property or group of properties, so it is going to be difficult to motivate a restriction on which properties these objects of thought really have.

These difficulties do not arise for nonliteralist Meinongianism, whose central claim is M_{non-L}.[12] There's no contradiction in representing something as having contradictory properties. On the other hand, nonliteralist

Meinongianism lacks some of the resources of the literalist kind. To maintain freedom from contradiction, it is likely to restrict the properties possessed by nonexistents to representational properties (like being represented to be a detective). Then it cannot offer a straightforward account of all the puzzle cases. It cannot explain how it can be true that Anna is more intelligent than Emma (the closest truth is that Anna is represented as more intelligent than how intelligent Emma was represented to be). The false reading of "Holmes is famous" is false for the wrong reasons (assuming that being famous is not a representational property, an assumption to be questioned in chapter 6 below). It also cannot readily explain the truth of such claims as that Conan Doyle created Holmes, since being created by Conan Doyle does not appear to be a representational property.[13]

The last point raises a more general question: how will any version of Meinongianism deal with authorial creativity? That's the question for the section that follows.

3.4 Creativity and nonexistent objects

> Sherlock Holmes = the object which has exactly those nuclear properties which he is understood to have in the Conan Doyle novels.
>
> Parsons 1980: 54

> The view that Dickens created Mrs Gamp by something more like discovering her in the realm of Sosein ... makes the creativity of the novelist seem very like the "creativity" of the flower-arranger.
>
> van Inwagen 1977: 308

All versions of Meinongianism face the problem of giving a realistic account of the creative process. Intuitively, authors of fictions create their characters, they bring them into existence. A Meinongian is barred from saying this, for the view is that fictional characters do not exist and so are not brought into existence. Moreover, intuitively an author develops his characters over time. That is, he introduces a character, and then adds properties to that very character. We'll see that many versions of Meinongianism require us to reject this as a correct account.

At a first attempt, a Meinongian might say that although she cannot regard the creation of fictional characters as bringing them into existence, she can make sense of bringing them into nonexistence. That's just what Conan Doyle did for Holmes. However, Meinongians generally accept the inference from "x does not exist" to "x is nonexistent", so presumably they would accept a time-relative version, and thus would accept: "Holmes did not exist in 1780" so "Holmes was nonexistent in 1780." If so, Holmes was nonexistent before Conan Doyle was born, which means that Conan Doyle could not have brought him into nonexistence; Conan Doyle was too late.

A more promising idea is this: nonexistent objects have no beginning in time, but there may be a time at which their Sosein undergoes enrichment. That's what occurs in the creative process: it's not conjuring an object out of nothing, but adding properties to an object that previously had only a minimal Sosein: whatever array of present-tense properties (nonexistence and other present-tense negative properties) that any nonexistent has. The trouble with this suggestion is that it remains unclear how the author is to add the properties to the right object: that's what I call the *selection problem*. Presumably, on Meinongian views, it is true of Holmes, before Conan Doyle started writing any Holmes stories (and so, we'll pretend, at any time before 1886), that he will be invested with the property of living in Baker Street, or perhaps simply that he will live in Baker Street.[14] This is not true of the equally nonexistent Anna Karenina, nor of a highly Holmes-like nonexistent who lived in Dover Street but otherwise was as like Holmes as can be. Conan Doyle needs to make sure he's creatively investing Holmes, rather than Anna or the pipe-smoking inhabitant of Dover Street, with the property of living in Baker Street, and it's mysterious how he could do that.

We can treat this issue adequately only in the context of some specific theory about what nonexistent objects there are and what kind of life history they have. Principle M_L was geared to ensuring that there were enough nonexistent objects for every thought to have an object. It resolves no questions about, for example, whether thinking about an F on one occasion and thinking about a G on another could be thinking about the same object. Intuitively, we need this sometimes to be possible if we are to have a realistic account of the making up of stories. It's an incremental process, for both reader and author. In *A Study in Scarlet*, we are first introduced to Holmes as "a fellow who is working at the chemical laboratory up at the hospital" and who might be in need of someone to share his digs. Details are added as the book progresses; intuitively these are details about a fictional character we have already encountered. Likewise the natural account of the creative process is that Conan Doyle thinks of his character, and then adds embellishments, adventures, a past, and so on as features of that very character; the character is fixed at an early stage in the creative process. A Meinongian must say something about these dynamics.

A classic Meinongian view is that objects, or at least nonexistent ones, can be individuated by collections of nuclear properties. (We must restrict to nuclear properties, since we don't want a property like existence in the collections.) One extreme possibility is that Holmes is to be individuated by all the nuclear properties that, as we intuitively say, have ever been ascribed to him, or ever will be.[15] This means his individuation is, in a sense, not yet complete, for who can say in how many future derivative fictions he will figure? Or how many philosophers and others will ascribe properties to him in the course of theoretical work?

On a less extreme option, we could think of Holmes as individuated just by the nuclear properties that are, as we say, ascribed to him in the Conan Doyle novels. This was suggested by Parsons in the quotation at the head of this section, and also seems to motivate Zalta:

> [T]he act of storytelling is a kind of extended baptism, and is a speech act more similar to definition than to assertion. ... It seems illegitimate therefore, in the case of storytelling, to ask whether the author is referring when he or she uses the name of a character before the storytelling is complete. (Zalta 2003: 8)

Whether we adopt the more or the less extreme of these views, it's not obvious how to accommodate the fact that story-telling is a doubly dynamic process. First, the narrative act unfolds through time. At later stages in the telling, our character will have been ascribed more properties than he had been ascribed at earlier stages. Second, there are the changes ascribed, the new scrapes and deeds the character is represented as involved in. It is the first of these that seems especially problematic for the Meinongian. If we take it at face value, it shows that we cannot think of the character at a time either as the bundle of properties ascribed by that time, or as the bundle of properties of the form: *having been ascribed such-and-such a property by that time*; later times involve the same character but different bundles. This blocks one route to giving an account of how thinkers are supposed to have one rather than another object in mind. The other route, the most natural one in the case of existent concrete objects, is causal. But nonexistent objects are supposed to be causally isolated from existent ones, so causation won't help explain how nonexistents get to be thought about by us.

The property-based view also raises a modal issue. Properties that individuate an individual are essential to that individual: having a different individuating property is being a different thing. Conan Doyle changed his mind about whether or not Holmes fell with Moriarty from the Reichenbach Falls. If the property of falling individuates Holmes, then the person Conan Doyle claimed did not fall was not Holmes. This is markedly at odds with what we in fact believe.

Zalta, though friendly to the Meinongian view we're discussing, thinks it has a consequence which, in my eyes, would constitute a definitive refutation of it.[16]

> The character Sherlock Holmes has so many properties that it may be unreasonable to think that Doyle ever has him completely in mind. (Zalta 2003: 9)

Of course Conan Doyle knows who Holmes was from an early stage, and we as readers can do the same. However, the absurd consequence does not follow: Zalta's move from the metaphysics (a fictional character is individuated by all his properties) to the epistemology (one can only have something in mind only if one knows all that thing's individuating properties) is unsound. That's a good thing, since it's plain that we can have something (a friend, a city) in mind in the sense of being able knowingly to refer to it, without knowing all or even many of its properties.

The unsoundness in Zalta's move is masked by two uses of "individuate": one is purely metaphysical, so that something's individuating$_M$ properties are those that make it what it is; another is epistemological, so that to individuate$_E$ something is to think about it as the individual it is, to single it out in thought. It's a plausible claim that individual animals are individuated$_M$ by their origin in certain gametes, but it's absurd to suggest that we can only individuate$_E$ an animal (that is, single it out) if we know which gametes it originated from. So one could hold the metaphysical aspect of Zalta's position – that fictional characters are individuated$_M$ by their properties – without accepting the absurd consequence that we cannot think about them individually without knowing all their properties.[17]

Even so, the view that a fictional character is individuated$_M$ by all the properties ascribed to him in the relevant stories is hard to swallow. The difficulty has two aspects: the view makes fictional characters "modally fragile"; and it returns us to the selection problem: how does the author manage to select the right character at the start of the creative process?

Intuitively, Conan Doyle could have written slightly different things *about* Holmes. If Holmes is individuated$_M$ by the properties he is in fact ascribed, this is impossible: being ascribed different properties would amount to being a different individual. This seems decisive against treating fictional characters as individuated by the properties their creators ascribe to them.

In any case, the selection problem is unresolved: how does Conan Doyle manage to bring Holmes, as opposed to any other nonexistent (or indeed existent) object, before his mind? Although we've allowed that one can individuate$_E$ something without knowing all its individuating$_M$ properties, even so it seems somewhat miraculous that, in composing *A Study in Scarlet*, Conan Doyle could bring before his mind an object which, unbeknownst to Conan Doyle, possessed the future-indexed property of struggling with Moriarty, given that Conan Doyle has not then thought of Moriarty. A natural move is to finger some primordial proper subset of the collection of individuating$_M$ properties as those which Conan Doyle can use as individuators$_E$ at an early stage. What might these primordial properties be? Perhaps they are the first to be mentioned. Then, for *A Study in Scarlet*, they would be drawn from a list which begins:

1 Being the first man today to use the expression "Looking for lodgings" to Stamford (an old acquaintance of Watson's).

2 Working at the chemical laboratory.

3 Having bemoaned not being able to find someone to share his lodgings.

4 Being Sherlock Holmes and not yet known to Watson. (The first use of the name is in Stamford's mouth: "You don't know Sherlock Holmes yet.")

5 Being well up in anatomy. (Or perhaps: being said by Stamford to be well up in anatomy.)

A structural question about primordial properties is whether they can be relations to other fictional entities. With the possible exception of (5), the listed properties are relational in this way: (1) involves Stamford, (2) involves the chemical laboratory (which is fictional as far as I know), (3) involves a relation to Holmes himself, through the possessive ("his lodgings"), (4) involves Watson. Yet it seems not unreasonable to require a Meinongian to give an account of what a "pure" act of individuation$_E$ would be like, one not dependent on prior individuation$_E$ of other fictional characters or objects. Unless there are such pure individuations$_E$, it's hard to see how there could be any impure ones.

In practice, we know perfectly well (though in a rough way) the sort of thing that happens when a story is made up. It's enough for Conan Doyle to muse: "I want to write about crime, but not from the police point of view. I'll have as my main character a private person who loves forensics, and ...." Intuitively, that's enough (with some filling of the dots). Assuming that Conan Doyle really thought something like this in 1886, he has, with no effort, thought about Holmes, and has started the process of creating his character. The present question is not how this is possible, but how a Meinongian can explain its possibility. For an irrealist, there's no question about how Conan Doyle comes to stand in any kind of relation to an object, Holmes. All that needs explaining is how a story gets written. Any kind of realist, by contrast, must represent story-writing as standing, or coming to stand, in relations to real objects.

Let's sketch a non-Meinongian view. There are two issues to address: one is the apparently effortless way in which we can understand new singular expressions; the other problem, the selection problem, is how, and under what conditions, this understanding connects us with objects.

A striking phenomenon, common to factual and fictional narrative, is that one can move directly from indefinite to definite forms of speech: "Last night I met a very interesting man. He's a lawyer." The first sentence contains only an indefinite specification of a man. The second sentence assumes that we can now move to a definite specification.[18] How is this to be explained? As far as understanding goes, I think we should say that a proper response even to an indefinite noun phrase in this kind of use is to introduce an individual concept. Interpreting the first sentence would in part involve using this concept to subsume the following information: was met by my interlocutor last night; is very interesting. The concept is then available for use in interpreting the second sentence, which demands the thinker to subsume under the concept the further information: is a lawyer. Understanding can occur regardless of whether or not there is an object. The speaker might have spent the evening alone. Understanding does not raise the selection problem.[19]

The selection problem arises independently of understanding. Suppose the speaker spent the evening alone, and was simply fabricating her meeting with the lawyer. Then there is no object that either party can be said to "have in mind". Now suppose the speaker spoke truly, and the lawyer she met is called Alex. We can reasonably ask: did the hearer succeed in getting Alex "in mind"? Or did the hearer manage to individuate$_E$ Alex? The question is perhaps a bit vague, but a sensible answer is Yes: there was a suitable causal chain leading from Alex, via the speaker's words, to the hearer, the kind of causal chain that knowledge could travel along. There is no need to go into detail to see that, for an irrealist about fictional entities, this is a phenomenon that cannot arise for fiction: since there are no such entities, no one can ever, in this sense, have them "in mind". The greatest achievement available is understanding the fiction. There are no objects to link up to. The selection problem is specific to realist theories of fiction, but they typically deprive the theory of the usual causal way of dealing with it. For realists, there is always a further question to be asked, even once understanding has been secured: does the thinker have any nonexistent object in mind, and if so, which? Nonexistent objects, lacking causal power, cannot help answer this question in the causal way familiar when the question arises for actual existent concrete objects.

Part of what an author has to do to "create a character" is to "get the character in mind". An irrealist can treat getting a character in mind as no more than thinking some intelligible thoughts which exploit an appropriate individual concept with no referent. A realist must allow for a strong reading of "having in mind" according to which the thoughts link up with one among the vast cloud of nonexistent (or nonconcrete or nonabstract) objects. I confess I don't see how a Meinongian can offer any sensible account of how an author's or reader's thoughts are supposed to engage with one rather than another nonexistent entity; and that is a strike against the theory as a theory of fictional entities.

3.5 Other problems for nonexistents

A point in favor of realist views in general, and of literalist Meinongian views in particular, is that we are supposedly inclined to believe that Holmes lived in London. Literalist Meinongians may have an advantage over other realists in doing justice to this supposed belief. For them, some actual object, Holmes, had the property of living in London. By contrast, nonactualist views (introduced in detail in the next chapter) hold only that a nonactual object lived in London, which is hard to distinguish from the mere possibility that some object lived in London; whereas our belief seems more than this. If Holmes is a mere abstraction, then he cannot literally have lived in London, and a more complex story has to be told. Meinongians, by contrast, seem easily able to accommodate a literalist perspective.

I've already said that we should not place much weight on our supposed inclination to believe that Holmes lived in London, or that the sentence "Holmes lived in London" is absolutely true (see chapter 2 above). But let's set that observation to one side, and agree that it counts in favor of Meinongian views that they can do pretty straightforward justice to such supposed truths. These views deliver the verdict that "London was inhabited by Holmes" is no less true; but this is hard to swallow. If it's true of London that it was inhabited by Holmes, why did his habitation leave no traces? Why did he not figure in the census? In the electoral roll? And so on. To say that it's because Holmes didn't exist seems, at first sight, like a retraction of our starting point: if he didn't exist, he didn't (really) smoke a pipe or live in London or .... As we saw in chapter 2, it might be best for the Meinongian not to place too much weight on the supposed intuition that ordinary fictional claims (like the claim that Holmes lived in London) are true. Best to explore nonliteralist versions of the view.

Fiction within fiction poses a structural problem for the Meinongian. Fictions can embed fictions to any desired depth. In *Hamlet*, Hamlet is a real person whereas Gonzago is fictional. Or compare the dagger at Macbeth's belt with the dagger he hallucinated: the former is, according to the fiction, real, whereas the latter is not. Intuitively we need three distinctions or levels: reality (no Hamlet, no Macbeth), the first level of fiction (Hamlet but not Gonzago, the dagger at the belt but not the hallucinated dagger) and the second level of fiction (Gonzago, the hallucinated dagger). Meinongians distinguish between nonexistents and existents, but this is just a two-way distinction and cannot do justice to the three-way distinctions just mentioned. Hamlet and Gonzago, the dagger at the belt and the dagger hallucinated, are all nonexistents; and Meinongian theory as such has nothing more to say.[20]

No doubt epicycles can be added.[21] But the most straightforward approach is one that simply bypasses Meinongian ontology. There's how things are in reality: it contains neither Hamlet nor Gonzago. There's how things are according to the play *Hamlet*: Hamlet exists, but Gonzago does not. And there's how things are according to the play aimed to catch the conscience of a king: Gonzago exists. There is no end to the iteration of the operators: it can be so according to fiction-1 that there is a fiction-2, and that according to fiction-2 there is a fiction-3, and so on. What needs to be explained is explained in terms of different things said, by different fiction operators, and not in terms of objects of different kinds.

There is also a different kind of failure of existence which Meinongian theory cannot distinguish. Amie Thomasson points out that, in Jane Austen's novel, Emma Woodhouse has no "pesky kid brother" (2003: 205). Emma is a fictional character, and so is her sister Isabella. But there is no fictional brother. The Meinongian knee-jerk reaction is to represent the kid brother as a nonexistent object. How to distinguish him from Isabella? Both are nonexistent. The obvious answer is to distinguish between what is so according to the novel and what is not so: according to the novel, there is a sister, but no brother.[22] This distinction not only does not require the notion of nonexistence; nonexistence obscures it.

One well-known feature of intentionality is that it can take an unspecific form. As we've mentioned, I can want a sloop without wanting any sloop in particular: I want merely "relief from slooplessness" (Quine 1956: 177). I can also want a sloop even if there are no sloops, search for the fountain of youth even if there is no such thing, and think about Pegasus. We expect Meinongianism to come to the rescue in the last case: thinking about Pegasus is thinking about something nonexistent. Likewise, Ponce de León's search for the fountain of youth might be described as a search for something that did not exist. Can we bring Meinongian views to bear to explain the nonspecific character of some desires (and other propositional attitudes)? On the face of it, nonexistents don't come into the story, for we can want a sloop in the unspecific way even if there are plenty of sloops and even if I am acquainted with plenty. I still want a sloop, even though there's no sloop I want, and nonexistents don't in any natural way feature in an explanation of how this is possible.

The only way I know for Meinongians to propose a distinctive account, one essentially involving nonexistent entities, is for them to say that there are unspecific sloops. Unlike many specific sloops (for example, the one I own), unspecific ones don't exist. The idea is that my unspecific desire is a desire for one of these.[23] But this will not give the right answer. An account of what my desire is a desire for must specify something that would satisfy the desire. But only an existent sloop would satisfy the desire, and all existent sloops are specific.

Unspecificity features in another way, one which poses a problem for all realist accounts of fiction. The realist is naturally tempted to accept some form of exportation principle. Since she holds that fictional characters belong to our reality, she's likely to accept that if there is a fiction which concerns ..., then there is some (possibly nonexistent) thing or things ... that the fiction concerns. As we saw earlier, it's natural for a realist to move from "*Anna Karenina* concerns Levin" to "Levin is such that *Anna Karenina* concerns him." Unspecificity in fiction sits uneasily with any such principle.

Lewis reminds us that, according to HMS Pinafore, Sir Joseph Porter is attended by a chorus of his sisters and his cousins and his aunts. Intuitively, no sister, cousin, or aunt is a fictional character, since they have not been specified. A Meinongian who follows the naïve exportation principle can infer that there are cousins, sisters, and aunts that HMS Pinafore concerns. Yet intuitively there are no such things, for intuitively no cousin, sister, or aunt is a fictional character. Must a Meinongian say that there are nonexistent sisters but no nonexistent sister? Let's hope not.

Parsons (1980: 56, 181, 191) discusses two similar problems. According to some fiction, there is a crowd of many people. The crowd members are never specified. A Meinongian can be happy with exporting the crowd: there is a crowd that the fiction is about. But she should not be happy exporting any crowd member. So we have a nonexistent crowd without nonexistent members of the crowd. His other example is the hen that laid the egg that Holmes ate. Intuitively, the existence of this hen is entailed by the Holmes stories, but she is not a character in the story. Once again, exportation fails: the story says there's a unique hen, but there's no unique hen, not even a nonexistent one, that the story concerns.

Parsons himself turns our dialectic on its head, saying (very roughly) that we have a fictional character just if exportation seems intuitively correct for the case, and simply accepting that there can be nonexistent crowds without members and nonexistent sisters with no nonexistent sister. He thus dashes the hope I expressed two paragraphs back. Even if the position is technically consistent, it is highly unintuitive.

3.6 Retrospect on Meinongian views

Some people reject Meinongian views out of hand because of their "ontological extravagance". It's not clear that this reproach is justified. Meinongians agree with all theorists about what exists; and it's not clear that being "extravagant" about what does not exist amounts to deplorable lushness: if I think there are more things that don't exist than you think there are, it's hard to see why it's me that's especially extravagant. If you think I'm wrong to think they don't exist, is it that you think they do exist? Obviously not; this shows we are navigating treacherous waters.

Others accept Meinongian views without a murmur, thinking that they are established by the common-sense opinion that there are many things that don't exist. As we saw, this fails to take account of the fact that common sense also affirms that there are no dragons or unicorns, the very things that might be cited as examples of things that don't exist. Some resolution of common-sense opinion is required, and this is not to be attained by some simple observation.

There is no quick route to acceptance or rejection of Meinongianism. In this chapter, we have seen that although the position doesn't address all the problems of intentionality, and has a hard time with authorial creativity, it can offer an account of the truth of some sentences which certainly seem to be true. The main remaining problems we noted were: to find a consistent replacement for M_L, perhaps one exploiting the distinction between nuclear and extranuclear properties; a way of dealing with the selection problem; a way of doing justice to various levels of fictionality; and a way to integrate nonexistents into a complete account of the problems of intentionality (including the possibility of nonspecificity). Our view of Meinongianism is likely to be greatly affected by comparison with alternatives. We'll explore some of these in the two following chapters on realism (chapters 4 and 5) and the chapter on irrealism (chapter 6).

Suggested reading

Classic works, often classified as Meinongian, are Parsons (1980) and Zalta (1988). Both authors are sympathetic to the project of constructing so-called nonexistents as (existent) sets of (existent) properties; this would lead me to classify them as abstractists, though I do not discuss their views under that heading. They have many interesting things to say about the difficulties their proposals encounter. A firmly Meinongian text is Priest (2005), bold and elegant. The text usually cited for Meinong's own views is his *On Assumptions* (1910). A classic attack is found in Quine (1948), though there is no sharp distinction between an attack on nonexistents and an attack on nonactuals. (Nonactuals exist, though they don't actually exist.) For good surveys, see Jacquette (1996); Perszyk (1993). For a survey of contributions to the "puzzle of existence" see Miller (2002).

4

WORLDS AND TRUTH

FICTIONAL WORLDS, POSSIBLE WORLDS, IMPOSSIBLE WORLDS

> *Pegasus, Wyman maintains, has his being as an unactualized possible.*
>
> Quine 1948: 22

We happily speak of the worlds of fiction, thinking of them as peopled by characters from stories. In a fictional world, the events of the story occur as recounted, and the characters of the story live, move, and have their being. Philosophers have used the notion of possible worlds in giving accounts of modality, and in particular of modal logic. Can the philosopher's notion usefully be brought to bear to explain intuitive notions relating to fictional worlds and their denizens? Two main bases for an affirmative answer are considered in this chapter: one is the idea that fictional people and places are not actual entities, but merely possible ones, elements in nonactual possible worlds as understood in modal logic; I call realist views like this concerning fictional characters "nonactualist". Another basis for the appeal to the nonactual is the claim that we can regard fictional operators, like "According to *The Three Musketeers* …", as quantifiers over possible worlds as understood in modal logic, and so as saying something like "In every possible world in which things happen as in *The Three Musketeers* …." The first task is to give a brief overview of how modal logicians treat possible worlds (this should be skipped by readers already familiar with this approach). I'll then consider how worlds of this kind might figure in an account of truth in fiction, suggesting that they do not, and could not, deliver the kind of reduction that some theorists have sought. In the remainder of the chapter, I'll discuss how nonactualism might adapt to certain difficulties, and in particular I'll discuss a version of the view according to which some or all fictional objects are impossible, denizens of impossible or inconsistent worlds.

4.1 Possible worlds in modal logic

Omne possibile exigit existere.
(Every possible thing must exist.)

Leibniz 1686

As far back at least as Leibniz, philosophers have thought it useful to explain what it is for a fact to be necessary in terms of its holding in all possible worlds. This informal idea acquired some technical precision in 1963, when Saul Kripke used it to give model-theoretic semantics for modal logic. The central idea is that we replace the absolute notion of truth and falsehood by a relative one: truth at (or with respect to) a possible world. It is true with respect to the actual world that the state capital of Texas is in Austin; but there is a possible one (one in which Sam Houston got his wicked way) with respect to which this is false, and the state capital is in Houston. Some propositions, like truths of mathematics, are true with respect to every world, and so necessarily true; and their negations are true with respect to no world, and so necessarily false.

Logicians puzzle over questions like this: Is what is necessary necessarily necessary? Or could it have been that the range of necessary truths differed from what it actually is? Thus posed, it's hard to see how one might even begin to address such questions. Kripke showed that if we think of necessity in terms of possible worlds, and of a relation of relative possibility ("accessibility") between the worlds, we at least have another way of posing the question, even if not of definitively answering it.

For modal logic, we can start by making these minimal assumptions about possible worlds:

1 We can meaningfully speak of the set containing all of them.

2 Our world is one of them.

3   It makes sense to speak of a sentence as true or false *with respect to a world*.

4   At least some pairs of worlds are related by a relation of relative possibility, or "accessibility".

5   Worlds are complete: for every sentence *p* and world *w*, if *p* is not true with respect to *w*, then ¬*p* is true with respect to *w* ("¬*p*" abbreviates "not-*p*").

6   Worlds are consistent: for every sentence *p* and world *w*, if *p* is true with respect to *w*, then ¬*p* is not true with respect to *w*.

An example of relative possibility: given that it's not yet noon, I can still catch the 1 p.m. flight; but in half an hour that will no longer be possible. Catching the flight is a possibility relative to how things are now (not yet noon) but is not a possibility relative to how things will be in half an hour's time. A defining condition is this: w_2 is possible relative to w_1 only if anything true with respect to w_2 is possible with respect to w_1. Intuitively, every world is possible relative to itself (for anything true is possible), so the relation of relative possibility is reflexive.[1]

To arrive at definitions for the familiar logical sentential constants, one puts "truth with respect to a possible world" in place of "truth" in nonmodal definitions:

> for all worlds *w*, "¬*p*" is true with respect to *w* iff "*p*" is not true with respect to *w*

> for all worlds *w*, "*p* & *q*" is true with respect to *w* iff "*p*" is true with respect to *w* and "*q*" is true with respect to *w* ("&" abbreviates "and").

Likewise for the other familiar constants. The notion of relative possibility is used in defining "necessarily *p*" (abbreviated as "□*p*"):

> for all worlds *w*, "□*p*" is true with respect to *w* iff "*p*" is true with respect to every world *w'* that is possible relative to *w*.

Let's return to the informal question: is what is necessary necessarily necessary? We could represent this as the question whether this formula is valid:

$\Box p \to \Box\Box p$ ("$\to$" abbreviates "if ... then").

The answer is that it is, provided that the relation of relative possibility is transitive.[2] This does not give an unconditional answer to the question, but it suggests avenues to explore in order to reach an answer. For example, suppose relative possibility should be understood as similarity. Similarity is not transitive (A might be very similar to B and B to C, yet not A to C); on this view one would not expect relative possibility to be. The possible worlds account provides a new way of approaching some modal logical questions.

The consistency of possible worlds is required if they are to be possible, given the normal view that what is inconsistent cannot be so. Truth at a world would not suffice for possibility if some worlds were impossible. The completeness of possible worlds is not an absolute requirement on their use in modal semantics, but it is normally taken for granted in modal logic.[3] As we'll see, completeness is a serious barrier to identifying fictional "worlds" with standard possible worlds, for fictional worlds are evidently not complete. The stories do not tell us whether Holmes parted his hair to the left, to the right, or down the center, so neither the sentence "Holmes parted his hair to the right" nor its negation would be true with respect to "the world" of the Holmes stories.

If nonactual fictional characters are to be real, the worlds they inhabit also need to be real. The view that this is so is standardly called "modal realism", and derives from the work of David Lewis (esp. 1986). (The view is explained more fully in the next section. Fictionalism about possible worlds is the topic of chapter 8.) For purposes of modal logic, however, the metaphysics of possible worlds are of no significance: they play an essentially structural role, rather like truth values in standard propositional logic. Classical semantics for propositional languages interprets propositional letters (p, q) by assigning them one or other truth value, and interprets more complex formulae truth functionally (so, for example, "A & B" is assigned true iff both "A" and "B" are). The overall aim is to provide a definition of such notions as *tautology*: a formula is a tautology iff it takes the truth value true for every assignment of values to the propositional letters. If this is all we want from truth values, we do not need to wax metaphysically anxious about them. Any old objects will do the job: the numbers 1 and 0, or my left shoe and my right shoe. Structure is doing all the work. Suppose one accepts that there are plenty of numbers. Then one can use them to play the role of worlds. For example, one can regard "true at all worlds" as an unusual way of writing "true at all numbers", and the standard recursive definition will explain what it is for a sentence to be true "at" a number. All the usual questions about validity can be raised in this framework, and the answers will be no less valuable than had one spoken of worlds. The upshot is that modal logic as such has no need to take a view about the metaphysical nature of possible worlds.[4]

If this is how possible worlds help in modal semantics, modal logicians have no special reason to be modal realists in this sense. Rather than think of possible worlds as real but nonactual things, they can think of them as actual abstract things which provide the kind of structure required for modal semantics (this is the view Lewis [1986] calls "ersatzism"). They could just be numbers; or they could be maximal consistent sets of sentences, in which case being true with respect to a world is simply belonging to it. These options about possible worlds, however, will not deliver robust fictional characters as possible but nonactual objects. Nonactualism identifies fictional characters with real but nonactual inhabitants of real but nonactual worlds. Realism about possible worlds is an essential part of this thesis, and goes beyond anything required by modal semantics.

4.2 Realism about possible worlds (and their occupants)

> *Take, for instance, the possible fat man in the doorway; and, again, the possible bald man in that doorway. Are they the same possible man, or two possible men? How do we decide? How many possible men are there in that doorway?*
>
> Quine 1948: 23

> *How many possible men are there in the doorway? ... at least a countably infinite number.*
>
> Parsons 1980: 28–9

> *[T]he answer to the question "How many (merely) possible fat men are in that doorway?" is: Zero. ... a merely possible item cannot stand in entire physical relations ... to actual items.*
>
> Routley 1980: 417

> *How many possible men are there in that doorway? None. Being in the doorway is an existence-entailing property. So no non-existent object can have it.*
>
> Priest 2005: 114

What is a possible world? We ask the question from a realist perspective, that is, a perspective according to which possible worlds are real things. Otherwise we will not have the kind of account of possible worlds that will deliver fictional characters as real things, albeit nonactual ones.

The first part of the answer is that one of the worlds is special, for it is our world, and although opinions as to the metaphysics of our world differ, there is general agreement that it includes matter, people, thoughts, and so on. Now consider a possible world differing in some small way from our actual world: maybe when actually typing this sentence I left out the word "way" and had to scroll back and insert it, whereas in a similar possible world I put it in from the start. If this possible world is so similar to our world, then must it not also contain matter, people, thoughts, and so on?

"Yes", answers David Lewis, champion of what he calls "modal realism": possible worlds are real worlds, in which real possibilities are made actual, and many of them are very much like our world except that we do not see them as actual. For Lewis there's a crucial distinction between being real and being actual. Reality is very extensive, including all the possibilities and possible worlds. Actuality is a much narrower notion. We mean by actuality the world we inhabit. Inhabitants of other worlds will think of their worlds as actual, and they will not be wrong. Actuality is a relative notion.

At one point, Lewis argued as follows:

> I believe that things could have been different in countless ways; I believe permissible paraphrases of what I believe; taking the paraphrase at its face value, I therefore believe in the existence of things that might be called "ways things could have been". I prefer to call them "possible worlds". (Lewis 1973: 84)[5]

If fictional worlds are real but nonactual possible worlds, their denizens will include the fictional characters from the relevant stories; they too will be real but nonactual. The world of *Hamlet* will contain the Prince of Denmark and Ophelia and the murders and soliloquizings that are recounted in the play. Although robust fictional characters are real, their being nonactual explains why we can't find them no matter where we look in the actual world, and why finding more of them adds nothing to actual global warming. This species of realism about fictional characters differs from Meinongianism and from abstractism, for both these views hold that fictional characters are actual things (albeit nonexistent in the one case, and merely abstract in the other).

Can nonactualism about fictional characters be easily dismissed, for the kinds of reason suggested by Quine (in the quotation at the head of this section, and elsewhere)? Quine argued that merely possible objects lack criteria of identity, and this lack is meant to be revealed by our inability to provide sensible answers to the questions about how many possible men there are in the doorway. As the other quotations show, there is room for more than one response. Here are a couple of observations relevant to nonactualism about fictional characters. One is that since they are nonactual, they are not actually in any doorways (or anywhere else in the actual world). At least when thinking about fictional characters from a nonactualist perspective, we should side with Routley and Priest against Parsons.[6] The other observation is that questions of identity do arise for fictional characters, and even if they are sometimes tricky to resolve, the questions seem perfectly coherent and well framed. We ask whether Pierre Menard's Don Quixote is the same as or different from Cervantes',[7] and whether the Roman god Jupiter is the same as or different from the Greek god Zeus. Even when theorists disagree, it's not that they throw up their hands and say "This question lacks serious content." Such questions are standardly taken to be contentful and capable of being given correct or incorrect answers.

Nonactualists about fictional objects wish to locate these objects in possible worlds; so they need to be realists about the worlds (they need to be "modal realists"[8]), and realism can't be easily dismissed by questions about the possible men in the doorway. Holmes is to count as a real person, though not an actual one; likewise the events recounted in the stories. Though Lewis is the classic source of modal realism, it's not obvious that he is himself committed to nonactualism about fictional characters. The position sounds as if it would be congenial, but, in his work explicitly addressed to fiction (Lewis 1978), the metaphysical status of fictional characters does not occupy center stage. Rather, his official main target is the semantics of fiction operators, expressions like "According to the Holmes stories ...." As he puts it, his concern is with analyzing the notion of "truth in fiction" (what I have called fidelity), and we'll see that such an analysis has some independence from the question of the metaphysical status of fictional entities.[9] So we'll now take a quite lengthy detour to discuss the analysis, eventually returning to the question of how a modal realist might provide a nonactualist account of fictional characters.

4.3 Fiction operators as quantifiers over worlds

Is it faithful to the Holmes stories that Holmes has kidneys? They are never explicitly discussed. Unquestionably, according to the stories, Holmes is human. And, unquestionably, humans have kidneys. These two premises do not guarantee that, according to the stories, Holmes has kidneys; yet it seems a reasonable thing to believe. What is so according to a story may go beyond what is literally said by the sentences comprising the story. It may also fall short: if one of the sentences is intended ironically, or is a report of a character's speech, then it does not constrain how things have to be in order to be faithful to the stories.

We have, then, some vague ideas about what fidelity to a story involves. Becoming more precise proves very difficult. Ideally, we would like a precise and noncircular completion of the following schema:

1   (According to fiction F, p) iff ....

Lewis's idea is that the completion can begin "in every possible world at which - - -, p". This reduces the task of replacing the dots in (1) to that of replacing the dashes with expressions which help identify the relevant worlds.

Here is Lewis's first attempt:

> What is true in the Sherlock Holmes stories would then be what is true at all of those possible worlds where there are characters who have the attributes, stand in the relations, and do the deeds that are ascribed in the stories to Holmes, Watson, and the rest. (1978: 265)

In terms of our schema, the dashes are replaced by "there are characters who have the attributes, stand in the relations and do the deeds that are ascribed to them in F". Lewis gives two reasons for rejecting this account. First, "there is a threat of circularity" (1978: 265). We speak of worlds in which things occur as in the Holmes stories. But which worlds are these? In the present dialectic, we seem to have no answer other than the worlds which are faithful to the fiction, which is the very notion we are trying to analyze.

The second reason Lewis gives for rejecting the initial account starts with the premise that Holmes is purely fictional; he is not a real person around whom a fiction has been woven. However, it could happen, by an extraordinary coincidence, that our world contains someone called "Sherlock Holmes" who did all the things attributed to Holmes in the stories. On this supposition our world is one in which the plot of the stories is enacted; it would be what I'll call a Holmes world.

> It is false at our world that the name, "Sherlock Holmes," as used in the stories, refers to someone. Yet it is true in the stories that this name, as used in the stories, refers to someone. (1978: 265)

On the proposal to be rejected, "'Holmes' (as used in the stories) refers to someone" is true in the stories, yet there is a Holmes world (our world) at which it is false. Hence we can't equate truth in the Holmes stories with truth at every Holmes world.

Lewis says that we should think of stories in terms of acts of story-telling, rather than in terms of sets of sentences. This enables us to say that Pierre Menard's version of *Don Quixote* is not the original story, even if it matches Cervantes' version word for word.

Using the focus on acts of story-telling, the next suggestion Lewis considers is to restrict the relevant worlds to those in which the story is told as known fact (this is "analysis 0"). This eliminates our world, for that is not what happened here: the story was told as a story only. So the second of the problems is resolved. As for the first problem, Lewis's own criticism of analysis 0 shows that he thinks that it in effect defines truth in fiction as *explicit* truth in fiction. For example, he says that although we should believe that according to the Holmes stories, Holmes wore underpants, there are plenty of worlds in which the stories are told as known fact but at which Holmes did not wear underpants. Although, if he's right, this shows that analysis 0 is too restrictive, it also shows that the problem of circularity has been eased: perhaps we can help ourselves to the notion of what is *explicitly* so according to the fiction and use the notion of possible worlds to extend outwards and define what is *implicitly* so.

That's what Lewis attempts in analysis 1. It's inspired by the thought that the worlds we need to consider are those in which (a) the story is told as known fact and (b) there are no gratuitous changes (these worlds will differ no more from our world than is required for the story to be enacted). In our world, Baker Street is nearer to Paddington than to Waterloo. Although authors of fiction are perfectly entitled to ignore or alter such facts, nothing in the Holmes stories suggests that Conan Doyle is doing so: he doesn't explicitly say anything about this spatial relationship, nor is anything other than the actual disposition of the locations required for any of the plots. We should therefore conclude that according to the Holmes stories, Holmes lives nearer to Paddington than to Waterloo. In terms of analysis 1, we should exclude worlds that differ gratuitously from the actual world, and so should exclude worlds in which London's topography is different in the respects in question. In every world in which the stories are told as known fact, and which differ otherwise as little as possible from our world, Holmes lives nearer to Paddington than to Waterloo.

Lewis cautions against supposing that there is a *unique* "world of the fiction". There will be differences from world to world, differences which register the incomplete character of fictional objects. It's not the case that, according to the Holmes stories, Holmes had an even number of hairs on his head when he first met Watson. It's not the case that, according to the Holmes stories, Holmes had an odd number of hairs on his head when he first met Watson. There are worlds in which the stories are told as known fact, and which differ minimally from our world, in which the number is odd (guaranteeing the first point); and worlds in which the stories are told as known fact, and which differ minimally from our world, in which the number is even (guaranteeing the second). In effect, the incompleteness essential to fiction, which surfaces in the notion of a "fictional world", is being redescribed by quantification over complete worlds.

Analysis 1 in effect projects many features of our world into the stories. This would appeal to those who think psychoanalysis encodes truths about human nature. The analysis would justify the opinion that according to *Hamlet*, Hamlet suffers from an Oedipus complex, a result that some literary theorists may consider a point in its favor. However, the analysis faces difficulties. Suppose in our world that just 1,756 arrows were fired at the Battle of Hastings. Every world differing minimally from our world in which the Holmes stories are told as known fact will be a world in which there was such a battle, and just 1,756 arrows were fired. By analysis 1, it follows that, according to the Holmes stories, 1,756 arrows were fired at the Battle of Hastings. This is an undesirable result. Intuitively, the Holmes stories have nothing whatsoever to say about the Battle of Hastings.

Lewis recognizes that analysis 1 could be challenged (his counterexamples are more sophisticated[10]). He accordingly provides an alternative (and leaves the reader to choose between them). It is analysis 2, requiring that what is subject to minimal change, in determining which worlds matter to truth in fiction, is not how things actually are but how things are overtly believed to be by the story-teller and her intended audience (the "community of origin"):

> What is true in the Sherlock Holmes stories is what would be true, according to the overt beliefs of the community of origin, if those stories were told as known fact rather than fiction. (1978: 273)

Something is overtly believed in a community iff more or less everyone believes it and more or less everyone believes that more or less everyone in the community believes it. Only worlds in which all these beliefs are true are to be considered in the quantification. This would not be to the taste of those who wish to construct psychoanalytic interpretations (claiming, for example, that according to *Hamlet*, Hamlet had an Oedipus complex), since even if psychoanalytic theory is true, it was not believed by the community of origin of Shakespeare's play, and so the quantification will not be confined to worlds at which it is true.[11]

In many cases, the verdicts of analysis 1 will agree with those of analysis 2. For example, on both analyses, according to the Holmes stories, Holmes lives nearer to Paddington than to Waterloo. They will diverge on other cases. It's actually true that, indexing the tense to the time of the stories, London will come to levy a congestion charge on automobiles. It would be gratuitous to change this fact, when considering the worlds invoked by analysis 1; we don't have to change it in order to make sense of everything the story explicitly says. The unwanted upshot would be that, according to the Holmes stories, London will levy a congestion charge on automobiles. The example would not damage analysis 2, since in the community of origin no one believed that London would levy a congestion charge on automobiles.

A community may overtly believe something false, or something irrelevant to a story. Perhaps the community of origin for the Holmes stories overtly believed that there were no planets beyond Neptune. Then analysis 2 would have it that, according to the Holmes stories, there are no planets beyond Neptune. This result is counterintuitive. The Holmes stories have nothing to say about Neptune. In particular, it seems wrong to accuse them of commitment to a falsehood having nothing to do with the stories themselves. The case contrasts sharply with Russell's viper (discussed by Lewis 1978: 271): it seems reasonable to say that *The Adventure of the Speckled Band* is committed to the falsehood that a viper could climb a bell-rope, for this is what Holmes said explains the murder, and we are normally intended to suppose that Holmes does not err.

Some apparent counterexamples are common to both analyses. Since Lewis's worlds are closed under entailment, each contains every tautology, for example "If George Bush was elected for a second term in 2004, then he was elected for a second term in 2004." On both analyses, every tautology will be true in every story; and this is implausible (see Proudfoot 2006: 21–2).[12]

There is a problem which clearly worries Lewis, and to which he returned in a postscript to the paper: many fictions involve impossible happenings. Where this is simply authorial oversight, there are relatively easy ways of dealing with it. But where the impossibility is an integral part of the fiction, possible worlds accounts are at a loss. In chapter 3 we considered a time travel story along these lines: 26 years after his birth, our hero travels back in time and kills his grandmother, with the result that neither his father nor he himself was born. He was born, and he was not born.[13] In no possible world is a story to this effect told as known fact. Hence for an arbitrary sentence p, it is trivially true that it holds in every world in which our story is told as known fact; so, according to our story, p (whatever p may be); an undesirable result.

Lewis is well aware of the problem, the problem, in his terminology, of vacuous truth. In the main text of the paper, he is dismissive. Speaking of the result that "anything whatever is vacuously true in an impossible fiction", he says:

> That seems entirely satisfactory if the impossibility is blatant: if we are dealing with a fantasy about the troubles of the man who squared the circle, or with the worst sort of incoherent time-travel story. We should not expect to have a non-trivial concept of truth in blatantly impossible fiction. (1978: 274–5)

Ray Bradbury's story (cited in note 13) clearly has a nontrivial concept of truth. It is not true in it, for example, that Eckels is identical to Keith, or that there is no system of government, or that time travel is impossible. Lewis returns to the problem in more detail in the Postscript. He suggests that something is true according to an inconsistent story just if it is true in some consistent fragment of the story. The consistent fragments can be told as known truths in various possible worlds, and so deliver nonvacuous truths in fiction, which may be analyzed either according to analysis 1, or according to analysis 2. We would expect that, according to the inconsistent story, p, and also, according to the inconsistent story, not-p; but we will not have, according to the inconsistent story, *p and not-p*.

This division into consistent fragments is not always feasible. Proudfoot (2006: 27) invites us to imagine a story which introduces us to a circle-squaring character. She suggests that there's no way of separating out consistent fragments in such a way that putting the fragments together would reconstitute the story. She takes for granted, contrary to Lewis's explicit remark in the quotation displayed in the previous paragraph, that the story can be in some sense coherent. Priest's short story (2005: 125–33) is also designed to resist fragmentation into consistent streams, while being in some sense coherent: not everything is true according to it.[14]

Lewis's attempt to analyze fiction operators in terms of quantification over possible worlds is unsuccessful. Should we conclude that what is needed is further refinement? Or should we be skeptical of the project? I think skepticism is called for. Because of irony, perhaps lightly camouflaged irony, or irony camouflaged so deeply as to be detectable only by a small côterie of cognoscenti, we don't even have a simple recipe for determining what a story explicitly says. A fortiori, it's very unlikely that any single key will unlock the much trickier notion of a story's possibly implicit commitments. To start with a trivial example. Lewis is convinced that, according to the stories, Holmes wore underpants. Even setting aside my own ignorance of the history of these garments (which, for all I know, were not in common use until the twentieth century), and supposing that they were among the normal accoutrements of someone of the sex and class Holmes was represented to be, it seems to me quite unclear whether we should regard their use by Holmes as part of the story. We could well imagine a plot development in which Holmes desperately needed something with which to make a tourniquet. Underpants would do, at a pinch, but (so we may suppose) he wasn't wearing any, and so had to adopt some other stratagem. However silly, this plot development was not barred to Conan Doyle by the earlier stories. Hence the earlier stories do not have it that Holmes wore underpants. If this test is apposite, we could not even conclude that, according to the stories, Holmes had no third nostril. The test is: if something can be coherently added to the explicit content of the stories, it was not previously implicitly excluded.

It seems reasonable to feel in two minds about the test. On the one hand, the principle that we ought to allow for merely possible plot developments is quite appealing. On the other hand, as the third nostril illustrates, this would lead to a very narrow conception of what the story says. I think we should conclude that our standards are highly variable (and accordingly hard to pin down). If the question is what constrains someone wishing to extend an existing fiction, to tell a new tale about an old character, we are sympathetic to a very permissive answer, allowing the new story to attribute a third nostril. This pairs naturally with a rather restrictive conception of what is so according to the original story (it does not say that Holmes lacked a third nostril). On the other hand, if we're not thinking about possible developments but are just trying to immerse ourselves in the story as written, it seems that the only answer to the question whether, according to the story, Holmes had a third nostril is "No."

When serious matters are under discussion, greater freedom to "interpret" a story, that is, to draw out unobvious commitments, seems appropriate. Reading between the lines is often highly fitting (even if it does not lead to Holmes's underpants); and hermeneutics is supposedly a science, one which is hard to master even given a lifetime of study. The view that, according to *Madame Bovary*, Emma was subjected to anal sex by Rodolphe can be sensibly discussed, and it's unlikely that even the most ardent partisans of either view would suppose their case was decisive. Both parties would agree that it would have been impossible for Flaubert to describe this form of sexual contact explicitly; it would be common ground that it's an implicit part of the story, if it's a part at all. To have a worthwhile opinion one would need to know a good deal about the literary conventions that prevailed in nineteenth-century France, and also about Flaubert's own sensibility.

Here's a recent example of textual interpretation which shows how nuanced are the issues relating to what is so according to a story. Claire Messud, in a review of a collection of short stories by William Trevor, quotes the following passage from a story entitled "Faith":

> Then – as it happened, on a Sunday night – Bartholomew, with cruel suddenness, was aware of a realization that made him feel as if he had been struck by a blow so powerful it left him, though not in pain, without the normality of his faculties. This happened in his bedroom before he had begun to undress. The bedside light was on; he had closed the door, pulled down the two blinds, and was standing beside his bed, having just untied the laces of his shoes. For a moment he thought he had fallen down, but he had not. He thought he could not see, but he could see. A shoe was in one hand, which brought something of reality back, and sitting down on the edge of the bed did too. The clatter of the shoe on the linoleum when it slipped from his grasp brought more. Sensations of confusion lingered while he sat there, then were gone.

Messud claims that though we are not "told" that Bartholomew has experienced a sudden loss of faith, "we surmise that this is so because of the story's title, and above all because Bartholomew is a man of God undergoing an inexpressible revelation ... By what other life-shattering revelation would such a man be visited?" (New York Review of Books, February 14, 2008, 20–1). Messud says, in other words, that according to the story, Bartholomew suffered a loss of faith, though this is not explicitly said (we are not "told" this). The basis for the inference is subtle: we are to look for the best explanation of what might be happening to a character of the kind in question. We can use the title as a hint, though hardly as direct a hint as if it had been "Loss of Faith"; and titles are not always going to be helpful (think of movie titles like *Magnolia* or *Blade Runner*, or book titles like *Daniel Deronda* or *Zen and the Art of Motorcycle Maintenance*[15]). It's hard to believe that the inferential processes appropriate to determining what this story said could be captured in some formula that would apply as well to other stories. The best advice would seem to be that we have to use everything we have in the way of text, background knowledge, and our own experience to reach an account which, in some potentially unsystematizable way, is maximally coherent and satisfying. (In the last 50 years, many novels have deliberately set out to make it difficult for the reader to achieve this.)

The point is not just that there's room for well-informed disagreement about how things are in a story, but that the relevant considerations are of highly diverse kinds, and require sophisticated sensibility and literary skill to exploit properly. This is why there's no reason to expect that they can be captured in a neat formula of the sort we expect in philosophical analyses. This is consistent with the possibility of some delineation of the logical features of fiction operators, and some useful distinctions among them, as I mention in chapter 6. Our present concern is to provide a framework for the consideration of fictional characters as real but nonactual things, and we now return to that main thread.

4.4 Which possible object is Sherlock Holmes?

Lewis's account of truth in fiction does not as such constitute a nonactualist metaphysics of fictional characters. Suppose his account of truth in fiction is correct. That doesn't entail that fictional characters are nonactual objects. Compare Lewis's account of vagueness.

The reason it's vague where the outback begins is not that there's this thing, the outback, with imprecise borders; rather there are many things, with different borders, and nobody has been fool enough to try to enforce a choice of one of them as the official referent of the word "outback". (Lewis 1986: 212)

The upshot is a semantics for the word "outback": "It's easy to get lost in the outback" is true iff true of each of the precisely bordered outback-candidates, false iff false of all these things, and otherwise neither true nor false. There's no metaphysical answer to the question "What is the outback?" There are various things, no one of which is the outback, and we can draw on these various things in giving our semantic description. Likewise, Lewis could say that there are various possibilia, no one of which is Sherlock Holmes, and we can use these various objects in our account of truth in fiction. End of story.

As already noted, something like Lewis's modal realism is a prerequisite for nonactualism, since nonactualists need to say that fictional characters, though nonactual, are real. It would also be natural, though not mandatory, for them to adopt a Lewis-like account of truth in fiction. I'll now turn to nonactualism in its own right, without assuming it to be committed to Lewis's account of truth in fiction.

Nonactualist theorists say that Sherlock Holmes is a possible but nonactual object. Which nonactual object is he? Here is a natural principle to help us start on that question:

(*)   Holmes has F at a world at which he exists iff, according to the stories, Holmes has F.

The principle is supposed to reflect the idea that any relevant possible object will in some sense "realize", at its own world, the properties assigned to Holmes in the stories. The principle takes for granted the notion of what properties Holmes has according to the stories. If Lewis is right to say that, according to the stories, Holmes wore underpants, then only underpants-wearers are candidates for being Holmes.

(*) enshrines a literalist as opposed to a nonliteralist approach. A literalist about fictional objects takes them to have just the properties ascribed in the stories, whereas a nonliteralist takes the objects to have only properties of the form: *being ascribed such-and-such a property in the stories*. For a nonactualist, a nonliteralist approach is hardly an option. The reason for locating fictional objects at nonactual worlds was to make room for their bulky properties, like that of smoking a pipe. By contrast, if representations need objects at all, there's no need for them to be nonactual: they could as well be actual things which are nonexistent or nonconcrete. Whereas you need to exist and fill space to smoke a pipe, you don't need to do that in order to be represented as smoking a pipe. So I'll only consider literalist versions of nonactualism, the ones according to which Holmes is a detective and smokes a pipe.

Although the principle (*) is a natural one for nonactualists to adopt, it leads to serious trouble for simple-minded nonactualist views. Consider some property about which the Holmes stories are silent, in the sense that the property is neither ascribed to Holmes nor denied of him. For example, it is not the case, according to the stories, that Holmes is under 6 foot 2. And it is not the case, according to the stories, that Holmes is 6 foot 2 or more. It follows from (*) that Holmes is neither under 6 foot 2 nor 6 foot 2 or more. That's to say he has no height at all. But, necessarily, every physical thing has some height, and Holmes is necessarily a physical thing. So no possible object is Holmes.[16]

Rather different reasoning seems to have persuaded Saul Kripke that Holmes could not have existed, which presumably entails that no possible object is Holmes (and thus that nonactualism is false). He writes:

> The mere discovery that there was indeed a detective with exploits like those of Sherlock Holmes would not show that Conan Doyle was writing about this man; it is theoretically possible, though in practice fantastically unlikely, that Doyle was writing pure fiction with only a coincidental resemblance to the actual man. ... Similarly, I hold the metaphysical view that, granted that there is no Sherlock Holmes, one cannot say of any possible person, that he would have been Sherlock Holmes, had he existed. Several distinct possible people, and even actual ones such as Darwin or Jack the Ripper, might have performed the exploits of Holmes, but there is none of whom we can say that he would have been Holmes had he performed these exploits. For if so, which one?
>
> I thus could no longer write, as I once did, that "Holmes does not exist, but in other states of affairs, he would have existed". (Kripke 1972 [1980]: 157–8)

The first point Kripke is making is that the possibility that Holmes exists is not realized by there being an actual person having all the properties Conan Doyle ascribed to Holmes. Since Conan Doyle's intention was to write pure fiction, the existence of such a man would just be coincidence: he would not be the Sherlock Holmes of the stories. The second point he is making is that there are different possible people who have all the properties ascribed to Holmes. If any one of these is Holmes, all are. But that's a contradiction.[17]

One might think that the argument, and also the one I offered using principle (*), has to be fallacious, for it appears to infect the very idea of describing various possibilities for an individual in terms of variations between possible worlds. Socrates actually possessed a fine aquiline nose. But he might have been snub-nosed: there are worlds at which indeed he is. Now we seem to have a contradiction: our Socrates is not snub-nosed, the possible Socrates is, yet they are supposed to be the same Socrates.

Considerations of this kind led Lewis to counterpart theory, according to which nothing exists at more than one world. Then we have to understand the possibility that Socrates might have been snub-nosed as the fact that some counterpart of Socrates at another world is snub-nosed. The property of *being possibly snub-nosed* is interpreted as the property of *standing in the counterpart relation to someone who is snub-nosed at another world*. As Lewis was well aware, however, there is an alternative. We can understand truth at a world in such a way that it is quite consistent for the very same person to have a property at one world and lack it at another. "a is F and a is not-F" is, of course, a contradiction; but "At some world, a is F and at some world a is not-F" is not. It does the present dialectic no harm to depart from Lewis's counterpart theory, and take it that the same object can have inconsistent properties at different worlds.

On this way of thinking, Socrates has different and incompatible properties at different worlds. These consistently represent different possibilities for Socrates. So can't we defeat the earlier argument by saying that the different worlds which, according to (*), contain Sherlock Holmes represent different possibilities for Holmes? In some he is 6 foot 2 or more, in others he is less than 6 foot 2. But that doesn't show that the taller Holmes is distinct from the shorter one.

This misses the point of the original argument. The complaint was not that Holmes has inconsistent properties at different worlds, but that (*) ensures that he has inconsistent properties at any world, properties which nothing has at any possible world. The essence of the argument is simple: intuitively, and by (*), Holmes is incomplete. But every inhabitant of a possible world is complete. So Holmes is not an inhabitant of a possible world. So Holmes is not a possible object. Those who still doubt may check a slightly more explicit version of the argument in the note attached to this sentence.[18]

The nonactualist must regroup, moving away from the naïve position based on (*).[19] A radical move is to expand the range of worlds under consideration: if we add impossible worlds, we can identify Holmes with an impossible object, a denizen of one or more impossible worlds; if we add incomplete worlds, worlds not closed under some suitable relation of entailment, we can identify Holmes with an incomplete object, a denizen of one or more incomplete worlds. These approaches are considered in the section which follows (section 4.5). A less radical revision is to use supervaluational approaches.[20]

Adopting this latter option, we may define a *Holmes-surrogate* as a possible object having all the properties explicitly ascribed to Holmes in the story. There are many of these, representing what we earlier called the incompleteness of Holmes.

(**)   For all worlds w, objects x and properties F, x is a Holmes-surrogate at w iff

   (i) x has F at w if, according to the stories, Holmes has F and

   (ii) x lacks F at w if, according to the stories, Holmes lacks F

   (iii) either x has F at w or x has not-F at w.

(**) makes being ascribed a property F by the stories sufficient but not necessary for a Holmes-surrogate to have F. As originally intended, concerning properties about which the stories are silent, the various Holmes-surrogates are free to fill up as they wish, and each is required, by (iii), to attain completeness. Every Holmes-surrogate is complete, though none is Holmes.

The account gives truth conditions for sentences like "Holmes is a detective" by quantifying over Holmes-surrogates.[21] The sentence is true iff every Holmes-surrogate is a detective, false iff no Holmes-surrogate is a detective and otherwise neither true nor false. The truth-value gap marks the incompleteness of our hero. This is where, for example, "Holmes had a mole on his back" will fall, for some Holmes-surrogates have moles and others do not.

There are no doubt objections of detail to the semantics. (For example, as stated they are too literalist.[22]) Perhaps refinements can take care of these objections. However, given our current metaphysical concerns, the more striking fact is that the account says nothing about the metaphysical status of Sherlock Holmes himself, for he simply drops out of the picture in favor of his surrogates. The theory we have is simply not one according to which Holmes is a nonactual but possible object. Rather, it's a theory according to which we can replace or reconstrue talk of Holmes in terms of talk of other objects. None of the entities taken to be real (though nonactual) is Holmes, so the view does not meet the definition for being a nonactualist account of fictional entities.[23]

4.5 Strange worlds and objects: incomplete and impossible

Holmes is not a (classical) possible object, for every possible object is complete and Holmes is not. That is the problem for the version of nonactualism we reviewed in the previous section. This is enough to ground rejecting any straightforward version of the thesis that fictional characters are nonactual entities.

The rejection is overdetermined: some objects in fiction, like circle-squarers, and holders of Sylvan's box (Priest 2005: 130), are impossible in that they are ascribed properties which no possible object could possess. Hence not all fictional characters are possible objects, conceived as denizens of classical possible worlds. It would be acceptable to end our enquiry at this point.

However, impossible worlds have been studied with some care by Priest (2005), so I'll briefly mention this option. Applied to our metaphysical issue, it would enable us to say that fictional entities are nonactual things, some possible, others impossible.

If, as in classical logic, a contradiction entails everything, then there's at most one world containing a contradiction. A nonactualist classical theorist would lack the resources to distinguish a world in which things are as they are said to be in Priest's story "Sylvan's Box" (2005: 125–33) from a world in which things are as they are said to be in the story Proudfoot imagines about a circle-squarer (2006: 18, 27). Yet, as Priest stresses, a story containing a contradiction, like "Sylvan's Box", is in a sense coherent:

> There is a determinate plot: not everything happens in the story; and people act in intelligible ways, even when the inconsistent is involved. (2005: 121)[24]

Inconsistent or impossible worlds can play a significant role only if their logic is weaker than classical logic. Perhaps they are not closed at all;[25] or perhaps they are closed under a weaker-than-classical entailment relation. I'll assume that we take the relevant worlds to be closed under a logic (Priest prefers paraconsistent logic, but also considers relevance logic) which delivers a weaker-than-classical entailment relation, one which does not allow a contradiction to entail everything. We'll still have problems if we want to use worlds in an account of truth in fiction, for many weaker logics (including some paraconsistent logics) treat every instance of "*A* or not-*A*" as logically true; and we've already seen that this is problematic for truth in fiction (Proudfoot 2006: 11,16). But let's set this aside in our consideration of the claim that fictional objects are denizens of nonactual worlds some of which are impossible.

From the classical perspective, an incomplete object is an impossible object. Suppose Holmes is incomplete with respect to whether he has an aunt. Then neither "has an aunt" nor "lacks an aunt" is true of him, hence (classically) both are false of him, and so (classically) their negations are true of him, so both "Holmes lacks an aunt" and "It's not the case that Holmes lacks an aunt" are true: a contradiction. Weaker logics can allow truth-value gaps, rejecting the inference from "not true" to "false". Priest suggests that we do not need gappy worlds in order to accommodate the incompleteness of fictional entities, since we can do justice to it by supervaluating over complete entities. As mentioned earlier, even if this gets the truth values of relevant sentences right, it does not implement the envisaged metaphysics, according to which a fictional entity is some (one!) nonactual object. Let's see what happens if we have gappy worlds, as a way of making room for this metaphysical view.

Let's relax the condition that all worlds are complete, where a complete world is one at which, for every sentence, either the sentence or its negation is true. Take an incomplete world, say g, and suppose it contains a person called "Holmes" who has the properties ascribed to Holmes in the stories, lacks those which the stories says Holmes lacks, and for every other property neither has it nor lacks it. "Holmes is 6 foot 2 or more" is neither true nor false with respect to g, and nor is "Holmes is less than 6 foot 2." Why is not this object Holmes himself?

Let's first reconsider Kripke's objection within this new framework. There will be many other worlds, g', differing from g in the truth value they assign to some sentence, but agreeing with g on Holmes sentences. Does that make for too many candidates for being Holmes? That does not seem to be the immediate problem, for another one is more pressing. At every world, all the Holmes-candidates have all and only the properties ascribed to Holmes in the stories. It will be true that some worlds which contain a Holmes-candidate also contain you, and you are precisely 5 foot 10 tall. Holmes will not have any relational properties involving you, since you are not mentioned in the stories. So all these sentences are without truth value:

> Holmes is taller than you.
> Holmes is shorter than you.
> Holmes is the same height as you.

Yet the sentence "Holmes has some determinate height" is true at the world, since this is implied by the stories. Intuitively, the truth of this sentence ensures that one sentence of the displayed trio is true. If Holmes has a determinate height, then he must be either taller or shorter or the same height as you.

These remarks serve to highlight the strangeness of the conception of an incomplete object. With an incomplete representation, no one can possibly quarrel. Presumably all representations are in some way incomplete. The envisaged nonactualist metaphysics invites us to transfer the incompleteness onto an object. This is hard to make sense of.[26]

It's not an adequate response to say that incompleteness is unproblematic once we have included impossible worlds. In such a world the trio of displayed sentences can lack a truth value even though Holmes has some determinate height. But the point of impossible worlds was to do justice to impossible fictions. We shouldn't need them to accommodate just ordinary, humdrum consistent stories like the Holmes stories. How could a consistent story demand an impossible world?

This problem is a manifestation of the strangeness of incompleteness in objects. It's also a manifestation of a more general feature to which Lewis draws attention. It seems impossible for a literalist Meinongian to deny that the following argument is sound, yet its conclusion is intuitively false:

> Holmes lived at 221b Baker Street.
> 221b Baker Street is, and has always been, a bank.
> Holmes lived at a bank.

As Lewis puts it: "the Meinongian must tell us why truths about fictional characters are cut off, sometimes though not always, from the consequences they ought to imply" (1978: 262).

The literature is not rich in well-worked-out nonactualist versions of realism about fictional characters. It may well be that the obstacles I have uncovered can be overcome. Even so, other problems would remain.

There's the problem of making sense of authorial creation, which plays out in this case rather as it did with Meinongianism. Nonactual worlds are causally isolated from ours, so if fictional characters are nonactual objects they cannot be brought into being, or indeed affected in any way, by what we do here. We'd have to think of creativity as selection (or flower-arranging), and we'd have a hard job explaining how our minds connect with these causally isolated entities, which they do from the moment a story, or the telling or reading of it, is begun. There's also a special problem for nonactualist theories. We need the possible worlds to represent modal variation: Holmes couldn't have been an alligator, but could have moved into the lodgings at 221b Baker Street with only boxes and no portmanteaux. Should we allow that at some worlds Holmes has properties not ascribed in the stories? This would take us back to Kripke's worry that it's unclear what would make this individual Holmes as opposed to some impostor. We have a familiar dilemma: either identify individuals by causal relations, which is unavailable for nonactual objects, or by properties. Taking the latter horn precludes us from representing, through the machinery of worlds, the variation in properties that we believe is available to real entities of the kind that, according to realists, fictional characters are.

Suggested reading

For truth in fiction, Lewis (1978) is essential. His view has sometimes been taken to entail a nonactualist metaphysics of fictional objects, but for reasons explained in the chapter, this is a confusion. This leaves nonactualist positions fairly hard to find. Priest (2005) is probably the most useful reading.

5
FICTIONAL ENTITIES ARE ABSTRACT ARTIFACTS

> [I]t is not unreasonable to regard fictitious characters as abstractions — as mere roles, or as classes of properties, or as some other kind of abstract loci of properties. After all, what else could they be?
>
> Deutsch 1991: 210

Probably the currently most popular version of realism is the view that fictional characters are abstract artifacts. They are abstract not in the Platonic sense of being eternal and immutable,[1] but simply in that they are nonspatial and nonmental. They are artifacts because they are human creations, generated by the activities of authors.[2] Given that the versions of realism discussed in the previous two chapters had special problems with authorial creation, it's appropriate to approach the abstract artifact theory with hearts aglow and spirits racing. I'll start by setting out one version of the theory (based on Thomasson 1999, 2003). Then I'll look at the data that have been used to vindicate it. Finally, I'll give some reasons for rejecting the theory.

5.1 Abstract artifact theory

Think about contracts and marriages. They have no spatial location. A marriage ceremony is performed in a particular place, but the marriage itself is not confined to that place. It's not right to say that as the happy couple leave the place at which the rites were performed, the marriage moves with them. It's not the sort of thing that can move (or be still). Marriages and contracts are not purely mental: a contract or marriage may obtain even if all parties have totally forgotten about it. Yet they are produced by human activity, governed, as most activity is, by norms and conventions. If you have gone through a certain procedure, signed your name in certain places, said certain things in the presence of witnesses, then you are married, like it or not, and whether you or anyone else knows it or not. A marriage has been brought into existence. It may or may not be your first: marriages can be counted. It may not have come into existence until you were adult: marriages have starting dates. It may be dissolved: marriages may have ending dates (even before death do us part).

The abstractist idea is that we should think of fictional characters as abstract artifacts like marriages and contracts. Several questions need to be answered:

1   How do they first come into existence?

2   Can they go out of existence? If so, how?

3   Can the same fictional object occur in different works? If not, why not? If so, under what conditions?

Initial answers might be as follows:

1'   They come into existence thanks to the actions and intentions of story-tellers and related artists.

2'   They go out of existence if all relevant texts and memories are destroyed.

3'   The same fictional object can appear in distinct works if, and only if, one author defers to the intentions and creations of another.

We'd also need to say how fictional objects feature in the things we say and think: if we think that Anna Karenina deserved her fate, is the object of our thought something abstract? (Being under a train doesn't seem a possible property for an abstract thing.) What if we think she was more intelligent than Emma Bovary? (Being intelligent doesn't seem a possible property for an abstract thing.) And if we think she did not really exist? (The relevant abstract things presumably do exist, according to the abstract artifact theory.) As these questions suggest, developing the theory requires attention to a number of significant and detailed issues.

You have to be a space-occupier to smoke a pipe. If Sherlock Holmes is an abstract artifact, he's not a space-occupier, and so did not smoke a pipe. Yet the stories say he did. Like many stories, they speak falsely, and we should not be surprised, since truth, or at least humdrum everyday truth, is not a goal of fiction. Here we encounter the first rough edge of abstract artifact theory: fictional characters are abstract but are written about as if concrete. They are ascribed properties appropriate to concrete things, not to abstract things. One way to deal with the problem is to say that properties can be related to abstract artifacts in two ways. An abstract artifact can *exemplify* a property. For example, all abstract artifacts exemplify the property of being abstract and of having been created by human agency. An abstract artifact can also *encode* a property:[3] for example, the Sherlock Holmes abstract artifact encodes the property of being a detective and playing the violin, properties which it could not possibly exemplify. The encoded properties are those ascribed in the story, the exemplified properties are those the entity really possesses. Sherlock Holmes encodes but does not exemplify the property of being a detective. It follows that he exemplifies the property of encoding being a detective. He exemplifies but does not encode the property of having been created by human agency. He encodes the property of having been born, a physical process available only to occupiers of space.

Abstract artifact theorists will find it tempting to see some kind of ambiguity in predication. Read as exemplification "Holmes smoked a pipe" is false; read as encoding, it is true. This has its advantages. For example, the ambiguous sentence "Holmes is famous" can be regarded as ambiguous precisely between exemplifying and encoding: Holmes exemplifies being famous but does not encode it. As we will see, the ambiguity is also the focus of various problems.

The selection problem which dogged both Meinongian and nonactualist theories seems not to arise for abstract artifact theories. Meinongians and nonactualists are committed to there being a cloud of nonexistent or nonactual objects at the time of the creation of a fictional character, and the problem was to say what made it the case that the author selected one rather than another of these. (Think how terrible it would have been if Conan Doyle, by some ghastly accident, had lighted upon Kilgore Trout, and said it was he who lived in Baker Street, smoked a pipe, and so on.) By contrast, for abstract artifact theories there are no relevant objects around just before the creative moment. The objects begin to exist only as the author starts to tell the story. She does not have to select, only to narrate. Abstract artifacts are individuated by the act which brings them into existence. As we've seen, we intuitively count Menard's Don Quixote as distinct from Cervantes'. No problem: they are created by different people at different times, so of course they are distinct.[4]

Are impossible fictional characters, time travelers and circle-squarers, impossible abstract things? If so, then surely they cannot exist. An abstract thing cannot exemplify a property and its negation but it can encode such a pair. There's no contradiction in that. Similarly I can make this very piece of paper encode something impossible, by writing something of the form P and not-P, but this does not make the piece of paper itself impossible.

Are incomplete fictional characters (every character is an example) incomplete abstract things? If so, then surely they cannot exist. The same answer is appropriate as to the question about impossibility: an abstract thing is not in itself incomplete, since for every property, it exemplifies that property or its negation. But it may encode incompletely, neither encoding having an even number of hairs nor encoding having an odd number.

That is a first rough account of the nature of abstract things (or the nature of them according to the version I wish to discuss). Now let's see how it is to be applied.

5.2 Applying abstract artifact theory

Once we have abstract artifacts to work with, we can ask in more detail how they relate to our thought and talk. How exactly do they feature in the creative act? How do they connect with language?

Some creative acts involve assembly. Might we use this as a model for the creation of abstract fictional characters? Kit Fine entertains the thought that we can:

> [T]hey come into being as the result of [the appropriate activity of the author], in much the same way as a table comes into being as the result of the activity of a carpenter. (Fine 1982: 130)

The problem is to say what analogue of planks and glue is available to the author. There are words, of course, or images, or paint; but these do not end up as parts of the abstract object, as planks and glue end up as parts of the table. Perhaps the author assembles properties, bundling them together to make the character. Are the relevant properties things like *being a detective*? Or are they things like *encoding being a detective*? An abstract artifact exemplifies the second kind of property but not the first. Authors, if they take themselves to be dealing with properties at all, take themselves to be dealing with properties like the first: *being a detective*. The abstract artifacts don't exemplify these properties, so it's unclear in what sense they are constituted by a bundle of them. In any case, nothing in authorial activity amounts to the mere mention of a property; in the creation of fiction, properties are *ascribed* (or at least the author goes through the motions of ascribing them). In standard cases, there needs to be an object to receive them, so it's hard to think of that object as somehow constituted by the properties ascribed, since the object needs to be in place for the ascription to have a target.

Abstract artifact theorists generally think that creation is effortless, both authorially and philosophically. Here's an early account, by John Searle:

> [B]y pretending to refer to a person she [Iris Murdoch] creates a fictional person. ... she does not really refer to a fictional character because there was no such antecedently existing character; rather, by pretending to refer to a person she creates a fictional person. Now once that fictional character has been created, we who are standing outside the fictional story can really refer to a fictional person. (Searle 1975: 330)

And here, more recently, is Stephen Schiffer:

> [F]ictional entities are created in a straightforward and unproblematic way by the pretending use of names: the fictional entity Jonathan Pine was quite literally and straightforwardly created by John le Carré's use of "Jonathan Pine" in order to pretend, in the way definitive of fiction, to refer to a real person. (Schiffer 1996: 157)

One can question whether Murdoch or le Carré were *pretending* (at least intentionally) to refer to a real person. A paradigm way of doing that would be to engage in ordinary assertive behavior but slip in a name without a bearer, pretending that it has a bearer. By contrast, authors are engaged in the distinctive act of telling a story, inviting their audience to make-believe in Second Lieutenant Andrew Chase White and Jonathan Pine. They don't need to pretend that these are real people. Clearly, there's no real person that Murdoch or le Carré pretended to refer to.

What relevance does the "way definitive of fiction" have to the creative act? Suppose I wish to deceive you about my activities last night. I stayed at home working, but I want you to think I was out partying.

Me: I met Robert Smith at the party last night.
You: Who's he?
Me: A lawyer. Very interesting guy.

There is nothing problematic about this being a perfectly intelligible exchange, even though I met no one, and the name "Robert Smith" was a spur of the moment invention (perhaps transparently unimaginative). I did not have intentions definitive of fiction. I wanted you to believe what I said, whereas fictional authors intend only that their audience make-believe what they say. Does that mean I did not create an abstract object? Could such a nuanced difference in intention make the difference between whether or not I created a new object? We can continue to "talk about" Robert Smith, just as we can "talk about" fictional characters, and can correctly say things like: you just made him up; there's really no such person. So perhaps abstract artifact theory should extend its scope: perhaps abstract artifacts rush in wherever there is failure of ordinary reference. It would be structurally like Mill's view ("All names are names of something, real or imaginary": 1843: 27), with "concrete or abstract" replacing "real or imaginary".[5] We'll see that this extension of the theory exacerbates some of the problems that confront it.

Let's look more closely at authorial intentions. The abstract artifact Sherlock Holmes could not possibly have played the violin, since violin-playing involves occupying space. So what was Conan Doyle doing, ascribing *being a violin-player* to a kind of entity that could not possibly possess it? We all know that fictional sentences may well not be intended to be true, but this attribution seems more like a "silly mistake" (van Inwagen 1977: 306) than a careful piece of story-telling. And what are readers doing, when they think that, at least according to the story, Holmes plays the violin? Are they swallowing the same kind of nonsense as if they thought some story said that the number 2 played the violin?

The abstract artifact theorist can adopt one or both of two lines of defense. On the one hand, he can stress the distinction between de re and de dicto beliefs. General beliefs, like the belief that there are cats, are examples of de dicto beliefs. The target of a de dicto belief is simply a proposition. We can also form de re beliefs, beliefs whose target is some object: one believes, concerning that object, that it is thus-and-so. In the examples that follow, the first attributes a de re belief to Sally, the second a de dicto one:

> Concerning the evil man next door, Sally believes he is the soul of kindness.
>
> Sally believes that the evil man next door is the soul of kindness.

If the first attribution is correct, Sally has made a bad mistake, but it's an intelligible one: we are often taken in by appearances, and it may even be perfectly rational (and warm-hearted) to be so in this case (if the neighbor, cunning as well as evil, skillfully cloaked his true nature). The second attribution, by contrast, represents Sally as close to contradicting herself, and is hard to take seriously. (To take it seriously we feel we should insert inverted commas around "the evil man next door" to indicate that what Sally really believes is something like: The man next door that people say is so evil is the soul of kindness.) Abstract artifact theorists can say that authors and audiences don't have to think of abstract artifacts *as* abstract artifacts in order to say and think things about them, for the relation can be de re rather than de dicto. Nathan Salmon puts the point like this:

> In reading a piece of fiction, do we pretend that an abstract entity is a prince of Denmark (or a brilliant detective, etc.)? ... Taken *de dicto*, of course not; taken *de re*, exactly. That abstract entities are human beings is not something we pretend, but there are abstract entities that we pretend are human beings. (Salmon 1998: 316 n.45)

That's the first line of defense. It won't work for the creative act itself, since until the creation has occurred there is no object fit to be the target of a de re belief, or of the de re ascription by an author of a property to a character. Setting that aside, Salmon's view still involves attributing error to ordinary people, producers and consumers of fiction alike. For people do take it that, in thinking and talking about fictional characters like Sherlock Holmes, they are thinking and talking about concrete things, things who could in principle be detectives or play the violin.

The other line of defense plays up the distinction between exemplifying and encoding. If we refer to the abstract artifact Sherlock Holmes and say he encodes the property of being a detective, we make no mistake. He does encode it, though he doesn't exemplify it. This means that once Holmes is on the scene, we can understand attributions to him as the correct attribution of encoded properties rather than the "silly" attribution of exemplified properties. Likewise with the creative process. When Doyle writes for the first time "Holmes played the violin" we should regard him as attributing the encoding of the property of playing the violin. As a result, the abstract artifact comes genuinely to exemplify the property: *encoding playing the violin*.

True enough, even with this line of defense the theory must be fairly lavish in its ascription of error, for neither producers nor consumers of fiction think of things like Holmes and Kilgore Trout as abstract. But what would be the point of doing philosophy if we were not open to the thought that we have hitherto been wrong about something? We don't have to think of something as what it is in order to think of it and talk about it.

Some versions of abstract artifact theory (e.g. van Inwagen's 1977) dispense with these entities in an account of the creative process, and introduce them only for critical purposes. It's in the mouths of critics (amateur or professional) that purely fictional names come to have abstract things as their referents. What's true is that when we turn, as we shortly will, to considering what role abstract objects can play in semantics, it's in the context of critical discussions that they are most needed. So the bulk of the evidence is drawn from that region of speech. We should not conclude, however, that we ought to see some kind of ambiguity or polysemy in fictional names, sometimes (in story-telling) used with no semantic referent, at other times (in critical talk about the fiction) with an abstract artifact as referent.[6] In Salmon's image (1998: 298), now we have our "expensive Italian sports car" (the abstract artifacts) we should drive it as much as possible. As he puts it:

> One need not claim, as Kripke does, that a name like "Sherlock Holmes" is ambiguous. ... the sentences of the Sherlock Holmes stories ... literally make reference (although their author may not) to the fictional character, and literally express things about that character (mostly false). (1998: 298, 302–3)

It's not merely that we might as well see reference to abstract artifacts everywhere if we see it anywhere. There are at least two further reasons not to ascribe polysemy or ambiguity. As Kripke himself says elsewhere, one should not posit ambiguity unless the data directly confirm it.[7] In the present case, speakers have no conscious awareness of ambiguity, and have no problems, or sense of zeugma, confronted with anaphoric linkages across what ought to be distinct uses of the name, as in "Kilgore Trout is a writer, and one of Vonnegut's most engaging creations." Secondly, one would miss out on what to me is one of the most attractive features of abstract artifact theory, its ability to explain authorial creation as literally bringing something new into existence. It's authors who do that, not critics. If we adopt the more uniform picture of fictional names as having abstract artifacts as their referents wherever they occur, then we have to say that, for example, Conan Doyle genuinely ascribed the property of being a violin-player to Holmes, and, from the point of view of abstract artifact theory, to say that Holmes encodes this property is to say no more than this.

5.3 Motivating abstract artifact theory

Much of the motivation comes from the general features of our discourse which seem to demand realism of some kind. The specific motivations are those that distinguish the abstract artifact version of realism from the others.

One quite elaborate series of motivating considerations has been provided by Peter van Inwagen. As set out in "Creatures of Fiction" (1977), his view can be summarized as follows:

1. There is no good ground for adopting Meinongian views. On the contrary, everything exists. Although van Inwagen is not entirely explicit, he's probably disposed to take a similar line against nonactualism: everything is actual. Putting these views together yields: everything is an actual existent.

2. He gives examples which, he thinks, can only be accommodated by adopting a realist ontology of fictional characters. We've encountered some of these already, and we'll shortly look at them in more detail.

3. Putting these claims together ensures that fictional characters are real, actual existents.

4. Since they are not mental and are not in space, they count as abstract entities.[8]

I mentioned (in passing) that van Inwagen's version of abstract artifact theory has it that authors of fiction do not express propositions, true or false, which suggests that he does not see abstract artifacts as the referents of fictional names as these are used in story-telling. He seems to infer this from the fact that, in telling a story, authors don't make assertions. But people can say things without asserting them (jokes, for example), and if someone says something he expresses a proposition and may refer to a particular thing. Accordingly, I will bracket that aspect of his account, and will focus on the examples he gives which he thinks favor realism.

Here are the first two (numbered as in his 1977 text, p. 301):

(2)   Mrs. Sarah Gamp was, four-and-twenty years ago, a fair representation of the hired attendant on the poor in sickness. (Dickens, preface to an 1867 edition of *Martin Chuzzlewit*)

(3)   Mrs. Gamp ... is the most fully developed of the masculine anti-women visible in all Dickens's novels. (Sylvia Bank Manning, *Dickens as Satirist*, New Haven, 1971: 79)

Van Inwagen stresses that these are not examples in which "Mrs. Gamp" is used within the fiction, as part of the telling of a story. Thus used, there would typically be no commitment to truth. By contrast, standard uses of (2) and (3) are about the novel, and are used assertively: when Dickens wrote (2) and Manning (3), they thereby committed themselves to speaking truly. The assertions seem to be about someone called "Mrs. Gamp". Van Inwagen says we should take this appearance "at face value": (2) and (3) (and similar sentences) can properly be used assertively, and their truth requires that there be an entity called Mrs. Gamp. Given van Inwagen's refusal to accept Meinongian views, and his implied actualism, this entity has to be existent and actual, and hence nonconcrete.

Rather than spend much time trying to justify the literal truth of (2) and (3) directly, and their entailment of Mrs. Gamp's existence, van Inwagen (1977) turns to a more general realist claim, that *there are such things as characters in novels*. With this in place, he thinks one can but interpret (2) and (3) as involving reference to such things. This strategy of making generalizations the first wave of the defense of realism is also at work in a later paper (2003). Here are the examples:

(4)   There are characters in some nineteenth-century novels who are presented with a greater wealth of physical detail than is any character in any eighteenth-century novel.

(5)   Some characters in novels are closely modeled on actual people, while others are wholly products of the literary imagination, and it is usually impossible to tell which characters fall into which of these categories by textual analysis alone.

(6)   Since nineteenth-century English novelists were, for the most part, conventional Englishmen, we might expect most novels of the period to contain stereotyped comic Frenchmen or Italians; but very few such characters exist. (Van Inwagen 1977: 302)

Van Inwagen insists that these sentences are true, are to be interpreted "at face value", and entail that there are characters in novels. If that's so, then, he argues, it cannot be disputed that Mrs. Gamp is one of them, so we can see each of the earlier singular sentences ((2) and (3)) as requiring the existence of a fictional entity.

Van Inwagen sometimes expresses his desired conclusion in terms that an irrealist can happily accept:

> There are such things as characters in novels. (1977: 302)
>
> There are fictional characters. (2003: 137)

An irrealist can regard "in novels" as functioning as a fiction operator, in which case the 1977 conclusion is, to a first approximation, nothing more than the uncontroversial one that, in novels, there are characters. As for the 2003 conclusion, an irrealist, as we have already seen, can say that "fictional" functions as a fiction operator, so that, to a first approximation, "there are fictional characters" says no more than that, according to some fictions, there are characters, and this is no basis for realism.[9] If his paper is to be of interest, we need to regard his conclusion as what we earlier expressed by the sentence: there are *robust* fictional characters, objects that belong to our reality, and not merely to whatever scenes are portrayed in the fiction.

The irrealist's deflating paraphrase is not quite accurate, and may best be presented as replacement rather than paraphrase (see chapter 6 for the distinction).[10] The alleged paraphrase is consistent with the fiction taking an entirely general form, not using proper names or other definite expressions. If a fiction says that on a bleak day in December, lots of people were gathered on the Glienicke Bridge, but mentions no person in particular (and never offers anything singular in the rest of the tale), then according to the fiction there are characters. But that's not what people have in mind when they say that there are fictional characters. They have in mind fictions with specific singular terms, like "Sherlock Holmes" and "Kilgore Trout". A fully correct fictionalist account needs to recognize this specificity. I think it can be done quite easily: according to some fiction, there are *specific* fictional characters.[11]

There's also a question of whether what the irrealist offers meets a certain familiar but very demanding notion of paraphrase, according to which a paraphrase should not only have just the same truth conditions as its target sentence, but should also reveal the semantic mechanisms or logical form of the target. In the present context, irrealists can work with a much less demanding notion. They can challenge realists to explain why anyone would wish to say more than that, in novels, there are specific characters, or more than that, according to some fictions, there are specific characters. The realist will no doubt rise to the challenge, offering some of the more problematic sentences we have been discussing, like the "Mrs. Gamp" sentences. The irrealist should accept that this is a proper response, but it's one that accepts that no significant probative force attaches to our inclination to affirm that there are fictional characters, or characters in novels. Otherwise the more detailed examples, like the Mrs. Gamp sentences, would be otiose. (Section 6.3 offers more explanation of various kinds of paraphrase.)

The sample sentences ((4)–(6)) are logically very complex, involving generics, plurals, a seeming fiction operator ("in novels"), and other tricky constructions. This makes it hard to see exactly what is supposed to be doing the pro-realist work. In the next couple of pages, I'll try to separate out the contribution of some of these various idioms.

Let's simplify (6) to:

6*   Few nineteenth-century English novels contain stereotyped comic Frenchmen.

On one reading, this is just a case of embedding in a fiction operator, brought out as follows:

6'   According to few nineteenth-century English novels are there stereotyped comic Frenchmen.

The irrealist has no problem with this for a familiar reason: the quantification over stereotyped Frenchmen occurs within the scope of a fiction operator. There may also be a distinct reading of (6*). It's one thing for a novel to present a character as stereotyped, another for a presented character to be in fact stereotyped. The former state of affairs uses the notion of a stereotype from within the world of the novel, and the relevant stereotypicality is what the author takes to be such; the latter uses it from outside, and the relevant stereotypicality is what we take to be such, even if this notion has not impinged on the author. (6*) is most naturally read as employing the notion of stereotypicality internal to novels, and this is captured by (6′). For a more external reading, I would suggest the following:

6″ There are properties, F, which are distinctive of stereotyped comic Frenchmen, and according to few nineteenth-century English novels are there characters with F.

It's hard to see any special problems for the irrealist in such examples. The ambiguous (6*) can be disambiguated precisely either as (6′) or as (6″).

Van Inwagen's (4) and (5) pose more severe problems for an irrealist. In these cases, I think we can bring out what is doing the main pro-realist work by focusing on these predicative expressions:

4* x is presented in novel y in more detail than x′ is presented in novel z.

5* x in novel y is modeled on z (an actual person).

It's natural to say that these predicates are (genuinely, not just fictionally) satisfied, and that means: satisfied by (genuine) entities. So there are genuine entities corresponding to the "x" variables, and it's these entities that are called fictional characters. That's a serious argument for realism.

But not necessarily a decisive one. The core issue (as I've identified it) is whether we can treat these predicates "at face value". Here's an initial reason for suspicion. No one would take the following seriously as an argument for the reality of unicorns:

Many unicorns are represented as about the size of a horse. Therefore, there are many unicorns.

A standard labeling of the phenomenon (it hardly deserves to be called an explanation) is that verbs like "is represented as", along with "thinks about", "looks for", and many others, are to be classified as "intensional verbs". The key feature is that sentences built from these can be true even though nothing satisfies the predicate. "John thought about Pegasus" can be true, even though it is not made true by some object that satisfies the expression "John thought about x"; likewise for the other cases.[12]

Even to describe intensional verbs in this way is controversial, for a realist will deny that the sentences built from them can be true even though nothing satisfies the predicate. Realists will insist that what we have is not absence of satisfaction, but satisfaction by exotic entities, ones that are nonexistent, nonactual, or nonconcrete.

A proper defense of irrealism must include an account of intensional verbs. If there is no account to be had, irrealism fails. But if there is a good irrealist account of intensionality, as I claim in the next chapter there is (chapter 6), then one cannot use the truth of sentences built from intensional verbs to argue for realism.

Returning to van Inwagen, the core components of his examples (4) and (5) are intensional verbs derived from "x is presented ..." and "x is modeled on ...". If these are to be taken at face value, then indeed realism is true. But we know from the example of the many unicorns that they are not to be taken at face value, or not always. Only a fairly lengthy discussion can resolve the issue, and that awaits the next chapter.

Van Inwagen's strategy was to use examples (4)–(6) to establish that there are robust fictional characters, and then return to (2) and (3). Even if one thought that this strategy is moot until the question of intensional verbs has been resolved, one might think that (2) and (3) already give powerful reasons for realism, with no help from (4)–(6). If (2) and (3) (repeated below) are subject–predicate truths, it seems hard to deny that there is such an entity as Mrs. Gamp.

(2)   Mrs. Sarah Gamp was, four-and-twenty years ago, a fair representation of the hired attendant on the poor in sickness.

(3)   Mrs. Gamp ... is the most fully developed of the masculine anti-women visible in all Dickens's novels.

The irrealist, however, will deny that they are subject–predicate truths. Once again the examples are quite complex, and many of the complexities are doing no special pro-realist work. Let's consider a simplified variant of (2):

2*   Mrs. Sarah Gamp was a hired attendant on the poor in sickness.

The irrealist will say that if we take this to be true, we are taking it to be implicitly qualified by a fiction operator ("according to *Martin Chuzzlewit*"). Unqualified, it can at best be faithful to the stories, and perhaps people sometimes use "true" to express this property. So far, no problem for the irrealist.

The actual example (2) is trickier, because it involves a fiction–reality comparison. What Dickens wanted to convey was that, when he wrote the novel 24 years earlier, the fictional character Mrs. Gamp was typical of the sort of person then hired to attend the poor in sickness. The essential apparent relation here is similarity: Mrs. Gamp is similar to the people typically hired to attend the poor in sickness. "Is similar to" is an example of an expression that has been categorized as intensional, and so as requiring special semantic treatment. It's natural to think that a cloud can be similar to a unicorn, even if there are no unicorns. Few would be tempted by the following argument: "Unicorns are similar to horses. So there are unicorns." We have made no progress: we know that realists can at least begin to tell a semantic story for intensional verbs in a natural way, based on the idea that the verb expresses a genuine relation, and that irrealists will try to resist, pointing out (as in some of my unicorn examples) that we certainly don't always want to draw realist conclusions from sentences built around such verbs.

(3) requires us to take into account a rather subtle distinction, which one might express as that between the operators "according to the novel" and "in the novel".[13] The latter can be followed by the kind of remark a literary critic could make. So we have as true

In the novel, Mrs. Gamp is a fully developed character

even though replacing "in the novel" by "according to the novel" yields a falsehood: according to the novel, Mrs. Gamp is a person, and not the kind of thing that can be "developed" or not (in the intended sense). We cannot assume that, just because "According to the novel, *p*" can be true when *p* is not, the same goes for "in the novel, *p*". Arguably, the sentence just displayed can be true only if Mrs. Gamp is a fully developed character (as this would most naturally be understood). Here "developed" is closely related to "represented": to be fully developed is to be represented in full detail. We saw that "represents" could plausibly be regarded as an intensional verb; the same classification would naturally be extended to "developed". We return to the familiar issue of intensionality.

To summarize van Inwagen's contribution, as I see it: he shows that discourse about fiction involves a number of intensional verbs. (This could be shown with much simpler examples than the ones he uses.) He takes it for granted that at least some such verbs demand realist semantics. He may be right, for all that has been said in this chapter; that question is deferred until the next.

Kendall Walton (1990: 416–19) has offered a different response on the irrealist's behalf. He says that the relevant sentences are not really true; it's just that we pretend they are true in complex games of make-believe. I share van Inwagen's view that this response will not work, though I don't share his reason. Van Inwagen says that it seems obvious to him that the relevant target sentences can be uttered in full seriousness, without any hint of pretense:

> [I]t simply does not seem to me to be *true* that the speaker who utters "If no character appears in every novel, then some character is modeled on another character" (assertively and so on) is engaged in any sort of pretense. (2003: 137 n.4)

I'm not sure that this is so obvious. There is certainly some distinctive attitude in question, even if it is not precisely pretense. Think again of our anthropologist who in full seriousness asserts that the difference between the fisher gods Atlaua and Chac Uayeb Xoc is that the latter was more concerned with the fate of the fish themselves, whereas Atlaua was responsible for the fate of fishermen. The speaker is not committed to there being any such gods, nor to his audience believing (or disbelieving) in such gods. Maybe we can't say that the speaker was just pretending when he spoke: he's at the dais at an important conference, and wants his claim taken seriously. However, he does know that he is speaking from within alien belief systems, not from within his own. Perhaps it's not entirely wrong to say that the anthropologist is pretending to accept the alien pantheon. And perhaps that's the kind of model we should have before us when we hear Walton saying that the utterance of "If no character appears in every novel, then some character is modeled on another character" involves pretense.

Yet I agree with van Inwagen that we do not need Walton's complex structure of pretense-based make-believe games to allow for the coherence of this kind of example, and Walton's approach has difficulty with the details. The crucial point is that it's under our control what to pretend, but we cannot control what is so in the kinds of examples under discussion. We saw earlier that Walton needs to explain why, if Charles's fear of the slime is part of an extended game of make-believe, it strikes Charles as completely out of his control whether to feel fear. If it's a game, why can't he pretend that he is so courageous that he overcomes his fear of the slime? It can't be just that some "rule" of the game prohibits this: rules can be broken, yet Charles cannot but feel afraid. Likewise, our anthropologist will take it that there's only one right thing to say about the Aztec and Mayan gods, however many things there are that could be pretended. Even if pretense is somehow involved in what happens at the anthropological meeting, it's quite wrong to say that our anthropologist pretends that the difference between the fisher gods Atlaua and Chac Uayeb Xoc is that the latter was more concerned with the fate of the fish themselves, whereas Atlaua was responsible for the fate of fishermen. The claim is one he's dead serious about.

There are many ways in which an assertion made in all seriousness may be devoid of ontological commitment. As we'll see in the next chapter, an irrealist has to pay close attention to these.

Thomasson justifies her abstractist ontology as a way out of apparent contradictions in our ordinary talk:

> [T]here are apparent inconsistencies in our ordinary ways of speaking of and thinking about the subject [of fiction]. We want to say, for example, in one breath that Frankenstein's monster was a creation of Dr. Frankenstein, in another that he was a creation of Mary Shelley. (2003: 205)

For an irrealist, there's no problem of contradiction. The context clearly suggests that fiction operators are at work:

> According to the story, Frankenstein's monster was a creation of Dr. Frankenstein, and the story according to which he is a monster was created by Mary Shelley.

In the present case, there's not even a problem about the pronoun. It's certainly dependent on the expression "Frankenstein's monster", but it's well known that it's an oversimplification to suppose that pronominal dependence always involves co-reference (in a sense which would be thwarted by there being no referent).[14]

The upshot of this section is that intensionality emerges as the true foundation of realism about fictional entities. If an irrealist can give an adequate account of this phenomenon, then irrealism will be available in an account of fiction; if not, it will not.

5.4 Problems for abstract artifact theory

Let's start with a difficulty that Thomasson herself, though a proponent of abstract artifact theory, has taken very seriously: how to do justice to the apparent truth of claims like "Sherlock Holmes does not exist." Sherlock Holmes neither exemplifies nor encodes not existing, so the sentence cannot be true if "exists" is treated as an ordinary predicate. Thomasson accepts that under some reading such sentences are true,[15] and proposes that we understand "exists" as a metalinguistic predicate, drawing on an idea she attributes to Donnellan (1974).[16]

> If N is a proper name that has been used in predicative statements with the intention to refer to some entity of ontological kind K, then "N does not exist" is true if and only if the history of those uses does not meet the conditions for referring to an entity of kind K. (Thomasson 2003: 217)

Thomasson begins with the promising thought that, at least in normal cases, negative existentials are dependent upon a previous usage, and the person uttering the negative existential is typically trying to debunk a presupposition of this usage:

> [N]onexistence claims implicitly comment on a prior range of uses (which the speaker supposes to be misguided) ... In making a nonexistence claim, the speaker does not herself intend to use the name "Santa Claus" to refer to a person; rather, she indicts prior uses of it that (she thinks) were made with that intention. (2003: 217)

Her approach aims to do justice to the fact that we need to make room for the falsehood of sentences like "The fictional character Emma Woodhouse doesn't exist." The account also needs to do justice to the fact that if a careless reader got the impression that, in the story, Emma had a pesky kid brother called Fred, we want "The fictional character Fred Woodhouse doesn't exist" to be true. In tablular form, the desired results are:

1	"The fictional character Emma Woodhouse doesn't exist."	F
2	"The fictional character Fred Woodhouse doesn't exist."	T
3	"Emma Woodhouse doesn't exist."	T

The aspiration raises problems, for, unless "doesn't exist" is ambiguous, the first and third sentences can differ in truth value only if the fictional character Emma Woodhouse is distinct from Emma Woodhouse, whereas presumably Thomasson should take them to be the same. Maybe it would be best for the abstract artifact realist to explore treating "exists" as ambiguous, or context-sensitive: sometimes when we use the word we mean to include everything, concrete and abstract, sometimes we mean to include only the concrete. The broader usage is at work in (1) and (2), the narrower in (3).[17] But that's not Thomasson's approach, so let's return to discussing her position.

The first difficulty is that a negative existential, uttered or not, can (apparently) be true even if there is no background of erroneous use. "Sherlock Holmes does not exist" is probably an example, for I doubt that anyone has used the name under the misapprehension that Holmes is a real person. In case I'm wrong about that, consider this example: I tell a story to my children about Fiamma, the fire-breathing dragon. They know it's just a story, and so know that "Fiamma" has no referent, and so they never use the name with a referential intention. Likewise I don't intend to refer to any entity of any ontological kind. So the condition under which "Fiamma does not exist" has a truth condition does not obtain. Hence the account assigns no truth condition to "Fiamma does not exist", yet this expresses a truth, whether uttered or not. Thomasson's account is at best incomplete.

The second difficulty is that Thomasson's account represents a mistake about ontological category as a mistake about whether something exists. A couple of examples. Consider someone who learns the name "Bush" in the usual way, believes Bush was president of the USA, and so on, but also believes that he is an angel not an organism, and that his seeming physical body is a supernaturally produced illusion. I take it that this deluded person uses "Bush" intending to refer to some entity of an ontological kind to which Bush does not belong (angelic), but that the history of this person's uses does not meet the conditions for referring to that kind (the semantic referent of the name, in the deluded speaker's mouth, is Bush). Since our speaker acquired the word in the usual way, the history is one appropriate to the name's referring to an organism, not an angel. On Thomasson's account, it seems to follow that "Bush does not exist" is true, or true in our speaker's mouth, which is the wrong result. For an example in which there can be no disputing the notion of "ontological kind", consider someone who learns the name "Coriolanus" from Shakespeare's play, and wrongly supposes that the name refers to a purely fictional general. (Confession: I was once such a person.) On the abstract artifact theory, this person uses "Coriolanus" with the intention of referring to an entity of the ontological kind "fictional character" (or "created artifact"). But in fact the person, whether she knows it or not, is referring to a fifth-century BC Roman general whose exploits were recounted historically by Plutarch as well as fictionally by Shakespeare. This person's uses do not meet the conditions for referring to a created artifact. So, by Thomasson's account, "Coriolanus does not exist" is true, or true in that person's mouth.

For Thomasson, the point of making the delivery of a truth condition conditional upon a specific range of speech acts, with intentions distinctive of some ontological kind, was to enable her to distinguish the first case in our table from the other two. "Emma Woodhouse" has been used with the intention of referring to things of the ontological kind *fictional character* and all the appropriate conditions for success in this intention have been met, so "The fictional character Emma Woodhouse does not exist" is false by Thomasson's account. By contrast, though "Fred" (we are to imagine) has also been used with these intentions, the conditions for their success have not been met, which explains why (2) is true. If we think of case (3) as somehow related to a situation in which "Emma Woodhouse" has been used with the intention of referring to a real person, then the appropriate conditions for success in this intention have not been met, and so "Emma Woodhouse does not exist" is true, according to the account. The problem is that there's no reason to suppose that "Emma Woodhouse" has been used, in any way relevant to our present discussion, with the intention of referring to a real person. It seems that the condition under which sentence (3) in the table is awarded a truth condition on Thomasson's account might not have been met, even if the sentence is in fact true.

Thomasson implicitly concedes as much. She writes:

> If prior speakers intended to refer to a person by using the name (e.g. "I think I'll hire Sherlock Holmes to solve this case"), then ... (in the context of those presupposed uses) "Holmes does not exist" is true. (2003: 217)

The problem is that the original intuition, that "Sherlock Holmes does not exist" is true, is quite unaffected by whether or not someone has endeavored to use the name with the intention of referring to a real person.

An abstract artifact theorist does not have to take these intuitions so seriously. Why not say that strictly speaking a sentence like "Sherlock Holmes does not exist" is false?[18] Someone using it in an effort to speak truly would be regarded as speaking loosely, and as really meaning something like "Sherlock Holmes is not a real person." People who say things like (1) ("The fictional character Emma Woodhouse does not exist") simply reveal that they have the wrong view of the ontology of fictional characters, (2) is fine as it stands, and (3) is a loose and strictly incorrect formulation of the truth that Emma Woodhouse is not a real person.

I see the problems for abstract artifact theory lying elsewhere, though perhaps unease at the treatment of existence is symptomatic of these other problems. They have the form: on abstract artifact theories, fictional characters just are not the kinds of things we want them to be. We want them to be as they are said to be in the stories, to be detectives and to play the violin, but they are said to be something of an entirely different kind. Let me elaborate.

1   When we think about fictional entities, we do not think of them as abstract. Authors, who ought to know, would fiercely resist the suggestion that they are abstract. Abstract artifact theory entails that producers and consumers of fiction are sunk in error. Fictional characters do not have any of the properties they are ascribed during their creation. This is mysterious: Conan Doyle stipulates that Holmes wears a deerstalker, there is such an entity as Holmes, yet that entity does not end up having (i.e. exemplifying) the property of wearing a deerstalker. He does end up having (exemplifying) a genuine property, that of encoding wearing a deerstalker, but this is not a property that's intellectually accessible to most authors. People can, of course, fail to understand what they are doing, but it's surprising to be told that so many authors, perhaps all, fail so often and so seriously.

2   Although the exemplifying/encoding ambiguity is essential for (this version of) the theory, it imputes too much ambiguity. Let's subscript verbs of predication with "X" or "N" depending as an exemplification or an encoding reading is salient (unsubscripted predicates retain their ambiguity). We don't want the ambiguity to be entirely general: for example, there's no false reading of "London is a city" as "London is$_N$ a city." Moreover, embedding in fiction operators needs to block the encoding reading, for stories tell us that their characters exemplify various properties. The theory does better to say that the predications unambiguously represent exemplification if either there's no fictional name in the vicinity, or the predicate is embedded in a fiction operator. Even with these restrictions, some unwanted ambiguities remain. For

example, it is hard to hear the *false* (N) reading of "Kilgore Trout was created by Kurt Vonnegut."

3 The encoded properties are typically encoded as exemplifications: it's *being$_X$ a detective* that Holmes encodes. But encoded properties may also be encoded as encodings, if there's a fiction within a fiction. Gonzago is encoded as being a fictional king, so presumably has$_N$ the property of being$_N$ a king. Since there's a fictional name present, the exemplifying/encoding ambiguity should kick in, so there should be up to four readings of the claim as expressed without subscripts. This is very implausible.

4 We get an excessive and weird literalism. The Holmes sentence ("Holmes lived in Baker Street") has a reading ("lived$_N$") on which it is absolutely and unequivocally true; that's excessive. Moreover, on this reading, it's not faithful to the stories; that's weird.

5 The distinction between encoding and exemplifying is one that is properly available for representational vehicles, but that's not what fictional characters are. They are what's represented. As an analogy, consider a spot of green paint on a canvas. It represents the emerald on the ring on the empress's finger: so it encodes being an emerald. It exemplifies having been squeezed from a tube. We can happily use an unadorned form of the verb "to be" to express either kind of relation: Yes, it's her emerald; and yes, it was squeezed from a tube. For literary fiction, the corresponding entities are the words or sentences: they can encode living at Baker Street and exemplify having been put together by Conan Doyle. That's all fine, but it's plain that the things that do the encoding are not fictional characters; rather, they are whatever is used to represent them. That shouldn't come as a surprise: to encode is to represent. The abstractist's fictional characters become representations, not the things represented.

6 The encoded representations can't be propositional: Holmes may encode being a detective, but can't encode that Holmes (he himself) is a detective, else it becomes obvious that it is representations and not fictional characters that do the encoding. So encodings are all subpropositional (e.g. being a detective). This means that nothing singular is represented; and this in turn is inconsistent with any normal understanding of what's going on in fiction. I'll conclude this chapter by elaborating this thought.

Singularity is an important feature of fiction: we are introduced to specific people, places, and events, and we engage in singular thoughts about them.

A proper account of fiction must do justice to this, and whereas realist ontology seems in general well adapted to meet this demand, the abstract artifact version, for all its other merits, fails to do so.

Singular thoughts are ones expressed using definite singular expressions like proper names and definite descriptions (as opposed to merely indefinite or general expressions). It's quite natural, though I happen to think incorrect, to suppose that singularity requires an object, and that's certainly an encouragement to realists. The right view in my opinion, though I can't argue for it here, is that singularity requires that thoughts have the right shape for thinking about individual objects even if, as in the case of fiction, they don't in fact introduce objects. Many fictional thoughts have the right shape, and are expressed by sentences containing, paradigmatically, proper names. Let's see if the abstract artifact theory does justice to this singularity.

The problem I see is that all encoding is subpropositional, and is done by objects that are inappropriate targets of the singular thought that fiction needs. What are encoded are properties, not propositions. How do we get from an encounter with a property, as encoded, to an encounter with a fictional character? That which does the encoding is typically not an exemplifier of the property in question, so the fictional character itself, as viewed by the abstract artifact theory, seems to be the wrong kind of entity to be the target of singular thought.

The point can be made another way. Of course, it can't always be wrong to convict people of erroneous thoughts. But let's see how the production and consumption of fiction would look if all parties were conscious believers in the abstract artifact theory, so there are no erroneous thoughts. Conan Doyle wants to tell us that Holmes himself wears$_x$ a deerstalker. It's not that he wants us to believe this, only to make-believe it. While he would no doubt regard it as not really true, he doesn't regard it as a ludicrous falsehood, ascribing a property of a kind that the object of the ascription simply could not have. Likewise, as readers, we imagine Holmes in all his deerstalker glory. But wait: since we're assuming that we know what we're doing, we know that we're imagining an abstract object. An abstract object in a hat? That's absurd.

If we are to do justice to singularity in the realist way, the objects need to be ones that undeceived writers and readers can use as targets for their imaginations. That means that the nature of the objects should not be resistant to the possession of the properties imagination ascribes. Some versions of literalist Meinongian and nonactualist theories do well on this score. The version of abstract artifact theory that in other respects seems most promising fares badly.

Suggested reading

Thomasson (1999, 2003) is a classic source for abstract artifact theory. For some criticisms and a different development see Voltolini (2006). For a distinct argument against abstract artifact theory, see Friend (2007). For a criticism of van Inwagen, see Sawyer (2002).

6

IRREALISM: FICTION AND INTENTIONALITY

6.1 Options for irrealists

> [P]araphrasis ... can enable us to talk very considerably and conveniently about putative objects without footing an ontological bill. It is a strictly legitimate way of making theories in which there is less than meets the eye.
>
> Quine 1969: 101

An irrealist about fiction claims that there are no robust fictional characters; or, at the least, that we have no need to suppose that there are in order to explain fiction. An irrealist about intentionality extends this position to all cases of "aboutness". The central notion is *thinking about*. I can think about Pegasus (a fictional or mythological example) or about a cure for cancer or the brilliant book I never wrote (nonfictional examples). Ponce de León's search for the fountain of youth was "about" the fountain of youth. We may not want to say that this is an example of fiction, but much the same issues are at stake: can there be a search for the fountain of youth even if there is no such thing or no such fountain? Can there be a search for Tralfamadore, even though there is no such planet? If every search needs an object, then the objects of some searches will have to be what I call *exotic*: nonexistent, or nonactual, or nonconcrete (else we will be committed to the falsehood that there is an existent, actual and concrete fountain of youth). Other examples of intentionality are very diverse and widespread. I may need help, even if there is none to be had, may worship Zeus, even if there is no such god, may admire Phaeton, even if he never existed, may fear ghosts, even if there are none; and so on. Irrealists say that we do not need to recognize exotic objects as the objects of such states: in the use of "objects" which matters to ontology, they are states without objects.

Intentionality is typically a feature of mental states, their aboutness. Although usage is not entirely settled, we can use "intensionality" to mark a cluster of features of some expressions, features which make them especially apt to describe intentional states.[1] A central such feature, which justifies the use of the term "intensional", is that the truth or falsehood of a sentence built from such a verb appears to depend upon something other than the extension of the terms in the sentence. The extension of a name is its bearer, of a predicate the things of which it's true, and of a sentence its truth value. An intensional verb like "thinks about" can apparently be used to construct a truth even if one of the terms has no extension at all, as in "John thought about Pegasus" or "Sally thought about a witch." As I'll use the contrast between "intentional" and "intensional", your thinking about London is a manifestation of intentionality, and the verb "thinks about" is an intensional verb. An irrealist will be asked how to understand intentional facts, or sentences built from intensional verbs, without positing exotic objects.

A realist about intentionality and intensionality is one who thinks that intentional states always need objects, which must sometimes be exotic, and that true sentences built from intensional verbs likewise always need relata, which must sometimes be exotic. I think one cannot sensibly combine irrealism about fiction with realism about intentionality and intensionality. Some apparently true sentences in which fictional or mythical names occur are also ones in which intensional verbs are used: "the Greeks worshipped Zeus", "Peter van Inwagen wrote about Mrs. Gamp." We can't very well say that our irrealism about fictional characters does not extend to these cases. Were we to admit that they require fiction- or myth-specific objects (Zeus and Mrs. Gamp), there'd be no reason not to make use of these objects in other puzzling cases, like overt metafictional quantification ("Many fictional characters are rather sketchily drawn"). Once we have extended our irrealism to cases in which fictional expressions occur in the scope of intensional verbs, it would seem mad not to make the further extension to intensionality in general: sentences in which nonfictional expressions fall within the scope of an intensional verb. If we say that the fact that the Greeks worshipped Zeus involves no object, Zeus, we should also say that the fact that Leverrier thought about Vulcan, or that the team looked for a cure for cancer though there is none, involves no object, Vulcan, and no cure for cancer. An irrealist about fiction must deal with fictional expressions in intensional contexts, and this naturally leads to irrealism about intensionality (and so intentionality) in general.

Irrealists are on the defensive, for many idioms suggest realism. We've seen in discussing Meinongianism that it's hard to resist inferring from the many examples of things that don't exist that there are things that don't exist. Yet we've also seen that, on reflection, resistance is required: it's not that there are dragons having the strange property of nonexistence, it's just that there are no dragons. The defence of irrealism consists in stiffening that resistance, case after case. The upshot is not a positive argument for irrealism but, if all goes well, a case for saying that there are no good arguments against it.

I'll begin by listing some moves available to irrealists. Different problems will call for different moves.

1   Paraphrase: The problematic sentence is true, but is equivalent in truth conditions to a sentence which lacks its apparent ontological commitment.

An example is the sentence "There are fictional characters." An irrealist may claim that this is paraphrased by "In some fiction or fictions, specific characters are portrayed", and the latter sentence, it is agreed on all hands, is not committed to the real existence of fictional characters. Having the same truth conditions is a symmetric relation, and sameness of truth conditions ensures sameness of ontological commitment, that is, sameness of the things that must exist for the sentence to be true. The paraphrase strategy is thus in general subject to the response: I agree with your equivalence, but I disagree about which of the equivalent sentences is the best guide to ontology. Someone who agreed that "There's a good chance he'll come" is equivalent to "It's likely he'll come" might use the equivalence to infer that the second sentence was, despite appearances, committed to an ontology of chances. Others might use the equivalence in the other direction. In the present case, there's no disagreement about the noncommittal character of "According to some fiction, there are characters", so the problem does not arise in this form.

A familiar strategy for regaining some asymmetry is to claim that the paraphrase reveals the "logical form" of the original. A logical form is supposed to have entirely "perspicuous" ontology, and so it, rather than the original, should be our guide to the original's commitment. This is a theoretically highly loaded approach, and it would be best if a defense of irrealism could avoid appeal to it. I'll give an example all the same: an irrealist about fiction might claim that to the extent that we regard a sentence like "Holmes was a detective" as true, its logical form is the prefixed sentence "According to the stories, Holmes was a detective." Whereas the original sentence appears to entail that there is such a thing as Holmes, the alleged logical form does not.

2   Rejection: the sentence is simply false, or its supposed ontological commitment does not obtain, and this can be shown directly, without supplying replacement or paraphrase.

For example, some people deny the truth of "The Greeks worshipped Zeus" (while not taking issue with the nature of the Greek pantheon). They will need to explain why so many people think otherwise, but the explanation need not involve offering a replacement or paraphrase.

Another example: I've claimed that "There are examples of Xs" does not entail that there are Xs (replace "Xs" by "things that don't exist"). Some quantifiers are not "over" any domain of objects, as in "There's something John and Mary both are: friendly", so it's open to an irrealist to deny that a quantificational expression requires commitment to objects in a corresponding domain.[2] Paraphrase or replacement need form no part of the strategy.

Rejection can also be qualified in an interesting way. One can reject something as false absolutely, while holding that it is true under a presupposition one is frequently willing to make, even though one does not believe it. One may therefore sincerely assert something (under a presupposition) one rejects as false when the presupposition is absent.

Notions of presupposition have been developed in specific and fairly technical ways in both the philosophical and linguistic literature. An early idea is that a sentence, utterance, or speaker (theories differ on which is the right subject) presupposes something only if that thing must be so in order for the sentence or utterance to be either true or false, or for the speaker to have made a true or false statement. Standard example (Strawson 1950): "The King of France is bald" presupposes that there is a unique King of France. If there is not, one can say nothing true or false by an utterance of this sentence. If there is a unique king, a true utterance correctly predicates of him that he is bald, and a false one incorrectly predicates of him that he is bald. If there is no unique king, there's no predication of one, so neither truth nor falsity is possible.

The notion we need is somewhat similar, but broader. We need the notion of people presupposing something in the sense of taking it for granted for the purposes at hand. This will include the standard case: normally, one who uses "The King of France is bald" to make a sincere assertion presupposes that there is a unique King. But it will extend further, as illustrated by this example:

You: Suppose it's fine tomorrow. What will you do?
Me: I'll go for a walk.

My reply is a sincere assertion; in making it I presuppose that it will be fine tomorrow. But I may not believe it will be fine. How can that be so? For isn't sincere assertion the assertion of something one believes? If one does not believe a presupposition of what one asserts, it might seem that one does not believe what one asserts.[3]

The envisaged notion of presupposition brings with it a notion of relative truth (as we envisaged in the discussion of literalism in chapter 2). It may not be true that I'll go for a walk tomorrow, and I may not believe it's true when I sincerely assert it. That's because the context (in this case very explicitly) demands that I make a presupposition, and the effect of the presupposition is to allow us to relativize the notions of truth and sincerity. (We are not thereby required to relinquish absolute notions: they stand ready and waiting.) I'm sincere if I really believe that, supposing it to be fine tomorrow, I'll go for a walk. That I don't believe it will be fine tomorrow when I assert, under the presupposition, that I'll go for a walk does not convict me of insincerity. This shows that we need to evaluate my remark not for absolute truth, but for truth under the prevailing presupposition.

An irrealist may characterize some sincere assertions made using sentences with an ontology demanding exotic objects as ones made under a presupposition that need not be believed, and hence as assertions to whose absolute truth we are not committed. This may be appropriate to our atheist anthropologists, and to explaining the sincerity of assertions of sentences like "Holmes lived in Baker Street, not Dover Street."

3 Replacement: the problematic sentence does not have to be accepted as true. In its place, we can supply a sentence which serves all the purposes of the original but lacks the problematic commitment.

The replacement approach is less demanding than the method of paraphrase, since the replacement does not have to agree in truth conditions with what it replaces, let alone tangle with the obscure notion of logical form. There's just the vaguer equivalence: the replacement serves all the same purposes as what it replaces. The asymmetry may be said to consist in some more congenial attitude we take to the replacement: we are happier to assert it than the original, or we agree it's "strictly speaking" more accurate, or that "it's all we really meant".[4]

We considered an application of it on behalf of the abstract artifact theorist. While not being willing to say that "Emma Woodhouse does not exist" and "There was no such person as Emma Woodhouse" have the same meaning or truth conditions, the latter (clearly true in the abstract artifact framework) was offered as a replacement for the former (most naturally understood as false in the abstract artifact framework).

The replacement approach has distinct motivations, and also distinct subspecies.

a   *Epistemic motivation*   Russell said we should replace metaphysical monsters with logical constructions. By "metaphysical monsters" Russell meant what we think of as quite ordinary things (tables, rivers, mountains) but which Russell called monstrous because he thought they involved a mysterious or incoherent notion of *substance*. The idea was that the replacing sentences, which referred only to sense data, exhausted the knowable content of the sentences they replaced. The claim that mountains exist, as ordinarily understood, commits one to substances. One does better to replace it with the claim that there are logical constructions out of mountain-like sense data. This enables one to make all the claims to which one is entitled, without sharing the epistemic darkness of the "superstitions of savages".

b   *Ontological motivation*   One might have scruples about whether there are any average families, but it's hard to find a paraphrase for "The average family has 1.3 children." (Applying Russell's theory of descriptions will likely lead to something even more problematic.) Finding a replacement is easy: the number of children divided by the number of families is 1.3. This isn't an account of the meaning or logical form or perhaps even truth conditions of the original (if these commit to the existence of an average family), but operates as a fallback: if ever I am pressed on the ontology of the average family, I'll simply retreat to the replacement. It will serve me just as well, clearly won't commit me to there being an average family, and will bring pointless fretting about ontology to an end without my having to supply any theory about the semantics of "the average family".

Applied to fiction, an example of ontologically motivated replacement is a theorist who concedes that, for example, "Holmes was a detective" *does* require a robust fictional character for its truth, but affirms that it can always be replaced, if needed, by the prefixed version "According to the stories, Holmes was a detective." Believing what the original sentence says is, on reflection, entirely superfluous, for we don't believe that the Holmes stories are true. Everything we really cared about can be expressed by the uncommitting prefixed replacement. The prefixing strategy can thus be treated in different ways: as paraphrase, or as replacement.

c *Loose talk* Variants (a) and (b) address motivations. An orthogonal distinction is how a replacement strategy characterizes what's wrong with what's being replaced. One diagnosis is that it's loose talk: we speak loosely, with technical inaccuracy, but we and our assessors know that we can easily replace the loose talk with something more exact. In this category one could place heliocentrics who speak of the sun setting, special relativists who speak of simultaneous events, and those who, while not being panpsychists, talk of the thermostat knowing the room's temperature. *Loose* contrasts with *precise* or *careful*, so looseness is probably not the right category for talk of the average family or unqualified assertions of Holmes's address, and certainly not for the atheist anthropologists. From the point of view of an abstract artifact theorist, we saw that loose talk might be the right category for the claim that Emma Woodhouse does not exist. The stricter claim, the one that is true, is that there is no such person.

d *Pretense* The role of pretense is subtly different from that of presupposition. Pretense most naturally affects how the force of certain speech acts is to be understood, for example treating what looks to be an assertion as a mere pretend assertion. By contrast, presupposition may leave the speech act categorization intact, for example as genuine assertion, and address only the way an asserted content is evaluated. Reverting to the previous example, I claimed that I genuinely asserted that I would go for a walk. Applying the pretense view, this would be categorized as only a pretend assertion.

Pretense seems to be the wrong categorization for the example of the walk. It would be more appropriate for a case in which, playing (or even initiating) a stumps-are-bears game, I point to a stump and shout "Watch out! There's a bear over there." It seems natural, if not compulsory, to say I'm not genuinely asserting that there's a bear, but only pretending to assert this as part of the game. It seems to me that rather few serious arguments for realist semantics are appropriately addressed by this categorization: realists will (or at least should) offer sentences that we feel disposed to assert as true, not ones we only pretend to assert.

A partially irrealist strategy has been developed by theorists who hold that fictional names are meaningless, because they have no bearers (e.g. Adams et al. 1997; Walton 1990). They have provided some useful specific suggestions about how to deal with pressures towards assigning exotic bearers to fictional names, and I will adopt these at some junctures. For two reasons, I will not follow the general strategy. First, it is quite clear that fictional names prima facie are meaningful. The claim that they are not emerges only within a Millian theoretical framework, and is usually acknowledged as a difficulty for the framework (superable perhaps, but nonetheless a difficulty). Since I see no reason to accept the background Millian theory, according to which every intelligible name has a referent, I see no reason not to accept at face value the natural view that fictional names are meaningful despite lacking bearers. Second, the issue as I see it is set in the wider framework of intentionality, and involves expressions other than names, for example indefinite and definite noun phrases (as in "a cure for cancer" and "the brilliant book I never wrote"). It is obviously wrong to say that such expressions are meaningless, so a different approach will in any case be required to deal with them.

6.2 A first irrealist look at a problematic case

Realists use interfictional comparisons to ground their position. A standard example:

> Anna Karenina was more intelligent than Emma Bovary.

Neither Tolstoy's story not Flaubert's mentions the other, so according to neither fiction is the comparison true; mechanically applying the idea of fidelity will not serve. Realists say that we have to treat the sentence "at face value", as having the overall form "*Rab*", and this requires finding exotic objects as referents for the proper names, else we cannot recognize the sentence as true.

One response open to the irrealists is that, with a little more work (work that in any case needs doing) we can treat the case just like "Holmes lived in Baker Street." As it stands, the Holmes sentence isn't true but is faithful to the stories. If we want genuine truth, then we'd have to prefix it with a fiction operator. This can be thought of as implementing a replacement strategy; or, alternatively (and with a little elaboration) as implementing one of presupposition.

The additional work is to show that fiction operators can agglomerate. Just as we can agglomerate the evidence from witnesses to generate a larger story than that told by any one of them, so we can agglomerate fictions, considering how things are according to both *Anna Karenina* and *Madame Bovary*. The two stories together make it fictionally the case that Anna and Emma both exist and stand in some relation, for example, the one being more intelligent than the other. Writing "F_x" for the preferred fiction operator, F, followed by an indicator (in the "x" position) of a specific story, or text, or suite of stories, or whatever, and enclosing the fictional content in square brackets, the agglomerative stipulation is this:

if $F_a[p]$ and $F_b[q]$ then $F_{a,b}[p$ and $q]$.[5]

When we agglomerate information from several witnesses, it can be the case that, according to the total testimony, p, even if no witness testified that p. Rather similarly, "$F_{a,b}$" is intended to represent what is so according to story a and story b, without assuming that there is a single conjoint story. Agglomerations of this kind are marked by this possibility:

$\lozenge$ ($F_{a,b}[p$ and $q]$ and not-$F_a[p$ and $q]$ and not-$F_b[p$ and $q]$).

Our comparative example could then be regarded as elliptical for:

> According to *Anna Karenina* and *Madame Bovary*, Anna Karenina was more intelligent than Emma Bovary.

We need have no fear that this will have the unwanted entailment that either work says anything about both women. Rather, just as a single work may explicitly say things which commit it to something not explicitly said, so the things said by Tolstoy and Flaubert commit them to assigning levels of intelligence to their heroines which verify the comparison. Analogously, a remark can be faithful (as I believe our target comparative sentence is) to an agglomeration of more than one fiction.

If one is at all sympathetic to the agglomeration approach, I think it should be preferred to a familiar alternative. Perhaps comparatives in general introduce degrees, so that "x is more F than y" should be treated as saying: there are degrees i and j of Fness, x has F to degree i, y has it to degree j, and i > j. The immediate application to our comparison does not advance the situation, yielding the no less problematic:

> For some i, j, Anna Karenina has intelligence to degree i and Emma Bovary has intelligence to degree j, and $i > j$.

The needed further move is to assign the quantification over degrees wide scope relative to fiction operators:

> For some degrees of intelligence, i, j, such that $i > j$, according to Tolstoy's story Anna has intelligence to degree i; and according to Flaubert's story Emma has intelligence to degree j.

Even if we think of i and j as corresponding to imprecise ranges of intelligence, there's room for doubt whether our hard-working authors managed to make a de re affirmation concerning them, one which relates these real mathematical entities to the relevant heroines. In any case, the proposed approach will not generalize. Gregor Samsa was turned into an insect and so had six legs. But imagine a slight variant in which he was turned into some many-legged creature. We know he has lots of legs but not how many. He has more legs than me. But there is no number $i > 2$, such that according to (modified) Kafka, Gregor has i legs whereas I have just 2.[6]

I've shown that an irrealist option is to treat cross-fictional comparisons just as we would simple sentences like the Holmes sentence ("Holmes lived in Baker Street"). Although, as many realists agree, it seems obvious that an irrealist should not be bothered by these simple cases, I've been less than fully explicit about what strategy an irrealist should adopt. Should we say that the Holmes sentence can be *paraphrased* by an operator-prefixed, but ontologically uncommitting, literal truth? That seems to me wrong: the sentences clearly differ in truth conditions. Should we say that the right idea is not paraphrase but *replacement*? That seems better, but how is the replacement justified? Although ontologically motivated, it hardly seems a case of replacing loose talk by something more exact, or replacing something we should at most merely pretend to assert by something fully assertible. (It's true that the prefixed version is fully assertible, but not obvious or uncontroversial that this fails to hold for the unprefixed sentence.) Should we say that we ought to evaluate the Holmes sentence for fidelity rather than truth? Although I think we should indeed do this, it would beg the question simply to assert this to a realist's face. If she is a literalist, she might well agree that we can evaluate it for fidelity, but might be unhappy to agree that we cannot properly evaluate it for truth. We would need to appeal to the kinds of arguments against literalism I offered in chapter 2.

My own preference is to think that we should recognize presupposition-relative assertion and truth. This allows for fully sincere assertions of the Holmes sentence (say in a context in which a less well-informed person has asserted that Holmes lived in Dover Street), along with a matching notion of presupposition-relative truth (i.e. fidelity). The closest rival account would take pretense as the central notion.

Walton's version of a pretense account seems to me vitiated by his requirement that, in singular cases, we not only have to pretend that they are true (when they are not), but also have to pretend that they express propositions, which, according to Walton, they do not. We can elide this feature. Searle's and Schiffer's use of pretense seems to me vitiated by their requirement that the relevant speech act is pretend-assertion, which we have seen does not square with the facts. (There is genuine assertion.) This feature, too, can be elided. The resulting more plausible version of a pretense account entails that in asserting that Holmes lived in Baker Street we are pretending that this is so, and it's appropriate to evaluate our assertion "within the pretense". This is structurally quite similar to the present proposal, but the notion of evaluating within a pretense needs examining. If this means that the assertion must be evaluated for fidelity to the Holmes stories, my irrealist can agree with the account, though the notion of pretense now drops out of view: to pretend that something is so is to be explained as asserting that it is so, intending that the assertion be evaluated for fidelity to some contextually determined fiction. If, on the other hand, to evaluate within the pretense is to evaluate relative to whatever the speaker is pretending, then we lose sight of the constraints that in fact govern fiction-related discourse. We are free to pretend whatever we like, for example that Holmes lived in Dover Street. But if we assert that this is so, we are wrong.

I would extend the notions of presupposition-relative truth and assertion to cross-fictional comparisons. We presuppose that there are such people as Anna and Emma, without believing it, and so genuinely assert the comparisons. If we find ourselves in an unusual situation in which the rule is to say only what is absolutely true, it's handy to be able to fall back on the agglomerated fiction prefixes.

6.3 Marks of intensionality

It's no good being an irrealist about fiction unless one can extend the irrealism to intensionality more generally. There are two reasons for making this connection. One is that fictional or mythical names occur naturally in nonfictional intensional contexts ("I thought about Pegasus all morning"). If the truth of these sentences requires the existence of an exotic Pegasus, our main ontological question is resolved, no matter exactly what we say about "Pegasus" in the context of fiction. Second, fiction is simply a special case of intensionality. Intentionality is the power of the mind to think about things that may not merely be absent, but also, as we are inclined to say, may fail to exist. Intensionality is the linguistic manifestation of intentionality. Fictional writing is a special (systematic and somewhat conventionalized) form of intensionality. So it would not be much good to have an ontology that worked for fiction but not for intensional expressions more generally. Even if the account of fiction that did not extend to intensionality contained no error, it would be inadequate in not revealing fiction as a species of intensionality.

Standard examples of intensional verbs (sometimes referred to as "intensional transitives", on the assumption that they are transitive verbs) include the following:

> searches for, wants, fears, needs, worships, admires, resembles, represents.

Standard marks of the intensionality of a verb V are as follows:

1. (nonspecific reading) A sentence of the form "x Vs a G" has both specific and nonspecific readings. For example, "John wants a sloop" can be read nonspecifically (any old sloop will do) or specifically (John has a specific sloop in mind).
2. (nonrelational reading) On some but not all readings, sentences of the form "x Vs a G" fail to entail corresponding sentences of the form "There's a G such that x Vs it."
3. (object-independence) A sentence of the form "x Vs –" can be true when there's nothing in the extension of the expression filling the blank: if it's filled by a name, the name can be empty, if by a definite or indefinite description, "a G" or "the G", or by a quantifier phrase like "many Gs" or "all Gs", the predicate in the phrase may be true of nothing.

For example, "The Greeks worshipped Zeus" may be true even if there's no Zeus, "Ponce de León searched for the fountain of youth" may be true even if there's no fountain of youth, and "James needs many well-qualified technicians" may be true even if there are no well-qualified technicians.

4   (SI failures) Substitution of identicals may fail for the position that follows V. For example, it may be that I fear Jack the Ripper but don't fear my neighbor, even though Jack the Ripper is my neighbor.

5   (EG failures) Existential generalization into the position that follows V may fail to preserve truth.

One example is when what follows V is an indefinite used nonrelationally, as in one reading of "Jack wants a sloop"; then we don't have "there's a sloop that Jack wants". Another alleged example is "The Greeks worshipped Zeus", which, it is said, is true even though "There is such a thing as Zeus that the Greeks worshipped" is false.

Realists will regard (3) as question-begging. For them, the truth is that there's independence of ordinary objects, but not of exotic objects, which are needed to be what intentional states are about. So let's regard (3) as restricted to ordinary objects.

Quine's early and influential discussions did not distinguish the distinctions marked by (1) and (2). For Quine (in present terminology) all and only specific readings are relational. That misses an important kind of case, the specific but nonrelational one. Jack has envisaged a sloop in considerable detail, and has commissioned full plans and given her a name: the *Mary Jane*. No other sloop will do. Jack's desire is specific, in that it fails the "any old sloop will do" test: he doesn't want merely "relief from slooplessness" (Quine's mark of the unspecific, 1956: 177). Yet something goes wrong and the *Mary Jane* is never built, and so never exists. In this case Jack's desire has the specificity it would have had if it had been relational, even though it is not relational: there is no sloop he wants, no sloop that could satisfy his desire.[7]

The same pair of distinctions can be made for other noun phrases, like ones that begin with "every". Suppose Perseus is a real person who has been duped by a myth about gorgons (the examples borrow from Forbes 2006). In case A, Perseus ends up simply believing that there are some gorgons, dangerous creatures who need to be destroyed. He wants to rid the world of every gorgon, however many there are. A nonspecific reading is called for. In case B, Perseus learns more details: there are just three gorgons, Stheno, Euryale, and Medusa. Rashly ignoring the immortal character of the first two, he plans to kill each. He wants to rid the world of every gorgon; in this case a specific reading is appropriate, even for us who know that there are no gorgons (so the reading is not relational). The difference between case A and case B is that in the latter but not the former Perseus has specific plans and (false) specific beliefs: a belief about Stheno can be distinguished from a belief about Euryale, and so on. The specificity comes from the agent's beliefs, not from the agent's situation, objectively considered. Specificity does not require existence, so we can have specificity without relationality. The same goes for bare plural noun phrases like "gorgons" or "unicorns". In hunting unicorns, Ctesias might have very specific beliefs about which unicorns he was likely to encounter. If so, he would be engaged in nonrelational but specific hunting.

It may be that unspecific readings align with generic readings. In that case, we don't have to regard the availability of such readings as marks of intensionality; they just mark genericity. On the other hand, the distinctions can be straightforwardly represented in terms of nonactual world semantics, in a way that does not extend to other generic uses. Applied to desire, the distinctions are as follows:

- The satisfaction condition for a relational and specific desire for an F is: there is an actual F, x, such that, at every world at which the desire is satisfied, x satisfies it.
- The satisfaction condition for a nonrelational specific desire for an F is: there is a nonactual F, x, such that, at every world at which the desire is satisfied, x satisfies it.
- The satisfaction condition for a nonrelational nonspecific desire for an F is: at every world at which the desire is satisfied, there is an F that satisfies it.[8]

We need to exercise care in another respect with criteria (2) and (5). It may be that Jack wants a sloop even though there's no sloop he wants. But there's something he wants, viz. a sloop. If this counts as existential generalization in the sense intended in (5), then there's no evidence known to me that intensional verbs fail to support existential generalization. For an example with a different category of expression in the object position (a name rather than an indefinite): "Perseus sought to destroy Medusa" doesn't entail that Medusa is such that Perseus sought to destroy her (in the envisaged scenario, there's a real Perseus but no Medusa). However, it does entail that Perseus sought to destroy something (viz. Medusa). I'm inclined also to believe that it entails that there's something Perseus sought to destroy (viz. Medusa, or viz. a gorgon), even though I do not believe that it entails that there's a gorgon Perseus sought to destroy. The "something" quantifier (in contrast to the "a gorgon" indefinite) does not range over objects, in the way first-order quantifiers do. It's more like the "something", noted earlier, in "There's something John and Mary both are: friendly." Likewise, there's something Ponce de León sought (the fountain of youth), but no fountain he sought.

Here are some considerations relating to the logical connections between the last three:

- Suppose mark (3) obtains. Then "*a Vs b*" may be true when "*b*" has no referent. So the truth of this sentence must hinge on some feature of "*b*" other than what it refers to, call it feature F. It's possible that expressions which refer to the same thing differ in respect of F. So substitution of identicals may fail: (4).
- Suppose mark (3) obtains. Then "*a Vs b*" may be true when "*b*" has no referent. In that case, an existential generalization into the "*b*" position will lead from truth to falsehood: (5).
- Suppose mark (4) obtains. Then the truth or falsehood of "*a Vs b*" is sensitive to something other than the referent of "*b*". But this is not enough to guarantee either (3) or (5). (The possibility in question is said by neo-Fregeans to be actual for occurrences of names within propositional attitude contexts: they need referents, and support existential generalization, but don't support substitution of identicals.)
- Suppose mark (5) obtains for "*a Vs b*". The natural explanation is that the sentence can be true even if "*b*" has no referent: (3).
- Suppose mark (5) obtains for "*a Vs b*". There's no inference to (4), since existential generalization might fail even though substitution of identicals does not.

Marks (3)–(5), even taken conjointly, may well not entail (1). For example, "worship" does not have a nonspecific reading.[9] Should we say that it is "less" intensional than, for example, "looks for"? We certainly need to take care not to generalize too swiftly; the different aspects of intensionality relate differently to realist agendas.

Realists are happiest getting us to focus on (3) (object-independence). A realist can happily redescribe the phenomena as cases in which there is genuine relationality after all. In, for example, "Sally thought about Pegasus", a realist can take the appearance of relationality at face value. It's just that Pegasus, the object of the relation, is exotic: nonexistent, nonactual, or nonconcrete.

Realism as such has nothing to contribute to the discussion of either the specific/nonspecific or the relational/nonrelational distinction. Whatever Jack's desires, they are not desires for any exotic object: nonexistent, nonactual, or nonconcrete sloops simply will not satisfy.

Realism also faces a difficulty with (4) (SI failures). According to a realist, sentences built from intensional verbs introduce exotic objects. There's no reason within their perspective why SI should fail. After all, an object is just an object, exotic or ordinary, so it's natural to infer that if a mental state really relates to an object, even an exotic one, it stands in that relation to that object however the object is described. In some cases, for example Sally's thinking of Pegasus, it's natural to say that SI holds. A realist will allow that there are truths of identity relating to exotica, for example, it's true that Pegasus is the winged horse owned by Bellerophon. That Sally thought about the winged horse owned by Bellerophon would appear to be an acceptable consequence (and one rather hard for irrealists to explain).

Graham Priest, a nonactualist realist, accepts that he is committed to SI, and so he seeks to undermine (4) as a mark of intensionality. He assures us that, for example:

> we may insist ... that Oedipus *did* desire his mother. He just did not realize that the object of his desire was his mother. (2005: 62)

Oedipus did not realize that the object of his desire was his mother, though Jocasta was his mother and he desired Jocasta. Intensional operator contexts, like the context induced by "realized that", are ones in which it is widely agreed that substitution may fail, and it fails in Priest's semantics. We should not expect to be able to infer that Oedipus realized that the object of his desire was his mother from the fact that he realized that the object of his desire was Jocasta, even given the fact that Jocasta was his mother. Priest gives one other example (Lois Lane does prefer Clark Kent to Clark Kent, but doesn't know she does this), and invites us to accept that in general substitution is valid for intensional transitives, even though it fails for nominative positions falling in the scope of intensional operators. That's what makes it consistent to hold that Lois Lane does not know that she prefers Clark Kent to Clark Kent, even though she knows that she prefers Superman to Clark Kent.

Perhaps fear is a more challenging candidate counterexample to substitution. Consider how Sally might speak after learning that her neighbor is the

Ripper: "I thought my neighbor was really nice, wasn't afraid of him at all, but if I'd known he was the Ripper, and living right next door, I'd have been terrified." She wasn't terrified of her neighbor, because she didn't know he was the Ripper; that seems an entirely consistent description of a state of mind. But if substitution holds in these cases, it is not. We have to say that, in reality, she was terrified of her neighbor, even when engaged in amicable chats over the fence.

The example is muddied by a contrast between occasion-specific and dispositional conceptions of fear. Sally is afraid of the Ripper, but she's not trembling all the time. Maybe she sweats and becomes nervous when she reads news reports of his crimes against women, but she's not in that state at all times: not when she's concentrating on her work, and not when she's having a friendly chat with her neighbor the Ripper over the fence. Occasion-specific fear involves having fear-sensations; dispositional fear is just being disposed to have those sensations under suitable conditions. Conditions in which an object of dispositional fear is presented in a benign light will not be ones which elicit occasion-specific fear. Sally dispositionally fears the Ripper, and dispositionally fears her neighbor, in that there are situations in which her neighbor is a source of her fear (he is a source of the news reports that make her tremble). But when she is having the friendly chats over the fence, she does not suffer occasion-specific fear either of her neighbor, or of the Ripper.

Using this distinction, we can make sense of Sally's claim without imputing substitution failure. She thought her neighbor was really nice. On the occasions on which they interacted, she experienced no occasion-specific fear of him (or of the Ripper). If she had known her neighbor was the Ripper, there would have been occasions on which she experienced occasion-specific fear of her neighbor (and of the Ripper). But she didn't know. In chatting over the fence, she experienced occasion-specific fear neither of her neighbor nor of the Ripper. This suggests that occasion-specific fear doesn't lead to substitution failure. More controversially, one might be able to extend the result to dispositional fear, though I'll not pursue that.

How should irrealists approach the problems of intensionality? On the assumptions made throughout this book,[10] that empty names can be intelligible, that is, contribute to the expression of a content, and that propositional attitudes are attitudes to contents, irrealists have no problem with occurrences of empty names embedded in sentence operators that express propositional attitudes: believes that ..., hopes that ..., and so on, where the dots are filled by a complete sentence. An empty name in the dot-filling sentence may still contribute to a content, and all that's needed for a (propositional) belief or desire to exist is that the subject be appropriately related to a content. It's therefore natural for irrealists to draw upon the acceptable species of intensionality, the kind found in sentences containing intensional sentence *operators*, to explain the problematic species of intensionality, the kind found among sentences containing intensional *verbs*. Subsequent sections consider ways of implementing this strategy.

6.4 Operator and predicate intensionality: reduction

> Quite typically, intensional transitive constructions have a close paraphrase involving a clausal, or clause-like construction.
>
> Larson 2002: 5

Quine thought that at least some sentences built from intensional verbs could be reduced to sentences built from intensional operators, a view we can label propositionalism about intensional verbs. To the extent that propositionalism is correct, irrealist problems are resolved: assuming the correctness of RWR (reference without referents – see appendix to section 2.4), irrealism has no trouble allowing for the truth of sentences dominated by intensional operators.

Quine claimed that where we have opacity, that is, failure of substitution of identicals, we do not have relationality: a term in an opaque position does not require an object, exotic or ordinary. Intensional verbs, in their problematic form, manifest opacity; Quine explains the fact that they are also not relational by their reduction to sentences with only operator-induced intensionality.

> In the ... opaque sense ["want"] is not a relative term relating people to anything at all, concrete or abstract, real or ideal. It is a shortcut verb whose use is set forth by "I wish myself to have a sloop", wherein "have" and "sloop" continue to rate as general terms as usual but merely happen to have an opaque construction "wish to" overlying them. This point needs to be noticed by philosophers worried over the nature of objects of desire. (1960: 155–6)

The claim is that "I want a sloop" reduces to "I want to have a sloop", which can be regarded as a more idiomatic variant of "I want that I myself have a sloop." In the reduction, "a sloop" occurs only in the scope of an intensional operator, and so the sentence needs no sloop in order to be true.

Pursuing the reduction, Quine suggested that

> The commissioner is looking for the chairman of the hospital board,

in its opaque reading, can be "expanded into" something along the lines of

> The commissioner is endeavoring that he himself should find the chairman of the hospital board.[11]

In these cases, according to Quine, we can have truth even if the hospital board lacks a chairman.

If Quine is right, we do not have to give a direct semantic account of intensional verbs like "want" and "looks for". All the necessary semantic work is done, so long as we can provide a correct account of the operators "– wants that" and "– endeavors that" (1960: 154).

Quine extends his propositionalist hypothesis to lion-hunting, for "hunting is endeavoring to shoot or capture" (1960: 154). He suggests that

> Ernest is hunting lions

reduces to one or other of the following, depending on whether the opaque or the relational reading is salient:

> Ernest is endeavoring that Ernest shoots a lion.
> For some lion, Ernest is endeavoring that Ernest shoots it.[12]

The intensionality of the verb phrase "is hunting" is relocated in the intensionality of the operator "Ernest is endeavoring that". Since we have assumed that sentences in the scope of intensional operators require no exotic entities, the reduction would ensure that the same goes for intensional predicates.

There is room for concern about the details. One may hunt without a gun, so "shooting" is more specific than "hunting". Quine at one point tries "shoot or capture", but there are still other ways of hunting (spears, arrows). Maybe "kill or capture" might be an improvement, though there are perhaps ways of hunting as yet undreamt of (trying to wound without killing or capturing?), so the lesser specificity of the intensional verb, as compared to the operator constructions, is an obstacle to reduction.

A recent defense of propositionalism points to facts about adverbial modifiers. The following is ambiguous:

> Max will need a bicycle tomorrow. (cf. Larson 2002: 233)

It can be read as saying that Max will tomorrow need it to be the case that he has a bicycle (at some future time or other, maybe much later than tomorrow). Or it can be read as saying that Max will (perhaps as early as later today) need it to be the case that he has a bicycle tomorrow. As the disambiguations illustrate, if we gloss the verb "need" in terms of the operator "– needs that" we find two slots in which to insert the adverb: either as qualifying the needing, as in the first reading, or as qualifying the having, as in the second. This may be taken as an argument for the view that, at least in these cases, what we really have before us is an intensional operator rather than an intensional verb.

The argument is interesting but, as Larson notes, somewhat limited in scope. It's hard to get the ambiguities for sentences built from "fears" and "worships", used as intensional verbs. So at best it will deliver a somewhat restricted propositionalism.

At least for Quine, the "reduction" (or as he sometimes says "expansion") is not the demanding "logical form" kind of paraphrase envisaged earlier (though this may be right for Larson's 2002 account). On a logical form proposal, semantic theory would not have axioms for intensional verbs, only for intensional operators. A kind of preprocessing would transform every sentence containing an intensional predicate into its "reduction", containing intensional operators but no intensional verbs. The resulting semantic description of the reducing sentence would then be regarded as providing semantics by proxy for the reduced sentence. Alternatively, and closer to Quine, a replacement strategy would be less demanding, and involve less semantic implausibility. Worried about commitment in your assertions using sentences built from intensional verbs? I'll show you how to use a sentence in which the only intensionality is operator-induced, rather than verb-induced, and which will serve every purpose you were concerned about.[13]

The most favorable cases for the propositionalist strategy are marked by two features. (i) Some verbs, like "fear", can happily take both noun phrases ("fears a unicorn") and sentential complements ("fears that a unicorn will trample her"), so they serve both to build intensional verbs and as intensional operators. (ii) Some verbs, like "wants" and "seeks", suggest end states that can be specified sententially: wanting is wanting that one get, seeking is trying to find, and so on. Favorable as these features are, problems of detail remain. Fear of ghosts does not specify any particular sentence-sized *fear that*: one may be afraid of them without being afraid that they will harm oneself or others, etc. Rather similarly, though wanting a unicorn might be wanting to have one, it might also be wanting one's child to have one, or wanting a unicorn to occupy an empty place on a canvas. In general, the sentences formed with intensional verbs are less specific than those formed with intensional operators, and this is enough to ensure that propositionalist reductions are not universally available. The point affects a weak replacement strategy as much as a strong paraphrase strategy. If you don't know the more specific operator-built fact, then you can't use it to replace the less specific verb-built claim.

Priest urges a restricted propositionalism: it is to apply just to sentences built from intensional verbs which admit nonspecific readings. He thinks that "hallucinates" is a potential counterexample: he concedes that there's no propositionalist reduction, but denies that there are nonspecific readings:

> If I say "I hallucinated a monster", the question "What was *it* like?" is always appropriate. (2005: 67)

The suggestion is that the appropriateness of the question shows there's no nonspecific reading. However, that's not a good test (and also not his own test, earlier in his text). Even for the nonspecific reading of "Mary wants a sloop", the corresponding question is appropriate: what's it like? As Priest implied by his earlier remarks (2005: 64, discussing "Which penny?"), the right diagnostic question is not "What was it like?" but "Which monster was that?"; this should be fully felicitous for all and only specific readings. In the hallucination case, the following answer is entirely appropriate: "No particular monster. Just some horrible monster or other." Compare: "No particular sloop. Just some gorgeous sloop or other."

Priest assures us that "Hallucinating a monster is irredeemably hallucinating *something*, not F-ing *that* anything" (67), so that propositionalism has no toe-hold for this case. But that seems strange. Why shouldn't the case be one in which I hallucinate that I am in the presence of a monster, or that there is a monster before me? This reduction to facts expressed by intensional operators seems as good as any of the others Priest proposes.

Even so, there are many cases in which propositionalism looks very unpromising. Take verbs like "admires", "worships", "paints". Neither on their own nor with the addition of other words do they naturally form expressions which take sentential complements. Admiring, worshipping, and painting cannot exist unless the agent has some suitable propositional attitudes, but no specific attitudes are needed. Hence no sentence dominated by an intensional operator is salient for a propositionalist reduction. We should not count on propositionalism in order to justify a blanket move from irrealism concerning discourse using intensional operators to irrealism concerning discourse using intensional predicates. However, reduction seems appropriate in at least a couple of absolutely central cases.

The first concerns thinking about. To think about something is to entertain a suitably related internally singular propositional content. For example, for John to think about Pegasus is for John to stand in some attitudinative relation to a propositional content expressible using "Pegasus". The content might be that Pegasus flies, though no restriction is placed. The attitude might be that of believing or imagining or simply entertaining the proposition; again, there's no restriction.[14]

One could present the proposed reduction schematically. The proposal is that sentences on the same row in the table below are equivalent:

X thinks about n	For some attitude A and some property F, X As that n is F
X thinks about the G	For some attitude A and some property F, X As that the G is F
X thinks about a G	For some attitude A and some property F, X As that a G is F
X thinks about many Gs	For some attitude A and some property F, X As that many Gs are F

The equivalences are significant because they show that what many people rightly take as the central case of intentionality does not require exotic objects. The possibly empty "intentional object" in the grammatical sense has been safely relegated to an embedding under an intensional sentence operator. Thinking about an object reduces to a proposition-related activity. If the proposition involves an object, as it will if it is expressed using a non-empty name, then the thinking about will also involve an object; if not, not.

Might one not just think about, say, Paris, without thinking any specific thing about it? "Ah, Paris ...!" It seems to me that thinking about Paris must put the city in some kind of light, as attractive, expensive, or whatever, evoking memories, hopes, or plans (the ellipsis in the quoted phrase is not without point); likewise for any object. The light in which my thought places the object provides the predicative material for the propositional content. It does not follow, and is not always true, that what I am thinking, when I think about something, is as salient to me as the fact that I am thinking about it. Maybe I have a hard time recalling what I ascribed to the object, or the light in which I was placing it, even though I am quite clear that I thought about it. The reduction is refuted only by a case in which someone thinks about an object without there being anything the person thinks about it. It's not refuted by a case in which someone thinks about an object without being vividly aware of what they thought about it. I claim that there are no refutations of the proposal.

The proposal says nothing about logical form or semantics. The claim is simply necessary equivalence: all and only the possible situations in which a sentence of the form specified in the left column is true are ones in which the corresponding sentence in the right column is true. For reasons to be amplified in the next section, this guarantees that the sentences containing the intentional verbs do not require for their truth the existence of any exotic objects.

The second important candidate for reduction is

Holmes is famous.

This is capable of being understood in two ways. On one reading, it makes a claim that is properly evaluated for its fidelity to the story, rather than for literal truth. Thus conceived, it's false, for Holmes shunned publicity and allowed the bumblers at the Yard to take credit for his successes. However, understood as a contribution to literary sociology, it's true: Holmes is, as theorists often remind us, more famous than any real detective. Doesn't this strongly suggest that realism cannot be avoided? In particular, it might seem that some kind of polysemous approach is required: on the false reading (the one in which it's a failed attempt to be faithful to the stories) it might be that "Holmes" has no referent, but the impression that it needs a referent for the true reading can be very powerful. Subject–predicate sentences cannot be true unless their subject expressions have a referent; right? And, on the relevant reading, isn't "Holmes is famous" just a true subject–predicate sentence?

I think not. Whatever one's final view about the syntactic–semantic parsing of the sentence, one must take into account the fact that for something to be famous is (and is nothing more than) for it to be thought about in the right sort of deferential way. We have a two-stage reduction: being famous is a special case of being thought about, and thinking about, by the earlier reduction, is essentially a matter of an attitudinative relation to a proposition.

These reductions should be significant encouragements to irrealists. The first is so central that its reducibility is highly suggestive. The target sentence in the second case initially strikes people (or at any rate struck me) as so problematic that it was hard not to see it alone as a sufficient basis for realism. The irrealist cause is well served by being able to put these cases to one side.

6.5 Operator and predicate intensionality: entailment

> [T]here are strong reasons for not regarding "X is thinking of Y" as expressing a relation between X and Y.
>
> Prior 1971: 112

Let's call sentences built from intensional operators "O-sentences" and sentences built from intensional verbs "V-sentences". Let's expand the class of O-sentences to include all ordinary sentences, that is, ones not showing any signs of intensionality, like "London is a city." Here's a two-part hypothesis:

(a) the V-sentences are entailed by the totality of the O-sentences, and so

(b) the V-sentences require no ontology not required by the O-sentences.

This section attends both to the claimed entailment in (a), and to the claimed ontological consequence of it in (b).

The realist about V-sentences who accepts the RWR picture for names in O-contexts is in a rather peculiar position. The RWR view ensures that non-referring names in these contexts are nonetheless intelligible, and can contribute to truths. The realist about V-sentences says that names in the relevant positions in V-sentences do have referents: they refer to exotic objects. If the realist combines this view of the V-sentences with the RWR picture of the O-sentences, she is committed to some thesis of ambiguity or polysemy for purely fictional names. Very likely, the realist would be better served by rejecting RWR. However, I am here taking the RWR approach as a premise.

The imputed lack of semantic uniformity might be discomforting in itself. It seems that once we've learned a fictional name, nothing in our understanding of the name stops us from understanding it either in ordinary sentences like the Holmes sentence, or in O-contexts or in V-contexts. If there's ambiguity here, it becomes mysterious how people in learning one meaning thereby learn another, just as it would be mysterious if somehow learning one meaning of "bank" was always associated with learning the other.

That's exactly why polysemy is a better option for the realist than ambiguity. The idea is that some doubtless implicit general principle gets us from any one of polysemously linked meanings to any other. Normally, coming to understand a new word that manifests container/contents polysemy equips one to use it in both ways. If I tell you that a jeroboam is equivalent to four normal bottles, you should be able to understand both "This jeroboam is made of glass" and "This jeroboam is ready to drink." The close relationship between the meanings of a polysemous expression explains how both (or all) of them can be acquired in a single act of learning. If the various meanings of names are polysemously related, they can be learned in a single act.

It might seem easy to refute the alleged polysemy by reflecting on anaphoric relations. In

Sherlock Holmes is a detective. He was created by Conan Doyle

it seems that our realist will have to say that "Sherlock Holmes" refers to nothing (acceptance of RWR approach) yet that "He" refers to an exotic object (to give a straightforwardly relational reading of the second sentence). If an anaphorically dependent pronoun had to agree in reference with the expression on which it depends, that would be a powerful argument. But we can see in other cases that the principle is false. For example, in

He drank the whole bottle and smashed it to the floor

"the bottle" has its contents reading whereas "it" has its container reading. There's been a shift in reference, despite the dependence. So we shouldn't attack realism on the grounds that its commitment to polysemy prevents it from giving an adequate account of anaphoric dependence.

There are many entailment relations from O-sentences to V-sentences. For example

> Leverrier believed that Vulcan was a planet

entails

> Leverrier thought about Vulcan.

According to the polysemous version of realism, the former sentence does not require for its truth any object, Vulcan, whereas the latter does. Yet the latter gives simply a much less specific description of the very same particular state of affairs as the former. It is impossible to see how the truth of the less specific sentence could involve an entity not involved in the truth of the more specific sentence. Being less specific is not a way to increase the number of entities needed for truth.

For the moment I'll set to one side the question how widespread these O- to V-sentence entailments are, and look more closely at the following general principle, which would vindicate the argument of the previous paragraph:

(*) If p entails q, then the ontology of q does not exceed that of p.

The notion of entailment I wish to invoke is just necessitation: p entails q iff every world at which p is true is a world at which q is true. The ontology of a sentence, as I will use that phrase here, consists in the things that have to exist for the sentence to be true.[15] Otherwise put, x belongs to the ontology of p iff every world at which p is true is a world at which x exists.[16]

(*) itself cannot be disputed, but there's room for dispute about its application. Let's consider an analogy. Quine (1960) aimed to persuade us that there were no such things as sakes. It's fairly easy to give sufficient conditions for the truth of a sentence "She did it for John's sake." For example, it would be enough that she did it to help John. On the other hand, it's hard to give a necessary condition, for there are so many more specific descriptions of activities that would make the sentence true: she did it to impress John, to honor John, or whatever. There's no reduction, yet intuitively, the existence of sufficient conditions in which no overt mention is made of sakes suggests that the apparent reference to a sake in the target sentence is illusory. Here perhaps the argument implicitly appeals to some principle like (*).

There is a familiar methodological difficulty. Perhaps we want to say that, since the entailing sentences don't have an ontology of sakes, nor does the entailed sentence (by (*)). But an objector may use (*) in the reverse direction: since the entailed sentence plainly requires the existence of John's sake if it is to be true, (*) tells us that the same goes for the entailing sentences. We reach a familiar impasse; (*) won't help us solve the general problem of ontological commitment.

The impasse does not arise in the present dialectic. That's because the agreed acceptance of RWR principles ensures that the entailing sentences in (1)–(3) don't have a realist ontology. The dialectic thus ensures we have a firm starting point, and (*) enables us to transfer this to the irrealist conclusion concerning V-sentences. Indeed, in very many cases, as we'll see shortly, we don't even need to appeal to RWR.

There's a small overstatement in the previous paragraph. What RWR ensures is that the names (and other relevant expressions) that tempt us to a realist conclusion for V-sentences don't have referents, exotic or other, as they occur in O-sentences. For most of us, there will be an insignificant gap between that point and the stronger point of the previous paragraph: the entailing sentences do not have a realist ontology. But suppose the exotic entities are necessary existents. Then they belong to the ontology of every truth; so they would belong to the ontology of the entailing sentences.

The view that exotica are necessary entities is not one that, as far as I know, has been taken seriously (though I don't wish to imply that it should not be), so I'm not going to take seriously the task of refuting it. I'll just note a couple of problems. One is that the nonactualist versions of realism cannot accept that the exotic entities are necessary, for our own world is a counterexample. The only theorists who could use the envisaged escape route are those who think of exotic entities either as nonexistent or as existent but nonconcrete. The second point is that the supposed exotic entities are clearly closely related to the contingent. The myth of Zeus does not exist in every world; even atheists who are realists, in that they believe there is such an exotic thing as Zeus (the mythical god) in every world in which the myth exists, might be reluctant to say that there is such a thing as Zeus (the mythical god) in a world that never has contained and never will contain intelligent life.

This is where we stand: we can use (*) together with RWR to establish that V-sentences that are entailed by O-sentences along with neutral sentences do not have an exotic ontology. Hence we can be sure that many of the examples that realists use in favor of their position have no force at all.

In the following cases, the entailed sentence (in italics) may initially seem to pose problems for the irrealist; but, given (*), the entailment shows that the irrealist has no case to answer.

1. "The Greeks thought that Zeus was powerful" entails "*The Greeks thought about Zeus.*" By RWR, the former does not require an ontology containing Zeus, so, by (*), nor does the latter.
2. "Ponce de León has summoned his men and told them that there is a fountain of youth (he heard it from a reliable source), that finding it would enable each of them to attain immortality, and wealth beyond imagination, that therefore they would be starting at dawn the next day, using a rough map drawn by the local informant. Next day at dawn, true to his word, Ponce de León led the expedition up-river" entails "*Ponce de León sought the fountain of youth.*" Since the series of sentences that does the entailing does not have an ontology that includes the fountain of youth, nor does the entailed sentence. This relies on the following assumption, which I take to be uncontroversial (and independent of RWR): it can be true that de León told his men that there is a fountain of youth without there being a fountain of youth.
3. "Conan Doyle wrote certain words (these are specified) with certain intentions (specified using O-sentences)" entails "*Conan Doyle created Sherlock Holmes.*" Since the entailing series of sentences does not have an ontology that includes Sherlock Holmes, nor does the entailed sentence.

Completing the argument requires showing that *every* V-truth is entailed by some set of O-truths (plus neutral truths). I don't know how to argue for that general claim in any tidy or interesting way. I've given a number of examples of the relevant entailments, including ones for what I take to be the trickiest cases (the two reductions of the previous section, and (1)–(3) above in this section). And I offered a general thought (which of course is not conclusive): V-sentences are used to provide an unspecific representation of O-facts. That's where I intend to leave it. However, there's an argument against this position that I'd like to rebut.

Consider those expressions, like "fears", which can be used to construct both V-sentences, like "John fears ghosts", and O-sentences, like "John fears that it will rain." These V-sentences don't seem to be entailed just by O-sentences built around the corresponding verbs. (We'll include the neutral sentences, neither O-sentences nor V-sentences, among the O-sentences.)

The sentence "John fears ghosts" might be true without any sentence like "John fears that ghosts will harm him", or "John fears that ghosts will make the horses bolt" being true. One can fear something in a nonspecific way without fearing that it will do damage or whatever. John just finds something spooky about ghosts, even though there is no truth of the form: John fears that ghosts .... The irrealist should not and need not deny this. The idea was simply that the totality of the O-sentences would do the entailing. There was no restriction to sentences containing operators, let alone to those operators involving only the key word in the V-sentence. In the case of a nonspecific fear of ghosts, the entailing sentences might include: "John avoids the prospect of spending a night in a supposedly haunted house", "If there's no help for it but to spend the night in a supposedly haunted house, John seeks out a companion or keeps the light on all night."

Here's a different argumentative use to which fears that are not fearings-that can be put. Suppose two people fear ghosts, in the unspecific way just envisaged. What, on my account, do they have in common?[17] I say: just that they both fear ghosts. It's true that there may be no overlap in the O-sentences that entail the two V-sentences ("John fears ghosts", "Sally fears ghosts"). That would be a problem were I offering some kind of reduction, but I am not. The claim is only that every V-truth is entailed by some set of truths each of which is either neutral or else an O-sentence. That's enough to do the required ontological work, establishing, by (*), that the V-truths do not have an ontology that includes exotica.

The irrealist can also make use of the entailments in a replacement strategy. If you accept the entailment thesis, you know that, for any V-truth, there are O-truths which entail it. Even if you don't know what these are, you can say: "by my assertion of the V-sentence it may look as if I am committing to exotic objects. But you, O realist, know as well as I do that this V-truth is entailed by some O-truths. So just take me to be committed to some entailing O-truths, whatever in this case they may be."

6.6 Presupposition and relative truth

We writers are privileged: readers take on our point of view with surprising ease.
Arturo Pérez-Reverte, The Queen of the South

So far we've taken for granted that the Greeks really worshipped Zeus, and that Jack really thought about Pegasus. In this section, this is questioned for at least some V-sentences.

"Worship" is standardly taken not to generate an unspecific reading.[18] If the Greeks worshipped a god, it can't be that they worshipped no god in particular. In the tradition of Quine, it's supposed that specific readings support existential generalization, the move from wanting a specific sloop to there being a wanted sloop. If this applies to the Greeks, then there's a god they worshipped. But now we appear to have vindicated the following argument, which has a premise my irrealist has hitherto been prepared to grant, and a conclusion he has denied:

1   The Greeks worshipped Zeus.

2   The Greeks worshipped a god.

3   There's a god such that the Greeks worshipped him.[19]

Perhaps (1) is false. Maybe the Greeks thought they were worshipping Zeus and went through the motions of doing so. Maybe we are sufficiently inclined to roll with their perspective to use (1) to report what happened. But the unvarnished truth is that they did not worship Zeus.

Support for this opinion comes from another feature of worship, already mentioned: it appears to support substitution of identicals (SI). Sally worships the man next door, who is, unbeknownst to her, the most evil person in the world. It seems we must conclude that Sally is in an unfortunate state: she worships the most evil person in the world. Although SI requires that substitution of identicals *always* preserves truth, and so cannot be established by a single case, this looks to be about as hard a challenge to its application to "worship" as one could find. Where substitution of identicals holds, one might well expect that an object is required for truth. The reasoning is not demonstrative, but it is suggestive: if SI holds for a position in a sentence, then what matters for that position is what object is referred to by the term that occupies it; so if we have truth, the term in that position must refer. More than one consideration, therefore, suggests that irrealists should explore the option of denying that the sentence "The Greeks worshipped Zeus" is true.[20] More generally, they should explore the option of denying that "worships" is an intensional verb. If that denial can be rendered plausible, more radical and exciting extensions suggest themselves: maybe even "thinks about" is not an intensional verb.

An irrealist should not simply declare that "The Greeks worshipped Zeus" is false. An explanation must be given of why it has so often struck both ordinary people and theorists as true. The suggestion I'll consider is that, for the purposes of conversation, and sometimes for the purposes of thought, we may presuppose things which we know are not true, and can evaluate other propositions as true or false relative to these presuppositions. In the present case, we presuppose something we know to be false, that there is such a god as Zeus; we can evaluate the sentence about the Greeks as true relative to this presupposition. (We can also bracket the presupposition, and then we evaluate the sentence as false.) By contrast, the Greeks didn't seem to pay much attention to Juno. So, even presupposing that there is such a goddess, we evaluate "The Greeks worshipped Juno" as false; a fortiori, it's false if we bracket the presupposition.

If one makes an explicit effort to block the relevant presupposition, the result is odd, for example:

> There's no such god as Zeus and the Greeks worshipped him.

This is evidence that one who without qualification asserts "The Greeks worshipped Zeus" presupposes that there is such a god as Zeus. Further evidence comes from the fact that one can always bracket the presupposition and say or think something true absolutely instead: the Greeks sincerely engaged in behavior that they would have described as worshipping Zeus, behavior governed by the belief that there was such a god.

Here's a familiar example of presupposition. You are telling your colleague about your departure next day. You know she has classes at the time you're supposed to leave, so you don't think of asking for a ride. However, she says "My sister's free then. She can take you to the airport." You had not previously known she had a sister; but, if the case is normal, you know it now. You would have reached the same state of knowledge had your colleague said: "I'm afraid my sister's busy then too." Either remark presupposes that your colleague has a sister, and you can come to learn the presupposition through hearing a remark which makes it.

Now for a variant that's relevant to the present discussion. Your colleague lives with a female lover. At the beginning, she falsely said the woman was her sister, to avoid scandal. No one cares any more, but she still refers to her as her sister. You know all this; you know she probably knows you know. When your colleague says "My sister's free then. She can take you", you need to be quite sure that this is true. Otherwise, by the time you realize she's not coming, it will be too late to order a taxi. So you press: "Are you quite sure? Can I really count on your sister coming for me?" Question and answer are to be understood as within the scope of the presupposition that your colleague has a sister, a presupposition you both know is false. But for both of you, presupposition-relative truth is a firm and significant notion. You have to explore it if you are to make your flight. You don't believe what you presuppose; you merely "accept" it (to use Stalnaker's term, 1973: 449).

The same account makes sense of the atheist anthropologists. They believe there are no gods, but they presuppose there are many. There is no inconsistency, for it is consistent to believe that p and, for some purpose, accept that not-p. In the heat of academic debate, their presupposition does not come up for evaluation; rather, it serves as a framework against which the various claims they make are evaluated, some as true, others as false. Most or all of the claims would be false if evaluated in the presupposition-free way.

Presupposition, as a theoretical concept, has from the beginning been closely linked with the operation of referring expressions, like proper names and definite descriptions. The present use of the notion connects with that tradition. In the examples, it's the presence of "Zeus" in "The Greeks worshipped Zeus" that makes one who uses the sentence in thought, or who hears it in conversation, roll with the view that there is such an entity as Zeus. In interpretation, one is normally right to take for granted that one's interlocutor's referring expressions have referents. Even in a case in which you know this is false, like the example of Hellenic worship, you still may be right to accept that there is a referent, if you wish to participate in the conversation, or even pursue your own thoughts (e.g. reflecting on the contrast between Greek patterns of worship and Christian ones).

As used in the present context, presupposition does more than simply invite acceptance of referents; it also invites acceptance of things introduced by quantifier phrases. You are a skeptical investigator of a spiritualist séance. The medium says "So many spirits are crying out to me from Lethe, aching for a chance to make contact." You respond: "Does every spirit speak English? Does each have the same accent?" You have presupposed there are spirits in order to open a line of questioning which may serve to reveal this presupposition as false.

Presupposition-relative truth is independent of fiction (as usually understood), as we saw in the case of my colleague's "sister". So it's not an ad hoc device designed to insulate an irrealist from problems special to fiction. How far should it be pushed? I think it makes good sense of literalist intuitions. Sure, we can hear "Holmes is a detective" as true. Earlier I suggested that in so doing we were hearing it in a way better described as faithful than as true. The alternative description is that we hear it as true relative to a presupposition (that there is such a person as Holmes), rather than as true absolutely. From the point of view of ontology, there is nothing to choose between these descriptions. I somewhat prefer the way in which the second so naturally supports interfictional comparison, and also comparison between fiction and reality. Given the presupposition, I can continue the quoted sentence: "and, moreover, a detective who is smarter than any real detective". The addition is not readily explained in terms of fidelity, because according to the stories Holmes is a real detective, and so his intelligence is not to be contrasted with that of real detectives. But the addition is very naturally accommodated within a presupposition-relative framework.

Or is it? Here's a difficulty (pointed out by Emily Caddick in discussion). If, in regarding the sentence "Holmes is smarter than any real detective" as true, we presuppose the existence of Holmes, we presumably presuppose his real existence. But then his fame cannot be greater than that of any real detective, else it would be greater than itself. This shows that an account of what is presupposed needs careful development. Most uses of "real" call for some kind of contrast; here, the required contrast is metaphysical. If we are to presuppose enough to make the sentence true, we must presuppose that there are unreal − here fictional − objects as well as real ones. We presuppose that there is a robust fictional character, Holmes, and it is he we say is more famous than any real detective. Does this sound rather like a realist view? The difference is that a realist says that the sentence is absolutely true, whereas the irrealist says it is absolutely false; and true only upon a presupposition that the irrealist takes to be false.

The example reveals something important about presupposition: its flexibility. There are two dimensions. (i) The presupposed content needs flexibly to adjust to context: in the Holmes example, sometimes we presuppose that Holmes is real, sometimes that he is a merely fictional character. (ii) What is presupposed may shift even within a single sentence. The latter is manifest when we think that the monster was created by Dr. Frankenstein, and is Mary Shelley's best-known character. The first part of the fact requires us to presuppose the monster and Frankenstein, the second shifts focus, and takes us back to presupposition-free reality. (Here I assume that being Shelley's best-known character is reducible along the lines of Holmes's fame.)

The phenomenon of how we can shift between various presuppositions deserves further study. I'll illustrate some of the complexities starting with fiction itself, for authors are adept at producing a kaleidoscope of shifts and turns in presupposition and perspective. (Difference in perspective involves difference in presuppositions.) Here are three examples taken from James Wood's study of how fiction works (2008: 14–22).

The first sentence of Chekhov's story "Rothschild's Fiddle" runs:

> The town was small, worse than a village, and in it lived almost none but old people, who died so rarely it was even annoying.

An annoying fact has to be annoying to someone. We are thus subtly – but irresistibly – shifted into the perspective of the mean coffin-maker for whom death is profit. Yet perhaps in the first phrase we are still within the neutral perspective of the omniscient author.

James Joyce's "The Dead" begins:

> Lily, the caretaker's daughter, was literally run off her feet.

The reader knows that Joyce would not be guilty of the vulgarism of using "literally" in this way, and so infers that we are being presented almost verbatim with a thought which runs through Lily's head. We are immediately within her perspective.

In Henry James's *What Maisie Knew*, Maisie is entrusted to the care of Mrs. Wix, whose own daughter, Clara Matilda, had died in childhood.

> Mrs. Wix was as safe as Clara Matilda, who was in heaven and yet, embarrassingly, also in Kensal Green, where they had been together to see her huddled little grave.

Wood comments:

> James's free indirect style allows us to inhabit at least three different perspectives at once: the official parental and adult judgment on Mrs. Wix; Maisie's version of the official view; and Maisie's view of Mrs. Wix.

"Huddled", as Wood says, is a word that belongs to James himself. It's not a word that either Mrs. Wix or Maisie would have used of the grave. Yet "embarrassingly" belongs to Maisie, who may be using it in a half-understood aping of her parents' being embarrassed by Mrs. Wix, or to reflect her own embarrassment when confronting the contradiction, offered by the "safe" Mrs. Wix, about Clara Matilda's location.

6.7 A final review

I think one should make one concession to realism about "fictional characters". There's a use of "character" on which we can compare people's characters: your character is to be thoughtful and caring, mine is to be impetuous and selfish. It is not part of the present irrealism to deny that there are characters in this sense. In this sense, Holmes too has a character (priggish and vain), and when we speak of character development in a novel, what we say is sometimes to be understood as involving this sense of "character". This notion is involved in the conception of an action or an actor being (or not being) in character.[21]

I believe I have now equipped the irrealist to handle every argument for realism. Let's see how some of these work out. The upshot of the earlier discussion of van Inwagen's arguments for realism (chapter 5) was that there are problematic intensional verbs, like the ones in the following:

1   Mrs. Gamp is similar to the people typically hired to attend the poor in sickness.

2   x is presented in novel y in more detail than x' is presented in novel z.

3   x in novel y is modeled on z (an actual person).

(1) could be regarded as true only relative to the presupposition that there is such a person as Mrs. Gamp. If one wished to say or think something true absolutely, one could replace (1) by something on the lines: the properties that, according to the novel, Mrs. Gamp possesses are similar to those of the people typically hired to attend the poor in sickness.

(2) is a case in which de re specification of levels of detail seems appropriate, for it is the speaker or thinker of (2) who is making an observation about detail. Then (2) is treated as equivalent to, or at least replaceable by: there are degrees of presentational detail, i, j, such that $i > j$ and in novel y, x is presented with degree of detail i and in novel z, x' is presented with degree of detail j. (The "in novel y" operator is, as we saw before, quite different from the "according to novel x" operator.)

(3) can best be understood by some account of the modeling relation as one that ensures matching properties. The account runs something like: z has some properties and novel y was written so as to ensure that, according to it, x has these too.

The following table reports claims made about some of the more simple sentences favoring realism. On the right is a view (or more than one view) that an irrealist can adopt (if there's more than one option, my preferred ones are asterisked).

Problem sentence	Irrealist treatments
There are fictional characters.	Paraphrase: There are fictions according to which there are specific characters.
Holmes lived in Baker Street.	(i) *Faithful but not true. (ii) *True under the presupposition that there is such a person as Holmes. (iii) Replaceable by: "According to the stories, Holmes lived in Baker Street".
Anna Karenina is more intelligent than Emma Bovary.	(i) According to the fictions *Anna Karenina* and *Madame Bovary*, Anna Karenina is more intelligent than Emma Bovary. (ii) *True under the presupposition that there are such people.
x represents Holmes (himself, the real Holmes).	For some F, according to x, Holmes (himself, the real Holmes) is F.
Sally thought about Pegasus.	For some F, Sally entertained a propositional attitude with the content that Pegasus was F.
Holmes is famous (as literary sociology).	Many people think about Holmes (in the properly deferential way).
The Greeks worshipped Zeus.	(i) *True only under the presupposition that there is such a god as Zeus. (ii) *Replaceable by: The Greeks sincerely went through the motions of worshipping Zeus.
Some characters in the *Classical Dictionary* are mythological, but most of them really existed.	Replaceable by: According to the *Classical Dictionary*, there are many characters, some did not really exist but many did.

Let me close by considering a passage Parsons offers as providing strong support for realism:

> I've dreamed about the same unicorn three nights in a row. It looks a lot like a dog I once owned, though the way it talks reminds me of my grandmother. Actually I'm growing quite fond of it, and I'm hoping that it will be back tonight. (Parsons 1982: 370)

The probative force of this passage as an argument for realism is undermined by the reflection that it could be sincerely and consistently asserted by one who does not believe there are any unicorns. This reveals the strength of the presupposition approach. There is nothing surprising in the idea that a vivid account of a dream should require me to presuppose things to exist which I do not believe to exist. It's not as if I take my dreams to be true.

Suggested reading

Forbes (2006) is probably the best starting point for a full-length treatment of intensionality. See also Crane (2001) and Richard (2001).

7
SOME FICTIONALISTS

[F]iction is a syphilis.

Bentham 1845, vol. V: 170

Fictionalists say that some thoughts or sayings are, or can be, or should be regarded as a fiction: the thoughts have value and importance, but, as with fiction in the ordinary sense, this does not consist in their being true. The contrast brings with it an essential contrast of attitudes: the valuable fictions are not or should not be *believed*, for they are false, or at any rate cannot be known to be true; instead the appropriate attitude is one of *acceptance*, a state that may guide action without amounting to belief. Fictionalist views have sprung up like triffids in the last 30 years or so, and have been applied to morals, mathematics, elementary physics, modality, composition, propositions, and even to truth itself.

One main source of fictionalism as discussed nowadays can be precisely dated to 1980, in which year were published two highly influential fictionalist theories: the constructive empiricism of Bas van Fraassen's *The Scientific Image*, and the mathematical fictionalism of Hartry Field's *Science without Numbers*. In this chapter I'll start by indicating some candidates for precursors of these towering works, and will conclude by giving a brief description of each. The focus is on what makes a position count as fictionalist.

7.1 Early history

Every philosophical view seems to have relevant predecessors (perhaps we have to exempt the pre-Socratics).[1] It might be argued that the pyrrhonists were fictionalists. While aiming to rid themselves of beliefs, even such ordinary beliefs as that the bread before them was nourishing, perhaps they held an attitude of acceptance towards such propositions. They thought it justifiable to act on them, even if they were not true. It is a matter of debate whether this is the right interpretation. Perhaps the fictionalist's distinctive contrast between acceptance and belief is missing, and it is not that pyrrhonists urged having an attitude other than belief to a proposition about bread, but rather that they urged believing a proposition other than one about bread, one merely about appearances. Here is the first hint of an important distinction: eliminativists about a region of discourse (for example eliminativists about "folk psychology") hold that the whole discourse has to be abandoned and replaced by something else (folk psychological talk about beliefs and desires should be replaced by talk of neurological processes). That is not a fictionalist attitude. Fictionalists hold that we should retain the discourse, and simply change our attitude to it, from belief to acceptance. (This contrast will be developed throughout this chapter.) A matter for debate is whether pyrrhonists were fictionalists or eliminativists about ordinary beliefs.

Copernicus's *De revolutionibus orbium coelestium* (1543) was prepared for publication by Andreas Osiander while Copernicus lay dying. Osiander included a preface in which he describes the astronomer's job as

> to think up or construct whatever causes or hypotheses he pleases such that, by the assumption of these causes, those same [observed] movements can be calculated from the principles of geometry for the past and for the future too .... It is not necessary that these hypotheses should be true, or even probable; but it is enough that they provide a calculus which fits the observations.

This is an early statement of the view that a scientific theory is adequate if it "saves the phenomena" (there is some doubt whether Copernicus himself accepted this). It also provides a very clear specification of one essential feature of modern fictionalism: something which is not true can be valuable. Even if the full astronomical claims about the movements of the heavenly bodies, and the causes of these movements, are false, this will not matter provided they enable us correctly to predict the observed positions of these bodies. What they get up to when we cannot observe them is of no consequence. This makes it close in some ways to van Fraassen's "constructive empiricism". To *accept* an astronomical theory (using the term in van Fraassen's sense) is to believe that it makes correct predictions about the observable behavior of the heavenly bodies, and to form no opinion about the correctness or incorrectness of what the theory says about their total movement or the underlying causes. In the sixteenth- and seventeenth-century context, this view of astronomy was appealed to in order to insulate it from theology. As Nicholas Ursus (1597) wrote:

> [H]ypotheses do not err in the least if they contradict the commonly held principles of other arts and sciences, or indeed, even if they contradict the infallible and certain authority of the sacred scriptures. (Jardine 1984: 39–40)

The fact that Galileo's insistence on the heliocentric view brought him into conflict with the Church shows that fictionalism about astronomy was not universally accepted.² Nonetheless, the view was certainly in the air, and arguably colored the meaning of "hypothesis" for more than a century, as in Newton's famous remark: "I frame no hypotheses; for whatever is not deduced from the phenomena is to be called a hypothesis, and hypotheses, whether metaphysical or physical, whether of occult qualities or mechanical, have no place in experimental philosophy".³ Newton can be construed as a realist who rejects anything that would require a fictionalist interpretation.

George Berkeley's "think with the learned, but speak with the vulgar" could be read as epitomizing a fictionalist stance: we can accept what we speak, but should believe only what we think (in our learned moments). His phrase was originally applied to his claim that spirits are the only causes, which seems to entail that "We must no longer say … that fire heats, or water cools, but that a spirit heats, and so forth" (1710: §51). By contrast, Berkeley says we *can* properly *say* the strictly false things, just as one who believes in the Copernican system can properly speak of the sun rising. The following quotation shows something in common with modern fictionalism:

> In the ordinary affairs of life, any phrases may be retained, so long as they excite in us proper sentiments, or dispositions to act in such a manner as

is necessary for our well-being, how false soever they may be, if taken in a strict and speculative sense. (1710: §52)

Falsehoods may sometimes properly guide conduct, because they can be useful to well-being. The strictly false judgment that fire will cause damage to your skin will help you avoid it, as you should; and will do this no less well, and perhaps better, than the true statement that god will damage your skin if you get it too close to fire.

Berkeley thought he could demonstrate that nothing could exist without the mind; this was the central tenet of his idealism. The positive corollary is that that what we call material things, like trees and chairs, are congeries of ideas, where ideas are essentially mind-dependent. It looks as if the thinking/speaking contrast could be applied here too. It may seem that the idealism entails that we must no longer say that trees can exist unperceived, for trees are ideas and ideas certainly cannot exist unperceived. Applying the thinking/speaking distinction, perhaps we can *say* things like this, and thus conform to vulgar speech, provided we think something more idealistically correct, perhaps that trees can exist unperceived by me, or unperceived by any finite spirit. Maybe we could think of this as a kind of fictionalism with respect to trees: there are, strictly speaking, no such things, though we can usefully speak as if there were.

In fact, Berkeley does not take this route.

> [I]n denying the things perceived by sense, an existence independent of a substance, or support wherein they may exist, we detract nothing from the received opinion of their *reality*, and are guilty of no innovation in that respect. All the difference is, that according to us the unthinking beings perceived by sense, have no existence distinct from being perceived, and cannot therefore exist in any other substance, than those unextended, indivisible substances, or *spirits*, which act, and think, and perceive them: whereas philosophers vulgarly hold, that the sensible qualities exist in an inert, extended, unperceiving substance, which they call *matter*, to which they attribute a natural subsistence, exterior to all thinking beings. (1710: §91)

About trees, Berkeley was no fictionalist. He held that ordinary speech does not entail the sophisticated and ultimately unintelligible philosophical theories concerning mind-independent substance. Claims about trees (so long as they do not attribute causation to them), for example the claim that there are ten trees in my yard, do not entail the existence of anything mind-independent, can be literally and straightforwardly true, can be believed, and are common ground between vulgar and learned. Only philosophers and atheists need the notion of material substance:

> Matter, or material substance, are terms introduced by philosophers; and as used by them, imply a sort of independency, or a subsistence distinct from being perceived by a mind: but are never used by common people. (1713: Third Dialogue)

To cast Berkeley as a fictionalist about material objects, we would need more than the texts yield. He might be expected to make the following claims:

1. The *correct* interpretation of sentences like "There are trees" is one on which they entail that there are mind-independent things. Hence all such sentences are false. [By contrast Berkeley says there is no such entailment, and the sentences are true.]

2. Taken at face value, the behavior of the vulgar shows that they are totally mistaken about the nature of their world. [On this issue, Berkeley is somewhat ambivalent. There are the ringing phrases proclaiming the naturalness of his view: "by the principles premised, we are not deprived of any one thing in Nature" (1710: §34). But he is inclined to admit there is error: "men may be said to believe that matter exists, that is, they act as if the immediate cause of their sensations ... were some senseless unthinking being" (1710: §54). On the other hand, men's actions can't be straightforward manifestations of belief, for what Berkeley took himself to have demonstrated was that we can make no proper sense of a "senseless unthinking being", so that there is no genuine content available for belief. We get the somewhat weasel conclusion: "upon a narrow inquiry, it will not perhaps be found, so many as is imagined do really believe the existence of matter or things without the mind" (1710: §54).]

3. We, the learned, can do better. We can prefix the mind-independent-object talk by a suitable operator, and so shift towards literal truth. (Optionally, we could say that the behavior of the vulgar is not to be taken at face value: beneath their coarse exteriors, they are in reality learned, silently prefixing their vulgar remarks by "according to the fiction of mind-independent things".) Or we can reconstrue mind-

independent-object talk as congeries-of-ideas talk. To accept a physical object statement is to believe its idealist reconstrual. [But this is not at all Berkeley's view. With one or two qualifications about causation, no reconstrual is needed.]

David Hume was strongly influenced by Berkeley, and he explicitly appealed to the notion of fictions of the imagination in discussing the problem of how we could form an idea of an "external thing", a mind-independent and enduring entity. His answer is that we cannot do so in any authentic way; the idea is nothing but a fiction of the imagination. Hume means by this something more literal than would be needed to make him a fictionalist. He does not say that external things are fictions, but that our ideas of these are fictions of the imagination, that is, made up by the imagination (which is guilty of various absurd confusions during the creative process). The contrast is with ideas formed in the authentic way, by copying impressions. We have no impression of external things (for all impressions are mind-dependent and ephemeral[4]), so we have no *authentic* idea of such things. Instead our imagination concocts an idea in a way which, once revealed, might well invite skepticism about whether anything in reality corresponds to it. But it is not this skepticism, or its subject matter, that Hume is labeling by the phrase "fiction of the imagination"; that labels only the process by which ideas of external things come into existence.

A fictionalist refrains from believing the distinctive claims of the relevant subject matter, but Hume is clear that this is not how he sees things: "we ... not only feign but believe this continued existence" (1739–40: 1.4.2). Moreover, a fictionalist regards acceptance as an attitude that does not require belief, but which can be stably combined with true beliefs about the same general subject matter. For example, van Fraassen's constructive empiricist might accept some claim about elementary particles without believing it; yet belief is not far away, for acceptance entails belief in the observable consequences of the claim. The combination of acceptance, disbelief in what is accepted, and belief in something closely related, is stable. By contrast, Hume's reflections on external things lead him to an unstable state: "there is a direct and total opposition betwixt our reason and our senses; or, more properly speaking, betwixt those conclusions we form from cause and effect, and those that persuade us of the continued and independent existence of body" (1739–40: 1.4.4). Fictionalism is designed precisely to relieve tensions of this kind (without Hume's resort to wine and backgammon): one set of opposed conclusions is relegated to the realm of fiction.

Some modern fictionalists mention Jeremy Bentham, who is famous for his discussions of "legal fictions": "By fiction, in the sense in which it is used by lawyers, understand a false assertion of a privileged kind, and which, though acknowledged to be false, is at the same time argued from, and acted upon, as if true" (1822: 267). Bentham probably intended this description of a legal fiction to bring it immediately into disrepute. In fact, his words capture some elements of one version of modern fictionalism. For example, a modal fictionalist may say that we can combine the acknowledgment that it is strictly false that there are nearby possible worlds at which my house is consumed by fire (for there are no possible worlds) with acting on it as if it were true (e.g. buying fire insurance), for we can transform the falsehood into a literal truth: according to the fiction of possible worlds, there are worlds in which my house is consumed by fire. Yet Bentham is not a happy choice of precursor for contemporary fictionalism, for he evinced the greatest antipathy towards legal fictions: "In English law, fiction is a syphilis, which runs in every vein, and carries into every part of the system the principle of rottenness" (Bentham 1843, vol. V: 170).

Bertrand Russell held that "logical fictions" or "logical constructions" could do duty for a whole variety of entities we normally treat in a more realistic way: space, material things, numbers, persons, and classes. Here is a characteristic statement of the program:

> You find that a certain thing which has been set up as a metaphysical entity can either be assumed dogmatically to be real ... or, instead of doing that, you can construct a logical fiction having the same formal properties ... to those of the supposed metaphysical entity ... and that logical fiction can be substituted for your supposed metaphysical entity and will fulfil all the scientific purposes that anybody can desire. (1918–19: 272)

The context is a discussion of matter, and is driven by epistemological concerns: "it is impossible that we should ever have any reason whatsoever for supposing that there are" the things physicists claim there are (1918–19: 272). This is because empirical knowledge is based on perception, and perception directly reveals only sense data or "appearances", "passing particulars of the kind that one is immediately conscious of in sense" (1918–19: 273). Knowledge of these, Russell believes, can never yield knowledge of things of a wholly different metaphysical character: lasting things not directly available to sense. Hence we do best to "replace" the supposed lasting unknowable things by logical fictions composed of passing knowable things. "What I can know is that there are a certain series of appearances linked together, and the series of these appearances I shall define as being a desk. In that way, the desk is reduced to being a logical fiction, because a series is a logical fiction" (1918–19: 273). A series is a logical fiction because it is a special kind of class "and classes are logical fictions" (1918–19: 270).

Russell's use of the word "fiction" may have its roots in the act of making, an interpretation supported by the seemingly equivalent use of "construction". This might make us think that the results of the construction would be something real, and so not a good resource for contemporary fictionalism. We should not rush to this view. The basis of Russell's position is the "no-class" theory of classes which "avoids the assumption that there are such things as classes" (Russell and Whitehead 1910–13: 187). On this view one can accept sentences which appear to affirm that classes exist, without being committed to their existence. This incorporates at least one aspect of contemporary fictionalism.

Russell's overall picture is that the simples are the fundamental reality: "simples have a kind of reality not belonging to anything else". The particular simples are appearances ("little patches of colour or sounds, momentary things" [1918–19: 179]); non-particular simples include simple properties and relations. Everything else is a logical fiction or construction out of these, that is, is a class-theoretic entity whose only ultimate members, if it has any, are simples. A tempting interpretive hypothesis is that Russell is a fictionalist, in more or less our contemporary sense, about everything non-simple. The justification is that according to Russell, classes are logical fictions. When we speak of them, we are fictionalizing; we are not genuinely committed to there being any such things.

Just about everything we pretheoretically say we know, for example that there are desks, is vulnerable to this dilemma: *either* we retain natural interpretations, according to which "desks" refers to enduring mind-independent objects which, according to Russell, cannot be directly known, in which case we "will have no possible argument either for its reality or against its reality" (1918–19: 272); *or* we reinterpret these claims as demanding no more than the existence of classes all or whose ur-elements (the things that don't themselves have members) are simple. Taking the second option, the no-class theory then kicks in to tell us that this demand can somehow be met even without our having to assume that classes exist.

It is a distinctive feature of fictionalism that there is no reinterpretation of the relevant discourse. The fictionalist about mathematics, for example, does not reinterpret the expressions that purport to refer to or quantify over numbers. Rather, she says that it is precisely because this is the right interpretation of the discourse that it is false (or that it cannot be known to be true), and so its value has to be found elsewhere than in its truth. Because Russell at this stage reinterprets claims about ordinary objects, he is not straightforwardly a fictionalist about them (in the modern sense). The reinterpretation implements a kind of elimination: properly speaking (with the learned) we should not assert that there are desks. We may use the expression "There are desks" (in conversation with the vulgar), but only if we understand it as meaning that there are series of classes of desk-like appearances. Desks (as ordinarily understood) are eliminated. Fictionalists, by contrast, characteristically distinguish their view from elimination.

When it comes to classes, however, the matter is less straightforward. On some exegeses, including at times (it must be said) Russell's own, the no-class theory is a reinterpretive theory: expressions which look as if they are to refer to or quantify over classes are to be understood to refer to "propositional functions", which seem sometimes to be understood as symbols and sometimes as part of extralinguistic reality. These words of Russell's, written many years after *Principia*, suggest a reduction to symbols:

> In the language of the second order, variables denote symbols, not what is symbolized. (1940: 192)

To make sense of the quotation, we have to understand Russell as saying that symbols are the values of the second-order variables, and nothing else is symbolized. This amounts to a reinterpretation of apparent reference to and quantification over classes as really reference to and quantification over symbols. Some support for this position can be found in the lectures from which most of my quotations have been culled. In a discussion following lecture 7 he says

> There are no classes really in the physical world. The particulars are there, but not classes. ... All those statements are about symbols. (1918–19: 268)[5]

On this interpretation, when he says that the no-class theory "avoids the assumption that there are such things as classes", he must be understood as meaning not exactly what he says, but rather something like: the theory avoids the assumption that there are such things as classes, if they are regarded as more than just symbols. Classes are reduced to symbols. (The structure of the position would be the same if the reduction were to propositional functions regarded as elements of nonlinguistic reality.)

An alternative view of Russell's position sees him as making a more radical claim which is not in this way reductivist. The more radical claim is that the apparently ontologically committing symbolism of his theory of classes is not really committing at all, not to anything. There is just symbolism; some of it, while seeming to refer to or quantify over classes, does not have to be regarded as referring to or quantifying over anything. This fits quite well with his early informal explanation:

> When two functions are formally equivalent, we may say that they *have the same extension*. ... We do not assume that there is such a thing as an extension. ... it is natural to regard the extension as an object, called a *class* ... This, however, is certainly not technically necessary, and we see no reason to suppose that it is true philosophically. (Russell and Whitehead 1910–13: 74)

It is not that extensions are being reduced to propositional functions or eliminated in favor of propositional functions. Rather, they are treated as superfluous.

If this interpretation is right, does Russell's no-class theory of classes count as genuine fictionalism? Suppose there are no classes. This is consistent, he wishes to assure us, with everything he says in his formal theories (including claims apparently about classes) being true. Knowing all the facts, he can use class theory in full sincerity without pretending, or engaging in fiction. Reading Russell this way, his no-class theory is not an example of fictionalism as it is understood today, despite his use of the phrase "logical fictions". It's an elimination: there are no classes (or, at least, we need not believe that there are).

7.2 Van Fraassen's constructive empiricism

According to van Fraassen, a realist about science makes three claims:

1. Scientific theories should be interpreted "at face value". If the theory includes the sentence "there are hadrons", it should be understood in the obvious, straightforward way, as claiming that there are hadrons; there is no reinterpretation.

2. Scientific theories purport to be true.

3   There is no obstacle in principle to our having good reasons for believing a scientific theory, that is, for thinking that it is true.

In van Fraassen's account, anti-realism (rejection of realism) can be divided into two kinds, instrumentalism and a form of fictionalism he calls constructive empiricism. Instrumentalists deny (1) while affirming (2) and (3). They say that "hadron" does not refer to a subatomic particle composed of quarks, but is a compressed way of speaking of observable features of various kinds of measuring devices.[6] Thus understood, scientific theories can indeed be regarded as purporting to be true (2) and we can have good reasons to believe them (3). By contrast, constructive empiricists agree with realists about (1), the face-value interpretation of scientific theories, but they disagree about the other claims. Constructive empiricists say that we should not regard scientific theories as purporting to be true. Rather "Science aims to give us theories that are empirically adequate" (van Fraassen 1980: 12), where a theory is empirically adequate just on condition that all its observable consequences are true. On (3), constructive empiricists believe that there is a principled obstacle to our having good reason to believe in the truth of a scientific theory, namely that we never have evidence that relates directly to unobservables. An appropriate attitude is not belief but *acceptance*: to accept a theory is to believe that it is empirically adequate, and to commit to allowing it to shape questions and research (1980: 12).

Van Fraassen considers a number of objections to his constructive empiricism, but he does not offer any direct argument for it. He more or less takes it for granted that one ought to prefer constructive empiricism to realism, if there are no cogent objections to it. This preference is presumably motivated by the thought that constructive empiricism is epistemically more cautious than realism. Whereas the realist who believes a scientific theory is committed to the unobservable entities and events the theory postulates, a constructive empiricist who merely accepts the theory is not. Hence, it may seem, the constructive empiricist is on stronger ground: he takes a smaller leap into the unknown regions that lie beyond the data.

Although that may seem obviously correct, there is room for doubt. Van Fraassen stresses that the observable phenomena to which one is committed in accepting a theory are not just those that have been observed; they include all possible observations, past, present, and future. The data are the actual observations, which we'll presume accord with the theory; the commitment is much more extensive. What epistemological considerations allow one to make this extension? Perhaps we are supposed to engage in a naïve form of inductive projection, as in this argument:

1   Up till now, all observational predictions made by theory *T* which have been checked have proved correct.

2   So (probably) all observational predictions made by theory *T* are correct.

Compare this with an argument made famous by Nelson Goodman:

3   All the emeralds I've examined up to now have been grue.[7]

4   So (probably) all emeralds are grue.

Most people think the argument from (3) to (4) is unsatisfactory: the premise gives no good reason to accept the conclusion. Should we be impressed by the constructive empiricist's structurally similar argument (1)–(2)? A standard move in discussions of the justification of induction is to say that inductive projection is justified only if the best explanation of the premises entails the conclusion. Inference to the best explanation is taken as the fundamental form of nondeductive reasoning, which stands in the background to vindicate those inductive projections which are in fact justified. No such inference to the best explanation is available to underwrite the grue argument: the best explanation of the premise is that the emeralds I've examined are green; unless my sample is skewed, this is some evidence (not conclusive of course) for the conclusion that all emeralds are green, which conflicts with (4). Scientific realists will say that the best explanation of the observations at issue in (1) involves the operations of unobservable entities, forces, and structures. These operations entail the conclusion, viz. that observations will continue to conform to the theory. If the appeal to explanation in justifying inductive projection is right, the question whether constructive empiricism is less epistemically adventurous than realism will be an issue that cannot be decided without deciding whether or not realism is correct, along with the picture of explanation it presupposes. We are thus left without an epistemic reason for believing in constructive empiricism.

Every theorist confronts the problem of induction. The point of these remarks is to show that constructive empiricists deprive themselves of one plausible way of dealing with it, namely, by treating inference to the best explanation as more basic than extrapolation.

Explanation will in any case be a critical issue between realist and constructive empiricist, since it seems that science, realistically understood, offers explanations of a kind it cannot do if it is understood in the constructive empiricist way. If this is right, we have a different reason, also based on explanation, to prefer realism. Van Fraassen takes the issue of explanation to be central to a defense of his constructive empiricism, and he offers a theory of it, which he calls pragmatist, designed to be favorable to the anti-realist.

Van Fraassen introduces the topic (towards the end of his chapter 4) by making three points that I think most people, and certainly many realists, could agree with:

1 An acceptable scientific theory doesn't have to explain everything (for example, Newton explicitly said he was not going to try to explain gravity[8]).

2 "[W]e don't say that we have an explanation unless we have an *acceptable* theory which explains". (1980: 95)

3 Explanation is not an overriding virtue: hidden variable theories of nonlocality phenomena don't trump quantum theories merely in virtue of the fact that the former provide an explanation and the latter do not.

Realists may make various kinds of connection between explanation and the value of a theory, for example:

> *A theory's explanatory power is evidence for its truth.* Van Fraassen (1980) cites Harman (98), Hempel (104) and Darwin (101) as theorists who have subscribed to this principle.
>
> *Explanatory power is a virtue.* A good scientific theory should explain the phenomena. In van Fraassen's words: "how well a theory is to be regarded depends at least in part on how much it can be used to explain". (1980: 103)

The first principle is quite contentious. The second principle, much less contentious, seems to pose a problem for constructive empiricism, despite van Fraassen's apparent endorsement of it in the quoted passage. If a theory posits unobservables, presumably they will need to be mentioned in using the theory to explain. This seems inconsistent with the agnosticism about unobservables championed by constructive empiricism.

Van Fraassen targets an argument which exploits a more general version of this idea. It crucially depends on the premise that only truths can explain.

1   Science aims to deliver explanations.

2   Only truths explain.

3   Hence science must aim to deliver truths. (cf. 1980: 97)

The conclusion is problematic for constructive empiricists, according to whom we should not believe theories (i.e. believe that they are true) but only accept them (i.e. believe their observable consequences). Van Fraassen says that the argument fails through insensitivity to the proper meaning of "explanation". Premise (2) claims that explanation is factive (as one might say), whereas, according to van Fraassen, its root meaning is or should be nonfactive: even a falsehood can be properly used in an explanation. For example, we can rightly say that Newton's theory explains the tides, even though we know that Newton's theory is strictly false (he gives several other examples: 1980: 98). So the argument just displayed fails in a straightforward way: it has a false premise. Van Fraassen enriches the diagnosis by saying that there are many contexts in which in *saying* that we have a theory that explains something we are thereby committing ourselves to the truth of the theory. This commitment is optional, not something delivered by the semantics, but an aspect of pragmatics, what Grice (1975) has called "conversational implicature". One sign that it is not part of the meaning of "explains" is that the commitment can be canceled without contradiction or retraction. As we've just seen, we can without impropriety or retraction claim in a single breath that Newton's theory explains, and that it is false. According to van Fraassen, the fact that the conversational implicature is often present helps explain why people have been tempted to believe the false premise (2).

Van Fraassen's own view is not entirely clear (at least to me). As noted above, he himself says that "we don't say that we have an explanation unless we have an *acceptable* theory which explains" (1980: 95). This suggests that only acceptable theories explain. (This is not entailed by his words: they are consistent with a pragmatic commitment to acceptability being triggered by *saying* we have an explanation, even though acceptability is not required for there to *be* an explanation. But there is nothing in the nearby text to suggest this interpretation.) The suggestion is inconsistent with van Fraassen's claim that Newton's theory explains, for, as he stresses, we know that it is not acceptable. Perhaps tense is important: "it was true then to say that Newton had an acceptable theory which explains the tides" (1980: 99). Newton's theory was acceptable relative to seventeenth-century data; so in the seventeenth century it explained the tides. It is not acceptable relative to our data. This invites the conclusion that for us it does not explain the tides. It is striking that all van Fraassen's examples supposedly of false but explanatory theories are in the past tense; they are examples of theories which once explained the data, that is, which in the past explained the data then available. It does not follow that any of these false theories can explain data now. So we don't have a counterexample to (2), the premise that only truth explains.

Even so, it's plausible that Newton's theory does explain the tides, even now; this seems a straightforward example of how a falsehood can explain. But it does not provide an appropriate model for a constructive empiricist. If Newton's theory explains the tides, that's because it's an entirely satisfactory approximation; its neglect of relativistic effects makes no significant difference (for almost all purposes). But van Fraassen could hardly say that some theory of particle physics was an entirely satisfactory approximation to the truth, for it contains endless claims about unobservables that he must regard as ones not to be believed: these, he must say, are very far from an approximation to the truth.

There would be little advantage in getting bogged down in nuances of our actual usage of explanatory vocabulary in English, so let us move at once to van Fraassen's specification of the form that claims about explanation are to take. Early in the discussion, the proposed basic form is: "fact E explains fact F relative to theory T" (1980: 101). Van Fraassen gives us no indication of how we are to de-relativize. Indeed, he firmly announces his intention to keep to the relative notion: "the topic of concern will be that basic relation of explanation, which may be said to hold between facts relative to a theory, quite independently of whether the theory is true or false" (1980: 101).

Yet de-relativize we must. We cannot treat "the fact that an old woman with a black cat mumbled some words explains the fact that the crops failed, relative to witchcraft theory" on a par with an acceptable scientific explanation. The quoted words may accurately report a theory-relative explanation, but we need more than that: we need a correct explanation, which is presumably an explanation given by a correct theory. We de-relativize "fact E explains fact F relative to theory T" when we have the premise that T is true.

Could we manage with merely the premise that T is acceptable, rather than that it is true? This seems hard to swallow. Consider van Fraassen's own way of showcasing the explanatory power of Bohr's theory of the atom:

> When the atom is excited (as when the sample is heated), the electron jumps into a higher energy state. It then spontaneously drops down again, emitting a photon with energy equal to the energy lost by that electron in its drop. (1980: 103)

It is hard to see how this could explain anything if there are no electrons or photons. In general, it's a lot easier to see how one could be agnostic about the unobservables posited by a theory if prediction was one's only concern than if one also cared about explanation.

These comments relate to the early phase of van Fraassen's account of explanation. By the end of his chapter 5, a new parameter has emerged, namely context. An explanation is relative to a question, and questions are often contrastive (why did this happen rather than that?) and are sensitive to local concerns and idiosyncrasies. Explanation relates three terms: theory, fact, and context (1980: 156). Van Fraassen explicitly addresses the question of how a constructive empiricist can invoke unobservables in explaining. The question "Why does the hydrogen atom emit photons with [just such-and-such] frequencies?" presupposes "that the hydrogen atom emits photons with these frequencies". Does not this "automatically make scientific realists of us all?" (1980: 151).

A negative answer starts by reminding us that constructive empiricists need only accept, rather than believe, this presupposition. That is, they need only believe that the claim has none but true observable consequences. Yet if they retain their agnosticism about unobservables, it is hard to see how they can agree that there is anything *about atoms* to explain. The only explanandum must take the form: why are things such as to make such-and-such observations as they are? No answer in terms of acceptance can address this. Consider any candidate answer, p, which is accepted but not believed. For constructive empiricists, the most that committing to p can amount to is committing to its observational implications. But we cannot explain observations merely by there being *something* which implies these observations. We have to say what that something is. In cases like the observations relating to photon frequencies, that must involve atoms, photons, and other unobservables.

The present aim is not to give a definitive evaluation of constructive empiricism but only to indicate some characteristic features of, and problems for, fictionalist theories more generally. No matter how a constructive empiricist responds to the problem of explanation, the general moral is that fictionalists typically take it to be incumbent upon them to give an account of the values that their target discourses have for us. In some cases, there may be dispute about what those values are. Is explanation an indispensable virtue in a scientific theory? Although van Fraassen is at pains to stress that it is not a pre-eminent virtue (1980: 95), and not a warrant-conferring virtue (1980: 100), I think he believes that it is a virtue, though less special than has often been thought. A more radical view, one still deserving to be called fictionalism, would be that it is not a virtue at all. Certainly van Fraassen holds that explanation wrongly understood, for example as essentially involving appeal to unobservable causal relations and processes, is just a "flight of fancy" (1980: 155). He will recognize explanation as a virtue only if it is something rather modest, information which provides an answer to a contextually salient question.

7.3 Field's mathematical fictionalism

"Nominalism is the doctrine that there are no abstract entities" (Field 1980: 1). The contrary view is Platonism: Platonists hold that there are very many abstract entities, including numbers, sets, and functions, and that they are just as real as concrete ones. Field aims to defend nominalism against the charge, made by Quine among many others, that we need to invoke abstract entities in order to give a proper account of the concrete world. In particular, Quine's objection continues, physical theories require mathematics, and mathematics involves reference to, and quantification over, abstract entities. A nominalist would have to reject physical theories, and this constitutes a proof that nominalism cannot be sustained.

One response to this argument is to reconstrue mathematics so that it does not involve reference to, or quantification over, abstract entities. (As I see it, Russell's no-class theory belongs in this category.) It is distinctive of fictionalism not to make this response, but to retain the "standard semantics" for the discourse in question. That is Field's approach. Many mathematical statements do require for their truth the existence of abstract entities. For a nominalist, it is precisely because there are no such entities that typical[9] mathematical statements are false. Field's project is to rebut Quine's objection by showing that mathematics is not needed for the theories of physical science: these theories (or at least some salient examples of them) can be reformulated in nominalistic terms; and even if we in practice use mathematics to draw consequences from nominalistically formulated theories, this is just for the sake of convenience: the consequences could be drawn, though more laboriously, without making any appeal to mathematics.

Field has two main claims to defend. The most difficult is the claim that there are nominalistically acceptable formulations of physical science. Field suggests that space (and space–time) can be thought of as made up of uncountably many concrete points. A Platonist (a believer in abstract entities) may wish to describe aspects of space–time in terms of isomorphisms to the real numbers. (For example, Newtonian three-dimensional space could be mapped onto triples of real numbers in such a way that spatial relations, like distance and betweenness, are mirrored by numerical relations. Such an approach appears to make full-blooded commitment to numbers.) Field says that a nominalist can happily accept that the concrete spatial points have a structure like those of Platonist numbers (they are densely ordered, etc.); this does not require commitment to numbers. Field goes on to offer a nominalization of a large part of Newtonian gravitational theory.

The other main claim Field makes is that mathematics is "conservative" with respect to nominalistic theories, theories that do not purport to quantify over, or refer to, abstract entities. Take a nominalistic theory, N (we assume that N is not "anti-Platonistic": i.e. it does not say there are no numbers), and add mathematics: the claim of conservativeness is that any nominalistic conclusion entailed by N plus mathematics is entailed by N alone. This is a very sharp formulation of the dispensability of mathematics to nominalistic reasoning. Field claims that "this claim [unlike the claim that extant scientific theories can be nominalized] is pretty much of an incontrovertible fact". In particular, he thinks it can't be disputed by Platonist mathematicians, for they take their theories to be true "at all possible worlds". A theory T entails a conclusion C iff every world at which T is true is one at which C is true. Adding necessary truths to T, that is, truths which are true at every world, cannot get it to entail conclusions not entailed without them: necessary truths do not restrict the relevant worlds. Let's use set-theoretic union to describe the effect of combining theories T and M: $T \cup M$.[10] If M (mathematics) is true at every world, the worlds at which T is true are just the worlds at which T ∪ M is true. So a Platonist (or anyone who believes that mathematics is made up of necessary truths) must agree that mathematics is conservative: adding mathematics to a theory does not add to its non-mathematical commitments.

From the variety of doubts and difficulties which have been raised for Field's approach, I'll pick three. The first raises the methodological issue of whether mere philosophers can sensibly challenge the views of Platonist mathematicians. The second raises doubts whether a completely nominalistic specification of scientific theories and their logic is possible. The third relates to the epistemological motivation for nominalism.

1   In a memorable passage, David Lewis suggests that it would be comically presumptuous of philosophers to tell mathematicians that they have been in endless error in believing in mathematical abstract objects.

> Mathematics is an established, going concern. Philosophy is as shaky as can be. To reject mathematics on philosophical grounds would be absurd. ... Even if we reject mathematics gently – explaining how it can be at most a useful fiction, "good without being true" – we still reject it, and that's still absurd. (Lewis 1991: §2.8)

Lewis goes on to contrast the ridiculous claims of philosophy – that motion is impossible, that we can have no knowledge of the external world, and so on – with the solid record of mathematics, and challenges a philosopher to dare tell the mathematicians that they are wrong.

This at first seems like fitting modesty, but on reflection it may seem to prove too much. Should philosophy never challenge current orthodoxy? Surely that cannot be ruled out in the global way Lewis suggests.[11] It's true that such challenges must be accompanied by an explanation of how the erroneous orthodoxies have grown up. But a fictionalist about mathematics has a range of possible stories to tell. The parties to the present dispute agree that in some sense mathematics presupposes the existence of abstract entities like numbers and sets. They can diverge about whether this presupposition is to be believed or is to be accepted. A fictionalist, who accepts these presuppositions without believing them, can be as adamant as a true Platonist that $5 + 7 = 12$, and that it's not the case that $5 + 7 = 13$, just as one atheist anthropologist can sincerely, indeed vehemently, insist to another that the difference between the fisher gods Atlaua and Chac Uayeb Xoc is that the latter was more concerned with the fate of the fish themselves, whereas Atlaua was responsible for the fate of fishermen. A fictionalist does not have to tell mathematicians that their mathematical claims are wrong: on the contrary, he accepts them (even while not believing them). When the philosopher aims for a totally presupposition-free position, she does something that she cannot expect mathematicians, in their professional capacities, to do. She does not quarrel with them from that perspective, for she takes it that it is a perspective that a practicing mathematician will, for good reason, not share.[12]

2 Field uses Newtonian gravitational theory as an example of a theory which can be nominalized. He is cautious on the question whether the whole of science can be treated the same way. There are many hairy problems: relativity theory, quantum mechanics, string theory. It has also been claimed that an early and relatively straightforward theory, Fourier's theory applied to vibrating strings, cannot be nominalized (Liston 1993).

An additional problem relates to the logic of theories, and indeed to logic more generally. A scientific theory is often thought of as a set of sentences closed under a relation of consequence. Sets are abstract things, as are sentences. (Theories must be allowed to have more consequences than those which have in fact been tokened, so we cannot use sentence tokens rather than sentence types.) Moreover, consequence is thought of either in terms of models (the semantic conception) or in terms of proofs (the syntactic conception). Models are set-theoretic structures, so they are abstract things. Proofs are sequences of sentence types, so they are also abstract things.

In later work, Field himself poses the problem very clearly (using "anti-realist" to encompass "fictionalist"):

> [I]t may seem unclear how a mathematical anti-realist could make sense of consistency and conservativeness. For consistency is usually defined as *having a model*, where a model is a set of a certain sort, and hence a mathematical entity; and since I defined conservativeness in terms of consistency, it will be defined model-theoretically as well.
> (1989: 249)

If that were the end of the story, fictionalism would be "self-defeating". Field's solution is to reconstruct the relevant notions on the basis of a *primitive operator it is logically possible that*. Sentences $A_1 \ldots A_n$ are (taken together) consistent just on condition that it's logically possible that A_1 & ... & A_n. A theory N is conservative with respect to a theory T iff, given that it's logically possible that T, for all A:

> It's not logically possible that (T & N & not-A) iff it's not logically possible that T & not-A.

Developing the solution requires it to be shown that there is a suitable reconstruction of the standard metalogical results (completeness and consistency of first-order logic, for example). We will not enter this very complex debate (see Field 1991, 1992).

3   A major motivation for nominalism is epistemological: how could beings like us, concrete elements in the causal order, possibly have any knowledge of causally inert objects of a totally different metaphysical kind? The problem, which dates back at least to Benacerraf (1973), is well expressed by Michael Liston:

> On our standard conception of mathematics, its objects are such that we do not perceive, observe, or in any way causally interact with them or with anything with which they causally interact. On the interactionist conception of epistemology, in order to have reliable beliefs about a class of objects or evidence that properly justifies those beliefs ... the beliefs and the evidence must be causally traceable either to those objects or to some objects with which they causally interact. If the epistemological conception is correct, beliefs reliably reflecting facts involving a class of objects must be informationally traceable to those objects; if our standard conception of mathematics is correct, no such connections are possible for mathematical beliefs; ergo, something has to give or be modified. (Liston 1993: 447)

Drawing on a picture of knowledge hostile to the possibility of mathematical knowledge, nominalists cling to the epistemology and abandon the mathematics. This may be a reaction in the wrong direction: perhaps a more sophisticated epistemology, departing from the crude interactionist model, would make room for the possibility of knowledge in the realm of mathematics (and other abstract realms, like logic). Indeed, many would regard failure to allow for the possibility of mathematical knowledge as a refutation of an epistemological proposal. There is a long history of noninteractionist accounts of a priori knowledge, and a burgeoning interest in recent years (see Bruce Russell 2007). These proposals undermine epistemological arguments for nominalism that are based on interactionist epistemology.

No matter how noninteractionist our epistemology, knowledge of Platonist mathematics poses a problem. There's a reliability conditional, which a Platonist might express thus:

> If mathematicians believe that p, then p. (cf. Field 1989: 230)

The question that arises is how this can be explained; and that question seems hard even if we are prepared to accept noninteractionist explanations. Suppose the question is hard because there is no explanation. According to Field:

> [W]e should view with suspicion any claim to know facts about a certain domain if we believe it impossible in principle to explain the reliability of our beliefs about that domain. (1989: 233)

It's not clear that this principle is correct, and not clear that the mathematical reliability conditional is the only one it's hard to explain. Many people accept that most instances of the following are true:

> If people come to the belief that p a priori, then p.

On most views, this subsumes the mathematical reliability conditional, and is no less hard to explain. Does that mean that we should view all claims to a priori knowledge with suspicion? That would apparently be self-defeating. So it might be that the envisaged epistemic motivation for nominalism would equally ground an unacceptable skepticism about any form of a priori knowledge.

7.4 Some features of fictionalism

It would take us too far afield (and be beyond my competence) to pursue the logical and epistemological issues raised by mathematical fictionalism. Instead, I'll close the chapter by listing some of the features of fictionalism that we have isolated through the historical review.

1   Fictionalists say that the sentences in a certain region of discourse (or a certain range of thoughts) are mostly false.

2 Fictionalism is distinct from reduction. From our perspective (though not from his) Berkeley reduced material objects to congeries of ideas. There really are such congeries. A fictionalist about material objects would say that there really are no such things, though the story that says there are has some value.
3 Fictionalism is distinct from one kind of elimination. As I understand Russell's no-class theory of classes, it claims that, properly understood, class theory has no ontology. We could call that view eliminativist; but not fictionalist. Many class-theoretic sentences are really true, just as they stand.
4 Fictionalism involves a kind of elimination. Field stresses that mathematics is to be interpreted "at face value", that is, as having an ontology of abstract objects. But on his fictionalist view, there are no abstract objects.
5 Fictionalism is often motivated by epistemological concerns. They are conspicuous in the case of van Fraassen and Field, and seem also to have played some role in views like Osiander's.
6 Fictionalism typically involves attributing some kind of error. For Field, Platonists are in error, for van Fraassen, scientific realists. The error may not be confined to theorists: no doubt ordinary people believe in electrons and numbers, so they, too, are in error, from a fictionalist perspective.
7 A fictionalist must find value in the supposedly fictional discourse. For van Fraassen, it's helping deliver observational predictions, which is fairly close in spirit to Field's views about mathematics, according to which math provides short cuts to nominalist conclusions. By contrast, Bentham's denial of the value of legal fictions makes it inappropriate to label him a fictionalist.

Suggested reading

On the history, Rosen (2005) is excellent. The *Stanford Encyclopedia* entries by Eklund, Balaguer, and Nolan should be consulted. For a general introduction to philosophy of science, locating the position of constructive empiricism, see Godfrey-Smith (2003). On Field's mathematical fictionalism see MacBride (1999) and on this and more general issues relating to fictionalism Burgess and Rosen (1997). For a collection of good articles on various kinds of fictionalism, and a useful editorial introduction, see Kalderon (2005b).

8

FICTIONALISM ABOUT POSSIBLE WORLDS

8.1 A partial taxonomy of fictionalisms

Let's say that a theory is fictionalist concerning some region of thought if it claims that thoughts in that region are, can be, or should be regarded as possessing this similarity with fiction: they don't have to be true to be good.[1] This already allows for three versions, depending on which similarity with fiction is selected: (i) the thoughts *are in fact* regarded as like fiction; (ii) the thoughts *can be* regarded as like fiction; (iii) the thoughts *should be* regarded as like fiction. The first version (i), that the thoughts are so regarded, claims that ordinary thinkers of these thoughts do (for the most part) regard them as not needing to be true to be good, or at least with modest Socratic questioning could easily be persuaded to appreciate that this is how they had been, perhaps implicitly, treating these thoughts. The third version (iii), that the similarity with fiction *should be* regarded as holding, makes an independent claim: given every relevant consideration, the best thing to believe is that this similarity holds. This might be so even if the ordinary thinkers of the thoughts in question did not regard them as like fiction, and it might fail to be so even if they did. In these two cases, ordinary thinkers will be in error. The second version (ii), that the relevant thoughts *can* be regarded as similar to fiction, requires elaboration: what constrains how the thoughts can be regarded? The initial vague answer is that the thoughts can be so regarded without detracting from the value (or the most important value) that they have. For example, in Field's fictionalism about mathematics, the "can" amounts to: can without jeopardizing the applicability of science to the world.

In my view, the *can* question is the crucial one, and makes us do some work on the value of the thoughts in question, the value that is supposedly preserved under a fictionalist interpretation, the "good" feature that supposedly does not require truth. Only if the thoughts *can* be so regarded is there any point in taking seriously either the *should* or the *are* questions. If the thoughts cannot be taken as relevantly similar to fiction (without some intellectual loss), then they should not be so taken; and if, under this supposition, they are so taken, then ordinary thinkers need some re-education, since they must be missing out something valuable about some of their thoughts.

A fictionalist must see something problematic about the relevant area of thought, though what is problematic varies from case to case. Field forthrightly declares that, as a nominalist, he holds that mathematics is false. By contrast, van Fraassen's view is not that the parts of physics dealing with unobservables are false, but that they cannot be known to be true, or even justifiably believed to be. This is the problematic feature that motivates his fictionalist stance.

On the other hand, the fictionalist must see something valuable about the relevant region of thought. That is the "good" feature that is available even when truth is absent. For Field, this feature of mathematics is its dispensable convenience for formulating scientific laws and deriving consequences from them. For van Fraassen, it's the possibly indispensable role played by the fiction of a structure of unobservables in delivering predictions about observables. The core fictionalist idea is that we can reap the benefits while avoiding the problems.

There are various options available concerning other aspects. How do ordinary users relate to the relevant region of thought? Do they recognize it as a fiction, possibly implicitly? If so, the fictionalism is sometimes called "hermeneutic" and if not "revolutionary" (see Burgess and Rosen 1997), corresponding to the earlier distinction between the claim that we *do* and the claim that we *should* regard some region of thought as fictional. A hermeneutic fictionalist does not have to impute error to ordinary thinkers of the relevant thoughts, whereas a revolutionary fictionalist does.

The question of how ordinary thinkers relate to their thoughts can progress up through several levels. Suppose they in fact treat the thoughts as fictions. Are they aware that they do this? The answers "Yes" and "No" give rise to two further versions of fictionalism. Likewise, suppose that the thinkers do not believe that their thoughts can or should be regarded as fictional. Are they aware that they believe this? Alternative answers give rise to further versions.

So far, we have considered only this similarity with fiction: the thoughts don't have to be true to be good, or useful. We can also ask whether they belong to a fiction, that is, whether they relate to some fiction in the way that the thought that Holmes is a detective relates to the Holmes stories. This requires that there be a fiction, an actual event of telling a story, and that the relevant thoughts are either recountings or reminders or developments of this story. Typically, fictionalists prefer not to demand this similarity.

Does the fictionalist draw upon a fiction operator? If he does, as do many fictionalists about possible worlds, he may face specific problems. Taken at face value, many fiction operators refer to fictions, in which case the fictionalist must, after all, say that, as a matter of historical fact, there were genuine acts of story-telling. This suggests that a fictionalist make use of "myth operators" (according to such-and-such a myth), for myths can come into being without a specific act of myth-making. However, both fictions and myths are most naturally thought of as abstract, posing a problem for fictionalisms driven by nominalistic preferences. Saying how fiction operators work typically involves some kind of modal closure (the simplest idea is that a thought is so according to a fiction iff it is *entailed* by something explicitly stated in the fiction – more sophisticated versions are discussed in section 4.3), and this may raise specific problems for fictionalists about possible worlds.

Whether the modal status of fiction operators poses a problem for modal fictionalism depends on a further distinction. Does a fictionalist aim to provide an *analysis* of the characteristic concept of the target thoughts? For example, does a fictionalist about possible worlds aim to analyze the notion of modality? If so, then this theorist, a "strong" modal fictionalist, will have to take note of the apparently modal nature of fiction operators and say, perhaps, that there is at least some value in reducing modal notions to a single one (e.g. Rosen 1990: 344–5, and discussion on ensuing pages). Fictionalisms which can be pursued without any attention to fiction operators, like Field's mathematical fictionalism, do not raise this kind of problem.

In my view, the crucial question is the *can* question: can we regard the relevant thoughts as fictional, without losing the characteristic value of these thoughts? Unless the answer to this is affirmative, the other issues are of little consequence. We can see the different varieties of fictionalism as differing in point of what they add to the *can*-claim.

8.2 Fictionalist values

"The thoughts don't have to be true to be good." What does "good" amount to? It's important for a fictionalist to be highly explicit about the answer to this question, else she ceases to occupy a position clearly distinct from eliminativism. An eliminativist will say that we can or should simply dispense with a certain range of thoughts (they are false, or unknowable); nothing is salvaged, though we are typically directed to alternative ways to meet the cognitive needs served by the eliminated thoughts. A fictionalist is less draconian, trying to claim a value for the thoughts despite the fact that they are not to be believed as true.

No doubt there will be variations from case to case, but one value that may be imputed is that a fiction can form a kind of inference bridge, enabling one to pass from genuine fact to genuine fact. This is more or less Field's view of the role of mathematics in the application of science to the world. Below is a toy example of how it might work. The column on the left contains falsehoods which are true in the tooth-fairy tale; the corresponding entry on the right, if there is one, is a real-world truth which ensures that what is on the left (if anything) is true in the tale.

Tooth-fairy fiction	Reality
	I have put a tooth under my pillow.
	I have been disobedient.
If you leave a tooth under your pillow, the tooth fairy normally replaces it with a 10-dollar bill.	If you leave a tooth under your pillow, a parent normally replaces it with a 10-dollar bill.
The tooth fairy keeps all the teeth she collects on the other side of the rainbow.	
The tooth fairy doesn't want teeth from disobedient little boys in her collection, because these teeth make the rainbow lose its color.	
In light of my disobedience, the tooth fairy will probably not replace it with a 10-dollar bill.	In light of my disobedience, a parent will probably not replace it with a 10-dollar bill.
	So there probably will not be a 10-dollar bill under my pillow in the morning.

The italicized entries are used by the little boy in his reasoning, which takes him (let's suppose) from italicized right-column truths to an italicized right-column truth in some suitably authentic way (maybe the premises entail the conclusion, or perhaps the reasoning is of a more probabilistic kind). The value of the tooth-fairy fiction is precisely that it enables him to learn a (real-world) truth which he otherwise would not have known. Ignorant of his parents' role in replacing the tooth, he could not have used the nonitalic truths in the right column to reach the conclusion. Yet intuitively his reasoning is, as I said, "authentic": he did a good job, given his unfortunate mixture of ignorance and false belief.

The reasoning is not sound, for it passes through falsehoods. A fictionalist can locate the value of the tooth-fairy fiction precisely in its making the reasoning authentic without making it sound (for soundness requires truth). There's a reliable route from real-world facts to a real-world fact that, for our hero, passes through the falsehood of fiction; in the circumstances, this does not undermine the value of the reasoning – it remains authentic, reliable. We can use this as a toy model for one way in which a fictionalist may distinguish herself from an eliminativist. It also serves to illustrate the fictionalist's need to make fiction–reality connections, as exemplified by sentences which share a row.

8.3 Fictionalism about possible worlds

I take it as given that we possess a great deal of modal knowledge.

Rosen (1990: 337)

Modal fictionalism, as this term is often used in recent writing, is fictionalism about possible worlds. In my opinion, the label "modal fictionalism" is more properly applied to fictionalism about modality, the claim that possibility and necessity are not real things, but are like characters in some fiction. Since I can't realistically hope to correct established usage, I'll refer to *fictionalism about possible worlds* using those very words, and I'll avoid the phrase "modal fictionalism".[2]

Fictionalism about possible worlds takes as central the idea that thoughts about possible worlds can be (or are, or should be) treated as thoughts within a story, in some ways on a par with the thought that Holmes is a detective. The selected story is often taken to be the one told by David Lewis, and called "modal realism" (introduced in chapter 4): possible worlds are real entities, maximal spatiotemporal regions. One of them is the one we inhabit, which we call actual. This marks a perspectival difference between our world and all the others, but not a metaphysical one: all are equally real, though just one is (from our point of view) special in that we inhabit it. Inhabitants of other worlds also think of theirs as actual, and with no less right. The analogy is with spatial position. Where I am, my *here*, is special to me. You call where you are *here* too, and that place is special to you. Your location is just as real as mine, so there's no difference of metaphysical status between where I am and where you are. But there's a perspectival difference: we each think of where we are as special.

Fictionalists about possible worlds are not fictionalists about modality: they hold that some modal thoughts, like the thought that there could have been talking donkeys, are literally, and not merely fictionally, true. However, they hope to have the benefits of using the notion of possible worlds to amplify our modal thinking and investigate modal phenomena without the ontological cost of belief in the reality of possible worlds: "paradise on the cheap", to use Lewis's words (1986: 136). The benefits of talk of possible worlds relates to the familiar paraphrases of ordinary modal talk: *being necessarily so* is paraphrased as being so in every possible world, and *being possibly so* as being so in some possible world.

Let's see how Gideon Rosen develops this kind of view:

> [L]et *P* be an arbitrary modal proposition. The modal realist will have ready a non-modal paraphrase of *P* in the language of possible worlds; call it *P**. The realist's assertions about possible worlds are guided by explicit adherence to the schema *P iff P**.[3] The fictionalist's parasitic proposal is therefore to assert every instance of the schema: *P iff according to the hypothesis of the plurality of worlds, P**. (Rosen 1990: 332)

The worlds are fictions, that's the first commitment. When talk of worlds is prefixed by the fiction operator "according to the hypothesis of the plurality of worlds", we can use this talk to express genuine modal facts; that's the second commitment.

Consider the thought that Socrates might have been snub-nosed. Realists about possible worlds, those who accept Lewis's picture of possible worlds as real entities, regard this as equivalent to some thought dominated by existential quantification over possible worlds, say "At some possible world, Socrates is snub-nosed."[4] So an example of the Lewis paraphrase schema

L   P iff P*

is:

Socrates might have been snub-nosed iff at some possible world, Socrates is snub-nosed.

Rosen takes the right-hand side of this alleged equivalence to be false, since its truth would require there to be at least one nonactual world. On the other hand, he takes the left-hand side to be true. So he rejects the Lewis paraphrase schema: it has false instances. Yet, with a shift in perspective, everything useful about these paraphrases can be harvested as fruit to the fictionalist, without the cost of commitment to possible worlds. Simply take the right-hand side to be implicitly qualified by a fiction operator, "According to the realist's hypothesis of a plurality of worlds", for short "According to PW". Then the schema will be construed as saying: "P iff, according to PW, P*", and our instance as:

Socrates might have been snub-nosed iff according to PW, at some possible world, Socrates is snub-nosed.

More generally, the realist's schema "P iff P*" becomes the fictionalist's equivalence:

FE   P iff, according to PW, P*.

For many propositions P, both the left-hand side and the right-hand side of FE are true. For example, applying the * function to "There might have been blue swans" (P) yields "There are worlds at which there are blue swans" (P*), and the latter is so according to PW. This allows a Rosen-style fictionalist to differentiate his position from that of an eliminativist: talk of possible worlds still has a role, and can be used in the statement of truths, though it needs to be brought explicitly under a fiction operator. While one could envisage a version of fictionalism about possible worlds which did not count on FE, I'll restrict attention to versions that do.

Rosen's fictionalism about possible worlds combines the following features:

1   Unreconstructed modal thoughts, like the thought that Socrates might have been snub-nosed, are strictly and literally true.

2   There are no nonactual possible worlds, and thoughts purporting to existentially quantify over these are false.

3   It is strictly and literally true that, according to PW, there are many worlds, and the specific things this story tells us are of value in our knowledge of modality.

4   FE: P iff, according to PW, P*.

By contrast, the fictionalist about modality denies (1), saying instead that unreconstructed modal thoughts, like the thought that Socrates might have been snub-nosed, are strictly and literally false (or at least incapable of being known), but can be understood as pointing us to truths. This poses the question of how we might have mistakenly believed all these falsehoods. One approach is to liken the situation to our attitude to fictional sentences like "Holmes is a detective." These are not true, though their embedding in a fiction operator is. The immediate analogy would be to say that "Socrates might have been snub-nosed" forms a truth when prefixed by "According to PW". This would not be quite right, since PW does not use those modal notions (*might*, *must*, etc.).[5] However, we can take advantage of PW in two stages: first, apply the Lewis paraphrase schema L to modal thoughts, transforming them into possible worlds thoughts. Second, treat possible worlds thoughts as implicitly embedded under the operator "According to PW". Suppose someone asserts that there could have been blue swans. This is strictly false for the fictionalist about modality, since there are no real modal facts. But we can explain our inclination to treat it as true in terms of our possibly implicit willingness to equate it with "According to PW, there is a world at which there are blue swans."

This fictionalism about modality can be summarized:

1   Unreconstructed modal thoughts, like the thought that Socrates might have been snub-nosed, are strictly and literally false (or at least unknowable).

2   There are no nonactual possible worlds, and thoughts purporting to existentially quantify over these are simply false.

3   It is strictly and literally true that, according to PW, there are many worlds, and the specific things this story tells us are of value (though not to our knowledge of modality, for there is none of that!).

4   L: P iff P*.

5   Rather than evaluate modal thoughts as true or false, we should evaluate them as faithful or not to PW. (We can, if occasion suits, "speak with the vulgar" and use "true" to mean "faithful".)

One contrast between fictionalism about possible worlds and fictionalism about modality is that the former sees our ordinary modal thoughts as literally true, because equivalent to truths about what PW says, whereas the latter sees these thoughts as literally false or unknowable, because equivalent to quantifications over worlds. Both positions deny that there are nonactual worlds (variants of the positions could be merely agnostic on that question). Fictionalism about possible worlds requires no reconstrual of ordinary modal thinking: so long as we keep to the modal concepts of *must*, *can*, and so on, we can quite well attain literal truth. By contrast, fictionalism about modality treats ordinary modal thinking as involving error, if taken at face value. Fictionalists about possible worlds accept FE; fictionalists about modality reject FE but accept L (though in the interesting cases, the equivalence will hold because both sides are false).

The contrast between hermeneutic and revolutionary fictionalisms does not apply very happily to fictionalism about possible worlds, for the correctness of ordinary modal judgments is not disputed. Ordinary thinkers do not use the theorist's notion of *possible world*. True, they speak of possibilities, possible situations, and so on, but these are not possible worlds as realists understand them, for they may well be incomplete, and perhaps even inconsistent. The only users of the theoretical notion of possible worlds are theorists, and it would be absurd to say that David Lewis, for example, was really a fictionalist about possible worlds, despite his strident contrary affirmations. Equally, the title "revolutionary" would not be fully apt, for disagreeing with modal realists is not the fundamental shake-up needed for a revolution.

By contrast, there is a real question for a fictionalist about modality: whether to offer his theory as hermeneutic or revolutionary. It is hermeneutic if it says that ordinary modal thinkers, who have all these strictly false modal thoughts, implicitly embed them in a fiction; otherwise it is revolutionary. Taken at face value, the data point firmly away from the hermeneutic version.

Rosen distinguishes strong from timid fictionalism about possible worlds. The strong fictionalist aims to say what the metaphysical nature of modality is in terms of fictions: true modal thoughts are made true by the existence and content of the selected modal fiction. This theorist aims to provide a reductive analysis of modality, and so should avoid drawing on modal notions in the analysis.[6] By contrast the timid fictionalist about possible worlds refrains from this commitment, attempting only to establish correlations. This timid fictionalist regards the fictionalist equivalence FE (P iff according to PW, P*) as true, but as "merely a theory linking the modal facts with facts about the story PW" (Rosen: 1990: 354). The timid fictionalist can say that the modal facts systematically match the facts about what is so according to PW, yet think of them as two ranges of entirely distinct facts.

One impact of this distinction relates to the fiction operator. The "story" of PW, perhaps contained in Lewis's Plurality of Worlds (1986), states explicitly some things about worlds, but leaves much merely implicit. The relation between what is explicit and what is implicit is likely to be modal (for example, entailment[7]). A strong fictionalist about possible worlds must find this worrying: he was supposed to be giving an analysis of modality, and should not rely on modal notions in so doing. This is not a problem for the timid fictionalist about possible worlds. More generally, one might call any fiction operator "modal", for "according to fiction F, p" means roughly: "if things were as told in fiction F, it would be the case that p", and this counterfactual can reasonably be counted as modal. (One will certainly be justified in counting fiction operators as modal operators if, like Lewis, one thinks they can be analyzed in terms of quantification over possible worlds, as discussed in section 4.3.) A timid fictionalist about possible worlds can just allow that fiction operators are modal and leave things there; a strong fictionalist about possible worlds cannot.

8.4 Comparisons with other forms of irrealism

Talk of possible worlds in the discussion of modality is clearly illuminating

Rosen 1995: 67

Nominalists believe there are no abstract things. This motivates something other than a straightforward view of mathematics: it must be reinterpreted, or treated as a fiction. There's a structural analogy with possible worlds. Actualists believe that there are no nonactual things. This motivates something other than a straightforward view of talk apparently of nonactual possible worlds. One option is reinterpretation. For example, possible worlds are picturesque ways of talking about actual maximal consistent sets of sentences. Or they are merely useful fictions. Fictionalism about possible worlds may be driven by actualism just as fictionalism about mathematics may be driven by nominalism. In both cases, fictionalism is not the only option. Let's look more closely at the alternative options for actualists.

One straightforward one is elimination: let's abandon the possible worlds vocabulary and express our modal opinions in the ways that come more naturally to us, using modal auxiliaries like *must* and *can*, perhaps formalized by the usual symbols box ($\Box$) and diamond ($\Diamond$). This version of actualism need not deny itself some of the formal benefits of "possible worlds semantics", for example those of the kind developed by Kripke (1963). We've already seen (in section 4.1) that we don't have to take the "possible worlds" mentioned in these semantics any more seriously than we take truth values in the usual truth-value semantics for propositional logic. All we need is a structure with certain structural properties. For all that it matters to Kripke-style semantics, the possible worlds can be points in space, or numbers. Only their structural properties matter. One can coherently combine an actualist elimination of possible worlds with the benefits of possible worlds semantics. In reflecting on modal issues, trying to imagine a possible situation is certainly useful, but an eliminativist can say that this is merely an exercise of the imagination: it's not like trying to read off the facts about some nonactual object, or relating in any other way to anything nonactual. Just as imagining a dragon does not have to be thought of as a relation to a special kind of dragon (a nonactual kind), so imagining a world does not have to be thought of as standing in a relation to a special kind of world (a nonactual one). To the extent that it's not clear what loss is incurred by eliminativism, it's not clear what is to be gained by fictionalism.

The strongest argument against elimination is that it makes it impossible for us to say some of the things we do (or should) want to say. For example, David Lewis has suggested that the eliminativist's language of boxes and diamonds is inadequate to express the thought: *it might happen in three different ways that a donkey talks*. The "ways" quantified over in this thought seem to be possible worlds, and Lewis claims that one cannot do justice to the thought using just *must* and *can* (or boxes and diamonds).[8]

If eliminativism is ruled out, some reinterpretive or reductive approach naturally suggests itself to actualists. As already mentioned, nonactual possible worlds might be identified with sets of actual things, for example sets of sentences. Sets which are both maximal (for every sentence, either it or its negation is in the set) and consistent (for no sentence is both it and its negation in the set) could arguably do the job of possible worlds, without invoking anything nonactual. Arguably; but Lewis (1986) has argued for the opposite conclusion, claiming that these "ersatz" worlds, substitutes for the real nonactual things, are inadequate in certain quite tricky technical ways.

Eliminativism is allegedly vulnerable to expressive inadequacy, reduction to technical defects; if either of these alleged vulnerabilities is genuine, fictionalism emerges as the best option for actualists.

8.5 Problems for fictionalism about possible worlds

As I've presented Rosen's view so far, his fictionalism is not an approach to possible worlds that has the same scope as eliminativism or reductionism. Those latter theories address all possible worlds sentences: eliminativists say that you should have no truck with any of them, and use only sentences constructed with modal operators; actualist reductionists say you can use the possible worlds sentences so long as you reconstrue talk of nonactual things in terms of talk of actual things. The scope of Rosen's fictionalism, as so far presented, is much less extensive, since the only world-theoretic sentences it addresses are those that translate modal sentences: they are those that are the P* to some modal sentence P. As Lewis stresses (1968: 117), one can say things in the world-theoretic language ("counterpart theory", in his terminology) which cannot be said in the modal language, so the P*s will not exhaust the world-theoretic language. Rosen's FE has nothing to say about, for example, the sentence "There are nonactual worlds."

Let's suppose (temporarily) that this nonmodal sentence translates into Lewis's language of counterpart theory more or less as it stands. The language has a primitive predicate "A" true of just those things that are actual, and an axiom which says that there is at least one actual world (a world containing all and only the actual things). It also has as an axiom that nothing exists at more than one world. It follows that there is exactly one actual world, for which Lewis uses the name "@". So it seems that "There are nonactual worlds" is easily expressed in the language:

Something is a world distinct from @.

On our present assumptions about translation, this sentence is P* to the sentence "There are nonactual worlds" as P. Although this P* is not technically a theorem of counterpart theory (as adumbrated by Lewis 1968), it's clearly presumed to be true. So we have:

According to PW, something is a world distinct from @.

FE, the central fictionalist claim, was:

> P iff, according to PW, P*.

On our assumptions, an instance is:

> There are nonactual worlds iff, according to PW, something is a world distinct from @.

We have seen that the right-hand side of this equivalence is true, and that the fictionalist must accept this. So the fictionalist is committed to the truth of the left-hand side, the view that there are nonactual worlds. But he was meant to be an actualist! Something has gone wrong.

We must drop our assumption about translation. What Lewis actually says is that a modality-free quantification should be translated with the quantifier restricted to the actual world, so "There are nonactual worlds" is translated as:

> Some actual things are nonactual worlds. (cf. Lewis 1968: 118)

Lewis would reject this: nothing actual is nonactual. What a worlds-theorist will view as a vernacular truth ("there are nonactual worlds") is translated as a falsehood, and translation should preserve truth value. This is a problem for the supposedly helpful PW, but it poses no threat to the fictionalist. It undermines the translational claim upon which the previous anti-fictionalist argument rested.

Lewis's precise instructions about translation protect the fictionalist from other potential disasters. Rosen, raising an objection for his own view, asks us to consider this possible worlds thought:

> At all worlds, there are worlds at which kangaroos exist and worlds at which they don't. (Rosen 1993: 75)

This is so, he claims, according to PW. And (to cut a longer story short) PW is supposedly thereby also committed to:

1 At all worlds, there are at least two worlds.

2   (1) is the output of the asterisk function applied to the modal thought in (3).

3   Necessarily, there are at least two worlds.

By FE:

> *Necessarily, there are at least two worlds* is true iff, according to PW, at all worlds, there are at least two worlds.

If the RHS is true, the fictionalist must accept the LHS, which entails that there are at least two worlds. But the fictionalist is an actualist who holds that there is just one world, the actual world.

Noonan (1994) says that Lewis (at least in the 1968 paper) will reject one or other of (1) or (2), hence the argument is unsound; and Rosen (1995) gratefully accepts this response. Lewis (1968) requires a quantification in the vernacular to be translated as a restricted quantifier in counterpart theory, the restriction being to things in the world that's in question. By contrast, vernacular modal operators are to be translated as quantifiers restricted only to worlds. Hence the existential quantifier in (3), on translation, will be restricted by the universal quantifier that deals with "necessarily". This is not reflected in (1), so (2) is false.

If we try to effect the relevant quantifier restriction in (1), we get something like this:

At all worlds, *w*, there are at least two worlds in *w*.

But Lewis holds that there are no worlds in worlds.[9] That's to say: anything in a world is not itself a world, for a world is maximal.

The upshot is that the quick refutation of fictionalism about possible worlds fails.[10] The discussion brings to light that we are walking on a tightrope: slight modifications in translation procedures may make a big difference. The idea that there is something intuitively appealing about fictionalism will tend to get lost in these technicalities. This brings to salience the question: why be fictionalist about possible worlds?

FICTIONALISM ABOUT POSSIBLE WORLDS 189

8.6 Motivations for fictionalism about possible worlds

[Y]ou can have all the benefits of talking about possible worlds without the ontological costs.

Rosen 1990: 330

Many fictionalists allude, without further specificity, to the "benefits" of possible worlds accounts of modality. What are they?

It seems to me that there are four applications of PW to which one could allude:

1   PW semantics for quantified modal logic (as in Kripke 1963).[11]

2   PW talk makes modal speculation vivid and systematic.

3   PW talk is expressively richer in desirable ways relative to talk using modal auxiliaries ("must", "can") or operators (boxes and diamonds).

4   PW tells us what to think about modality.

(1) We've already seen that the elements of model theory, truth values or possible worlds, play an essentially structural role. So we cannot base any preference for fictionalism, as opposed to eliminativism, on possible worlds semantics for QML. The semantics can be correct even if the elements that play the role of "worlds" are not really worlds at all, but are merely indices.

(2) It may be that possible worlds talk makes modal speculation vivid. But there's no reason to think there's anything serious, or ontologically committing, about this imaginative prop. One can as well invite people vividly to imagine it being the case that p, and use their success or failure in the attempt as a guide to whether or not p is possible.

(3) There's no disputing that PW is expressively richer than QML. (We have already seen that if our only modal resources are boxes and diamonds we cannot express the thought that there are nonactual things.) The question is whether PW's additional expressive power is significant to our talk of modality. It can hardly be disputed that the standard QML apparatus of boxes and diamonds needs to be supplemented with an operator to express actuality. (If "A" is such an operator, the thought that there are nonactual things could be expressed: There is an x such that not A (x exists).) But

it's an open question whether, once this supplementation has been made (perhaps along with one or two others), the additional expressive resources of PW have any value for expressing modal thought. Lewis thinks they do; but that opinion is not universally accepted.

(4) Rosen is willing to let his modal beliefs be guided by what PW says. Why should he? PW says that the accessibility relation between worlds (or the counterpart relation) is not transitive, so, applying the usual semantics to QML, it in effect claims that $\Box A$ does not entail $\Box\Box A$. Now consider PW', according to which the relevant relation is transitive, so that the usual semantics applied to QML ensures that $\Box A$ does entail $\Box\Box A$. How should we choose between PW and PW'? This is a general problem for a fictionalist. On the face of it, some fictions need to be accorded more respect than others, but it would seem that a basis for discrimination must come from outside the fictions themselves. In that case, fiction is merely a way of keeping track of opinions formed on some other, more realistic, basis. In the next section, we look more closely at the relation between fictionalism and the epistemology of modality.

8.7 Whence modal knowledge?

Fictionalists face a quite general problem: how to choose the *right* story, given how many actual and possible stories are available. The tooth-fairy story was a good choice: the structure of its fantasy matched reality in helpful ways, as we can see by comparing tooth-fairy-based expectations with what actually happens. How should we choose a good story about possible worlds?

Lewis (1968) gives a clear and definite answer: be guided by his counterpart theory, which is based on the notion of similarity. He writes, for example:

$$\alpha_1 = \alpha_2 \prec \Box \alpha_1 = \alpha_2 \ (\alpha_1 \text{ and } \alpha_2 \text{ not the same variable})$$

> The translation is not a theorem, but would have been under the rejected postulate that nothing in any world had more than one counterpart in any other world. (1968: 124)

Is identity a necessary relation? No; and what's the reason? It's that some things have more than one counterpart at another world. Why should that be? Because the counterpart relation is based on similarity. Something c at world w is a counterpart of an object y at another world just if c is similar to y and nothing at w is more similar to y. This allows y to have more than one counterpart at w. If we were antecedently convinced of the necessity of identity, we would conclude that the counterpart relation, understood in Lewis's way, was inadequate to represent modal thought. But Lewis drives the considerations in the other direction. Entering the realm of worlds in Lewis's spirit, similarity seems the only available relation to mark our modal distinctions. Similarity has various features, like not being transitive and admitting ties, hence modal logic must have corresponding features, like not validating necessitation (if $\Box A$ then $\Box\Box A$) or the necessity of identity (if $\alpha_1 = \alpha_2$ then $\Box\alpha_1 = \alpha_2$).

The stipulations or postulates of counterpart theory are held to deliver correct results for QML. Why should we believe this? Lewis is confident that the counterpart-theoretic approach gives the deepest insight into modality. A fictionalist cannot share this confidence, for counterpart theory has to be a mere fiction. A fictionalist should accordingly look askance at the inference Lewis makes in the passage quoted (and several others on the same page of that article).[12]

Telling a purely fictional story is a freewheeling activity; it's not purely fictional if it's constrained by the nature of real facts. If a fictionalist sees PW as purely fictional, its pronouncements can carry no epistemic weight. Perhaps PW is only partly fictional, like a historical novel: the main outlines purport to tell things as they are, and some telling details are supplied by fictional infilling. But the fictionalist about possible worlds cannot accept this version either, for it can hardly be doubted that the main theme of PW is that there are possible worlds, and the fictionalist must treat this as purely fictional, not as a mirror of reality.

As far as I can see, a fictionalist about possible worlds can give no adequate justification for taking PW rather than alternatives as the "right" fiction. Why accept PW rather than an otherwise similar story that replaces the counterpart relation by identity? Or that insists that the accessibility relation between worlds is transitive? Lewis has things to say about these questions, but his view makes sense only from his realist perspective. For a fictionalist, there seems to be no answer to the question what makes one of these fictions better than another.

There's a useful contrast between fictionalism about possible worlds and both constructive empiricism and mathematical fictionalism. Both the latter theories are firmly constrained: constructive empiricism by observations, mathematical fictionalism by conservatism. Only "stories" which have the right observable consequences, or which are conservative, are to be accepted. There may be more than one such story, in which case we can properly be indifferent about which to accept. What we can't do is to use a story about unobservables or about mathematical entities to help us determine which observations are correct, or which empirical theories are true.

By contrast, in the modal case there are uncertainties about what the modal facts are. Hence there must be corresponding uncertainties about which possible worlds story is to be accepted. We don't have a firm basis for the selection of PW as our story of possible worlds as opposed to other stories. This makes it much harder for the modal fictionalist than for the constructive empiricist or the mathematical fictionalist to identify the value of their favored fiction.

Suggested reading

Lewis (1986) is the source for modal realism. Rosen (1990) first proposed fictionalism about possible worlds. Nolan (2007) gives a masterly overview.

9
MORAL FICTIONALISM

Fictionalism about mathematics and about possible worlds is usually motivated by ontological scruples, nominalism and actualism. An analogous scruple could ground moral fictionalism: one might think, as John Mackie did (1977), that moral values are too "queer" or peculiar to belong to the natural order: how can they both be fully objective yet intrinsically motivating? How can simply appreciating that an action has a certain property (being right) thereby incline one to perform it? According to Mackie, our moral talk is, or risks being, committed to these unacceptable entities. A fictionalist tries to have the benefits of moral talk without incurring the ontological costs of commitment to values.

A recent version of moral fictionalism, offered by Kalderon (2005a), does not proceed on these lines. Instead there is an intricate argument whose main premise concerns the nature of reasons. It's based on a series of dilemmas. Here's a rough outline:

1   There are two kinds of view about the nature of our moral discourse: cognitivist and noncognitivist. There are arguments which show that we rightly reject cognitivist views.

2   There are two kinds of noncognitivist view: nonfactualist (for example, expressivist) and factualist. There are arguments which show that we should reject nonfactualist views.

3   There are two kinds of factualist view: error theory and fictionalism. There are arguments which show that we should reject error theories.

4   Hence we should accept fictionalism about morality.

The argument contains a number of technical notions from moral philosophy (more exactly, metaethics). The distinction between cognitivism and noncognitivism will be discussed in the next section. A factualist says that moral discourse is supposed to state facts, and a nonfactualist denies this. An expressivist says that the meaning of moral sentences is to be given by the attitudes or emotions they are generally used to express or arouse. An error theorist (the salient example is Mackie 1977) is a factualist who says that our typical moral beliefs are false.

No matter one's opinion of the soundness of the argument (I am going to suggest that it is unsound), it is indisputably of interest, especially in the present context. In discussing other fictionalisms, it has sometimes been hard, or at least controversial, to find an argument showing the costs of nonfictionalism (e.g., an argument against Platonism) or the benefits of the fictionalized discourse (e.g. why take PW seriously, rather than engage in reduction or elimination?). Hence detailed argument is especially welcome. I'll spell out one of the stages in more detail.

9.1 Noncognitivism

Cognitivism is the view that "moral commitments are best explained by moral beliefs" (Kalderon 2005a: 2). Noncognitivism is the view that moral commitments are to be explained not by moral beliefs but by other attitudes, for example feelings of approval or disapproval. Here's an outline of one of Kalderon's arguments for noncognitivism:[1]

1   If moral acceptance is cognitive, disagreement about reasons in moral cases generates a lax obligation to inquire further. (2005a: 27, 34)

2   It is permissible to be intransigent, that is, it is permissible not to inquire further in a case of moral disagreement about reasons. In these cases there is not even a lax obligation to inquire further.

3   Hence moral acceptance is not cognitive. In other words, we must reject cognitivist positions.

The distinction between cognitivist and noncognitivist views in ethics is often made to turn on whether or not moral opinions can properly be assessed for truth. For the sake of vividness, let's suppose that truth is correspondence to reality. A cognitivist sees moral opinions as beholden to that correspondence: they can properly be assessed as true or false, thanks to the existence of a moral reality which it is their job to match. Noncognitivists, by contrast, think of moral opinions in terms of attitudes or feelings. Although we ordinarily speak of our moral opinions as *beliefs*, this word is misleading, since it suggests a cognitivist position. Noncognitivists think that moral opinions cannot be properly assessed as true or false and so, in a strict sense, are not beliefs. For noncognitivists, it's wrong to say that, of people with opposed moral opinions, at least one must be guilty of error. Error, in the ordinary sense of falsity, is not an appropriate way to assess moral opinion. By contrast, cognitivists think that error must be present in every case of moral disagreement, just as it must be present in every case of mathematical disagreement, or disagreement over any matter of fact.

Kalderon's idea is that we can clarify this debate by studying the kinds of reasons that are appropriate for grounding moral opinions. Suppose two people disagree about whether to accept some sentence S. Some disagreements are relatively uninteresting. For example, the disputants may have different information relevant to whether S should be accepted. That can be a fully satisfactory explanation of their disagreement. Other cases are more difficult and more interesting, for example those in which both parties accept some other sentence, say R, but disagree about whether or not R counts as a good reason for accepting S. Two doctors might agree about what the symptoms are but disagree about the diagnosis, S. They both ground their diagnosis in the same reasons, R, yet not only do they disagree about whether S is true, they also disagree about whether R grounds S. This situation is familiar in moral cases. Both parties to a dispute about whether a particular woman would be right to procure an abortion might agree that doing so would prevent the birth of a severely handicapped child, but whereas one party might regard this as a reason for counting the abortion as morally permissible, the other might not. This exemplifies what Kalderon calls "disagreement about reasons".

Kalderon claims that if we are in a cognitivist region of discourse, parties to a disagreement about reasons always have some kind of obligation to re-examine their position, to enquire further. Assuming our doctors have a reasonable measure of mutual respect, it would be entirely fitting for each to reconsider. If it is A who regards R as sufficient grounds for S and B who demurs, A should see if he can make vivid to himself cases in which R holds and S does not, and whether the present case might be one of those. B, who treats R as in general insufficient for S, or even as sufficient for not-S, might wonder whether in the specific circumstances it is a stronger reason for S than he had originally supposed. These admirable reconsiderations are not unconditionally obligatory: either party might have something more pressing to do at that particular moment. Nor is it obligatory *always* to reconsider, any more than it is obligatory to give to *every* good charitable cause. But just as it is obligatory to do *something* for charity, so it is obligatory *sometimes* to reconsider when one has found oneself in a disagreement about reasons in a region of discourse governed by cognitive norms. This is what Kalderon calls, in his premise (1), a lax obligation to enquire further. Fulfilling a lax obligation is meritorious, single cases of failure to fulfill it may not be irrational or blameworthy, but consistent failure is.

He claims that this obligation fails when the disagreement is one about moral reasons, and this will deliver premise (2). The claim is largely based on an interesting example. Hilary Putnam and Robert Nozick, for many years colleagues at Harvard, had deeply different political opinions (Nozick inclined to defend conservative principles, especially property rights, Putnam inclined to defend a more left-wing position). Kalderon quotes this passage from Putnam:

> I don't think that it is just a matter of *taste* whether one thinks that the obligation of the community to treat its members with compassion takes precedence over property rights; nor does my co-disputant. Each of us regards the other as lacking, at this level, a certain kind of sensitivity and perception. To be perfectly honest, there is in each of us something akin to *contempt*, not for the other's *mind* – for we each have the highest regard for each other's minds – nor for the other as a *person* – for I have more respect for my colleague's honesty, integrity, kindness, etc., than I do for that of many people who agree with my more "liberal" political views – but for a certain complex of emotions and judgments in the other. (Putnam 1981: 165; quoted by Kalderon 2005a: 36)

Kalderon calls this a case of "moral intransigence": neither party has even a lax obligation to enquire further. "Putnam holds Nozick's moral sensibility in something akin to contempt", so "what motivation would *Nozick's* accepting an undermining reason provide *Putnam* for inquiring further into the grounds of moral acceptance? None" (2005a: 37).

If Kalderon is right about this, we have the two premises needed for the argument for the noncognitivist conclusion at (3). The argument is valid, so the only question is whether the premises are true. In my opinion, neither premise is quite correct. Once corrected, we cease to have an argument for noncognitivism.

Kalderon recognizes that the first premise is controversial (2005a: 21). Disagreeing with someone who believes that the earth is flat, a reasonable person might not be motivated to enquire further into her disputant's grounds for accepting the flat earth claim. (For this to be relevant, we need to assume that a reasonable person will lack motivation to behave in a certain way only if she is not under even a lax obligation to behave in that way.) This leads Kalderon to distinguish two ways in which a sentence can be accepted: for oneself or, additionally, for others. To accept for others is publicly to lend one's authority to the claim; but one might accept for oneself without being willing to do that. (For example, one might believe, and accept for oneself, that a certain stock will rise, but be unwilling to lend one's authority to this in a way which might guide the actions of others: unwilling, that is, to accept this for others.) Kalderon suggests that the lax obligation to enquire further arises only when two conditions are satisfied: (1) the dispute is in a cognitive region of discourse; (2) the acceptance in question is on behalf of others. Since he believes, and I agree, that moral acceptance is acceptance on behalf of others, the modification does not disrupt the argument.

Yet a problem remains. Let's go back to the flat earth dispute with the distinction between the two levels of acceptance in mind. I'm willing to lend my authority to the claim that the earth is not flat but ovoid; I accept that on behalf of others; but I see no reason to tangle with the confused absurdities of the flat-earther. In taking this attitude, I'm not guilty of ignoring even a lax obligation.

Turning to the second premise, although Kalderon praises Putnam's candor, and allows that Putnam would not be motivated to reconsider his reasons in the light of Nozick's familiar objections, he does not show that Putnam would be other than admirable were he to reconsider. In earlier discussion, Kalderon has allowed, as a sufficient mark of the presence of a lax obligation to reconsider, that it would be admirable to do so (2005a: 15). Since it's hard to deny that Putnam would be admirable to reconsider, it's hard to accept that he is not under even a lax obligation to do so.

Kalderon says, rightly enough, that Putnam's failure to reconsider is quite intelligible. He then invokes a suspect principle to draw the conclusion that there's no obligation to reconsider: "if the failure to adopt the end of further inquiry is intelligible, then we are under no rational obligation to adopt this end" (36). Alas, failing to live up to obligations is all too intelligible and familiar. The intelligibility of not doing something is no evidence that it should not be done.

We need a more dynamic picture of disagreement. Return to our disagreeing doctors. Suppose they are long-time colleagues, who have had this disagreement over and over again. They each know that nothing they can say will have any effect on the other: they have endlessly explored all the avenues, and have found their disagreement persists. It seems to me clear that, although the region of discourse is cognitive, and the relevant acceptance is on behalf of others, they no longer have any obligation, however lax, to re-examine.

It's not as if Kalderon can adapt his proposal to say that the first disagreement of the relevant kind induces a lax obligation to reconsider if, and only if, the region of discourse is cognitive. Nozick and Putnam certainly took themselves in the early days to be under an obligation to reconsider. Only when they became convinced that this was fruitless did they see themselves as not bound to do this. In this respect, they are just like the long-time doctor colleagues. First-time disagreement among those who wish to get things right induces an obligation to reconsider whether we are in a cognitive or a noncognitive region. I take myself to be an expert on wine, and I know that you are certainly one. If you declare a bottle excellent which I find indifferent, I am right to think I ought to take another sip, and reconsider my judgment.

The upshot of this rather brief exploration of Kalderon's system is that his argument fails at the first step: moral reasons do not license a distinctive form of intransigence. Given our concern with fictionalism, we will leave this aspect of his position there, though people concerned with the other views that he proposes to eliminate on the way to his fictionalist conclusion, and especially those with any inclination towards expressivism, will do well to take his arguments very seriously. Moreover, the fact that some argument for noncognitivism fails does not show that the view is incorrect.

9.2 Fictionalism and semantics

Moving to a broader perspective, Kalderon motivates fictionalism as offering an alternative to the following choice: "between a plausible semantics wedded to an implausible cognitivism and an implausible semantics wedded to a plausible noncognitivism" (2005a: 146). The alternative, moral fictionalism, is noncognitivist, but shares the ordinary "realist" semantics which cognitivists sometimes treat as their prerogative. It says that moral discourse is of the fact-stating kind, but that our attitude to its sentences is not belief, but an attitude that does not commit us to there being any such facts. This section aims to lay out these issues.

Ordinary naïve semantics for simple parts of English associate names with bearers, and predicates with properties. "Fido" names Fido, "barks" introduces the property of barking; these two facts somehow come together to deliver the meaning of "Fido barks". These semantics are not appropriate for ordinary fiction, for it contains names without bearers. As we saw earlier (chapter 2), this has historically functioned as an encouragement to realism, which supplies fictional names with bearers after all. In the moral case, applying these semantics would require even a fictionalist to admit the existence of those moral values needed as bearers for names like "evil" and "courage".[2] However, this semantic approach is quite unnecessary: the less demanding account provided by RWR semantics does just as well (indeed, better). RWR semantics allow us to treat names of virtues and vices in the moral vocabulary as meaningful, without commitment to there being virtues and vices. Naïve semantics require a bearer for such singular terms as "evil" and "courage"; RWR semantics can do without.[3] This is helpful to a moral fictionalist.

Kalderon finesses the problem of distinctively moral names by asking us to consider a moral language whose moral vocabulary is confined to predicates. The "plausible" semantics to which he refers sees predicates as introducing properties. Familiar noncognitivists, for example emotivists, deny that there are any moral properties, and say that the meaning of a moral term like "evil" is given by the attitude conventionally expressed by its use. This leads to well-known difficulties. For example, in a conditional like "If masturbation is evil, encouraging others to masturbate is evil", no attitude of any kind is expressed, so the emotivist is at a loss to say what "evil" means in such a context. By contrast, the plausible semantics to which Kalderon alludes will simply invite us to regard "evil" as introducing a distinctively moral property. Theorists can then disagree about whether the property has any instances. Kalderon's fictionalist will say it does not. So Kalderon's fictionalism says, not that there are no moral properties, but only that no moral properties are instantiated.

This is not an entirely happy upshot for a moral fictionalist. Anyone moved by Mackie's considerations about the "queerness" of moral properties might find this large-scale commitment to them unwelcome. And someone who thinks that predicates in general do not have bearers (as in RWR and many other approaches) will regard the commitment to moral properties as unmotivated. But let's leave these qualms to one side.

Kalderon's fictionalism combines factualist semantics with noncognitivism ("Moral fictionalism is noncognitivism without nonfactualism" [115]). On this view, moral acceptance does not consist in believing that a moral property is true of something, but rather in adopting a certain attitude. So a fictionalist can make room for our moral opinions without ascribing to us endless error.

As we saw, Kalderon attempted to establish fictionalism (notably its noncognitivist aspect) on the basis of facts concerning our use of moral language. Hence he is a hermeneutic fictionalist in this sense: ordinary users of moral discourse treat it as a fiction. As one might put it, Kalderon is hermeneutic at level 1. At the next level up, however, he is revolutionary: he thinks that people do not generally recognize that they are fictionalists, perhaps because they are lulled by the apparent objectivity of moral language: "competent speakers take themselves to believe the moral proposition expressed" by a sentence they accept (2005a: 153). Belief is a nonfictionalist attitude. So he is revolutionary at level 2.

The largest problem for moral fictionalism is to explain how a merely fictitious morality can be of value. It is conspicuous that there seem to be many moral fictions, stemming from different cultures and different convictions. Which should we accept? And how could accepting a mere fiction have a suitable influence on conduct? These questions are the subject of the next section.

9.3 The value of morality from a fictionalist point of view

> *The writer has no business making moral judgments.*
>
> J. G. Ballard, *Miracles of Life*

How should we choose between different moral prescriptions? That's a hard question for any theorist. It's especially hard for a fictionalist, for this theorist finds it hard even to make sense of the point of a choice. How can morality be useful if we don't believe it?

Kalderon's contribution to answering this question comes from his response to a related question. What's going on when people use moral sentences with apparently assertive intent? He says that we can help ourselves to any noncognitivist view we like. We can stress that "In uttering a moral sentence that he understands, a competent speaker conveys the relevant affect and implicitly demands that others come to respond affectively in the relevant manner" (2005a: 148). At the same time, the speaker or thinker must be engaging in an activity that constitutes an appropriate response to fiction (even if they do not realize that that is what they are doing). One could summarize that response as pretense. So Kalderon appears to be committed to the following position:

- In cases of apparent assertion of moral sentences we pretend that they are true.
- In fact, these sentences are false (for the most part).[4]
- We do not realize we are pretending: we think we are believing that they are true.
- The point of our activity is to convey the relevant affect and demand that others do likewise.

Some problems:

1   It seems hard to believe that we could be so radically mistaken about our attitudes to the sentences we apparently assert: we wrongly think we believe them when we do not. Kalderon's response is that our treating intransigence as permissible in moral cases shows that moral acceptance is not belief; but this is a position that's open to question, as we have seen.
2   An account is needed of what makes an affect relevant. How would outrage (for example) be relevant to a claim that something is evil, given that nothing is evil? (On this version of fictionalism we can't say that we falsely *believe* that some acts are evil, and that the outrage comes from such false beliefs.)
3   How are we to account for unuttered states of mind of a kind we are inclined to report as the belief that war is evil? These states are important to us (we usually call them beliefs), but in being in them we are not conveying anything and we are not demanding anything; we can properly be in them when engaged in no interaction with others. (This is a problem for every theory which gives pride of place to expression in its account of morality.)

I don't find detailed responses to these difficulties in Kalderon's book, but they are nearer to the surface in an article by Joyce (2005). His view differs from Kalderon's in that he defends revolutionary fictionalism, agreeing (at least for the sake of the argument) that while we have genuine moral beliefs, the better thing would be to abandon them in favor of fictionalist attitudes. The questions just posed are as salient for Joyce's fictionalism as for Kalderon's, and Joyce addresses them more explicitly. He asks us to imagine that we have agreed with Mackie that moral beliefs are in very bad shape: there are no moral values, so morality is a tangle of error. We might respond, as we do to claims about witches, by rejecting the whole discourse: there are no witches, so let's have no more witch-talk. But the point of Joyce's article is to explore whether there might not also be a coherent fictionalist response, according to which our moral thought and talk could be treated as a useful fiction. He sets his sights low, aiming to uncover at least one feature of fictionalized morality which makes it useful, without claiming that this utility will match that of nonfictionalized morality.

One option he considers, and rejects, is that apparently assertive utterances of sentences which are not really true (but true only in a fiction) should be regarded as genuine assertions of the original sentence prefixed by a fiction operator. One good reason he gives for rejecting this view is that it makes no room for a retrospective explanation of the kind: "What I said was strictly speaking false." Had the original assertion been prefixed by a fiction operator, it would have been true, and it's hard to see why the utterer could not have known that it was true. Then the later assertion is inexplicable.

Joyce takes it for granted, quite reasonably, that an interesting kind of fictionalism will not be what he calls propagandist. It should not involve a scenario in which the manipulative cognoscenti, realizing that morality is a tangle of error, go through the motions of making moral assertions in order to keep the *polloi* in their place. The search is for something that can make the kind of sense of moral discourse that would make it acceptable to decent people who are fully aware of its nature.

He disputes the common thought that without morality "all hell would break loose in human society" (2005: 12), claiming that much of the behavior we are inclined to regard as moral would be held in place by self-interest, in particular our interest in securing the co-operation of others, which we know we will typically forfeit if we do not co-operate in our turn. Prudential reasoning of this kind, however, is often thrown off course by the lure of immediate gain, leading to an underestimation of the risks of detection in some act of uncooperative knavery. One value of morality, Joyce hypothesizes, is that it lends additional affective weight to what is in any case the prudent choice: "moral beliefs function to bolster self-control against practical irrationality" (2005: 13). But Joyce acknowledges that it remains problematic how a mere fiction could have even this rather second-class role.

The essence of his suggestion is that fictionally conceived morality can function as a precommitment. Just as Ulysses, before he could hear the sirens' voices, instructed his sailors to bind him to the mast, thus precommitting to resisting their temptations, so, Joyce suggests, moral opinions may help combat weakness of will, presenting in a livelier light, as morally good or bad, actions which are independently prudent or imprudent, and so increasing the probability that we will do the prudent thing. More precisely, and departing from the analogy with Ulysses, who suffered at his mast, the moral fiction "can exclude from practical deliberation the entertainment of certain options: all going well, the fictional attitude blocks the temptation to steal from even arising" (2005: 19).

Joyce says that within the moral framework, regret can become guilt or penitence, and these feelings, or the prospect thereof, can be motivating. Yet he presumably must admit that these feelings would be the result of some kind of delusion. Keeping to our epistemically best form, when we see clearly that morality is nothing but error, we should regard these responses as irrational. Indeed, we must regard the whole fiction of morality as nothing more than a veil of self-deception. It may be that sometimes we have good reason to allow ourselves to sink into the irrational slough of self-deception. (Some atheists claim to wish they could believe in god, even if the belief were false.) And Joyce's aim is modest: to show only that there is at least one benefit to be salvaged from fictionalized morality, not that it can deliver all the benefits of the real thing. Even so, it seems that what is really happening is that we have to forget that morality is merely a fiction. Clearly understood for what it is, fictionalized morality can have no action-guiding force for a rational person. When we appreciate that morality is simply providing an irrational boost towards a prudent choice, a clear-thinking and rational person will weigh the prudential reasons for what they are, and act accordingly. The moral considerations, unlike the very real ropes that bound Ulysses, will have weight only to the extent that we can forget that they have no epistemic worth whatsoever.

Joyce's view of morality makes it a poor thing: a trick to get us to be more prudent. There is no room at all for the kind of moral admiration we feel for saints and moral heroes, or for the detestation we feel towards the tyrannical, destructive and cruel.

The moral fictionalist project has failed: we cannot maintain the action-guiding utility of fictionalism while not paying the ontological costs of treating some moral statements as genuinely true.

It's worth trying to understand the contrast between mathematical fictionalism and the other two fictionalisms on which we have focused, concerning possible worlds and morality. In the last two cases, the fictionalist had no answer to the question: why choose one relevant fiction rather than another? For example, why choose a possible worlds fiction in which the accessibility relation is transitive rather than one in which it is not? Why choose a moral fiction according to which abortion is sometimes permissible rather than one according to which it is never permissible? Field's choice of classical mathematics as the relevant fiction, by contrast, is tightly constrained: it has to deliver just the right consequences from the nominalized scientific theories (together with the bridge laws). In this context, mathematics has a highly constrained task. Likewise, as we saw in chapter 7, constructive empiricism tightly constrains its fictions by the requirement that they deliver only correct observational predictions. Fictionalism about possible worlds and about morality, by contrast, is subject to no analogous constraint. We have no grounds other than realist ones for choosing among the relevant possible fictions. If we hold to necessitation, we'll select a possible worlds fiction which validates it rather than an otherwise similar fiction that does not. If we are pro-choice, we'll select a fiction according to which there's a wide range of circumstances in which abortion is morally permissible. The choice can only be driven by nonfictionalist considerations. This makes the fictionalism just a sham.

Suggested reading

Kalderon (2005a) and Joyce (2005) are important recent sources. Mackie (1977) is recommended reading for anyone interested in this topic, though the main views are not presented using the label "fictionalist".

10

RETROSPECT

The overall plan was to get straight about the metaphysics of fiction before discussing fictionalism. To conclude the book, I offer a brief evaluation of how the metaphysics of fiction affects fictionalism.

Fictionalism is often motivated by ontological scruples. Mathematical fictionalists like Field are nominalists: they deny that numbers, along with all other abstract things, are real. Fictionalists about possible worlds are often actualists: they deny the reality of all nonactual things, including nonactual possible worlds and any nonactual inhabitants thereof. Moral fictionalists are sometimes motivated by the thought that our world, the natural world, could not contain such weird entities as moral values seem to be. The most obvious way in which the metaphysics of fiction can impinge on fictionalism is if some form of realism is true, and the fictional objects (nonexistent, nonactual, or nonconcrete) somehow get in the way of the fictionalism, or of the motivation behind it.

The obvious example is mathematical fictionalism. Suppose that abstractism is right, so that abstract objects are required as referents for fictional names. Then even if mathematics is a fiction, the numerals introduce abstract objects. These objects may not actually be numbers, just as, on the abstractist view we discussed, the fictional entity Sherlock Holmes is not a detective, but they will at least encode various numerical properties, and will exemplify such properties as being thought about. If abstractism is correct, mathematical fictionalism has exchanged one kind of abstract object, numbers, for another. No progress towards nominalism has been made.

A mathematical fictionalist cannot avoid the charge by reminding us that, on his view, there is no need for mathematics to be true. Realism about fictional objects is offered in full awareness of the fact that sentences within fictions are typically not true. Mathematical fictionalists need to hope that irrealist accounts of fiction are adequate, for any motivation for nominalism is likely to extend to nonexistent and nonactual things. If there is something obscure about how merely abstract things could affect our cognitive systems in a knowledge-conferring way, it would be at least as obscure how nonexistent or nonactual things could have this effect. Any kind of realism about the metaphysics of fiction would thus be abhorrent to one whose fictionalism was based on nominalism.

The adequacy of irrealism may be necessary but is not sufficient to satisfy full-blown nominalist aspirations. Mathematics is a fiction, a story. But what is a story? The most natural answer is that it is something abstract: something which can be told on different occasions, or written down in different copies and different languages. Nominalists have to try to account for fictions or stories in terms of their concrete tokens. I don't envy them. I suggest that mathematical fictionalists are well advised to do what some have done (e.g. Yablo 2005): replace talk of fiction by talk of myth. A myth is like a fiction in not having to be true to be useful, but unlike a fiction in being capable of originating without specific fiction-directed actions. It's a little hard to think of a myth as concrete: on the face of it, a myth cannot be reduced to occasions on which it is invoked in belief or action. But the task here is perhaps no harder than the task confronting nominalists about many other issues (sentences, proofs, classes, resemblances, and so on).

Fictionalism about possible worlds is rooted in actualism, the view that everything is actual. These fictionalists cannot be nonactualists in their metaphysics of fiction. It would be technically possible for them to be Meinongians. Possible worlds and their occupants would be actual but nonexistent. In practice, the distinction between possibilism and Meinongianism has not been much insisted upon. Indeed, Meinongians sometimes remind their readers that resistance to their position stems from a prejudice in favor of the actual. If realism is right, then fictionalists about possible worlds might hope that the correct version is abstractism, for the abstract fictional objects are straightwardly actual, and so should be acceptable to the actualist. Acceptable they may be, but they undermine a fictionalist approach. To say that the fictional objects of the possible worlds fiction are abstract things is essentially to embrace a form of what Lewis has called ersatzism: the view that possible worlds are not real concrete nonactual things, but real abstract actual representations of concrete things. Although this view is appealing, it is inconsistent with fictionalism, for it's a form of eliminativism. An ersatzist will say that, understood correctly, "there are worlds containing blue swans" commits only to there being consistent abstract representations of blue swans. That's not fictionalism about possible worlds. So this fictionalist, too, should hope that the right metaphysics for fiction is irrealist. I've offered arguments in favor of irrealism, so to that extent I should find favor with fictionalists. On the other hand, I've found other reasons for dissatisfaction with some forms of fictionalism.

The case of moral fictionalism, or at least of the version we have discussed, is different. Kalderon requires moral properties, though he says that they are uninstantiated. His moral language does not contain singular terms, like names purporting to stand for virtues or vices, so he does not have to ask whether these can be treated in an irrealist way. For Kalderon, the moral fiction is metaphysically like a fiction told about people and places all of whom are real. We have plenty of literal falsehood, but there is no question of worrying whether there are entities specific to the fiction. Kalderon's moral fictionalist agrees with the moral realist that there are a wide panoply of moral properties, and these can serve as referents for moral predicates, whether used inside or outside the so-called fiction. The disagreement between this moral fictionalist and a moral realist is not over whether there are moral properties (they both say there are), but over whether or not they are instantiated, the realist saying they are, and the fictionalist that they are not.

Other forms of moral fictionalism, however, will face the metaphysical issues. Mackie thinks that although there are no moral values it's acceptable, even valuable, to continue to talk as if there were. How should this talk be understood by a fictionalist? Mackie's rejection of moral values was motivated by a form of naturalism, the belief that everything has a place in the natural order. Naturalists might feel antipathy to nonexistent, nonactual, or nonconcrete things, though I'm not sure that there's a strong argument to justify this. If there is not, they can be indifferent to the metaphysics of fiction. Otherwise they too may wish to adopt my arguments for irrealism.

The notion of acceptance, as contrasted with belief, has played a role throughout. I said in the earlier chapters that one might accept that Holmes was a detective without believing it; more generally, that one might properly regard what one accepts as true, even though one accepts without believing.

We saw that van Fraassen uses the notion of acceptance for a specific attitude to scientific theories, one not to be identified with belief. The notion is clearly available to Field, to report an appropriate attitude to some mathematical claims. And Kalderon says that we can accept moral sentences without believing them. This notion of acceptance was, in the earlier chapters, linked with a notion of presupposition that was not described in detail. For example, the atheist anthropologists in some sense presuppose a pantheon in their disputes about Mayan and Aztec gods; they accept that there are such gods for the purposes of their work, without believing this. Their disputes in some ways resemble how disputes among particle physicists might appear from van Fraassen's perspective. Both fictionalists and theorists of fiction need to draw on notions of presupposition and acceptance, notions which, most theorists would agree, would benefit from closer and more systematic scrutiny.

GLOSSARY

abstract objects although these have sometimes been thought to be ideal, immutable, causally inert, and so on, all I mean by an abstract object is one that is nonspatial and nonmental.

acceptance a mental state that resembles, but falls short of, belief. Developed by Stalnaker in one context (applied in chapter 6 in saying that we should accept but not believe that the Greeks worshipped Zeus) and in another by van Fraassen (in saying that we should accept but not believe scientific theories that posit unobservables).

actualism the view that everything is actual.

closed world world closed under some consequence relation R (a relation holding between sets of sentences and sentences). A world is closed under R iff, if there is a non-empty subset of the sentences true in the world that is R-related to s, s is also true in the world.

cognitivist cognitivist theories of ethics hold that there are moral facts, so that moral knowledge is possible. In Kalderon's version, a cognitivist is one who holds that a moral commitment is a belief.

constructive empiricism a form of fictionalism developed by van Fraassen. Its main tenet is that we should not believe the things that physics says about unobservable particles, but should believe only the observable consequences of these theories. Contrast with instrumentalism.

contradiction conjunction one of whose conjuncts is the negation of the other: for example, "A and not-A". (A conjunction is an "and"-statement.)

conversational implicature technical expression invented by Grice. A conversational implicature of something said goes beyond the literal content, and can be detected by applying general principles of cooperation among participants in conversations. E.g. if in a letter of recommendation I say "The candidate has beautiful handwriting", and stop there, I implicate but do not say that the candidate should not be appointed.

counterpart theory language for modality based on the view that nothing exists at more than one world. That Socrates might have been snub-nosed isn't true if it's taken to mean that there's a world in which Socrates himself is snub-nosed, for he is not snub-nosed in the only world in which he exists (the actual world). The claim is true iff our Socrates has a snub-nosed counterpart at some world, where a counterpart of Socrates at a world w is someone who resembles Socrates, than whom no one else at w more closely resembles Socrates.

de re belief, de dicto belief a de re belief targets an object, a de dicto belief targets a proposition.

direct reference theories of names usually another term for Millian theories of names (q.v.) but sometimes used more widely for any view that denies that names are equivalent to definite descriptions. In the broader sense, RWR theory is a direct reference theory.

empirical adequacy used as technical expression by van Fraassen (1980): a theory is empirically adequate iff all its observable consequences agree with what is observed.

encode abstract artifacts *encode* all kinds of properties, like smoking a pipe, that they could not possibly exemplify (q.v.). Encoded properties are those ascribed in the fiction.

error theory a theory according to which we are systematically mistaken in some region of thought. For example, one error theory in morality says that we believe in the reality of moral values, but these beliefs are false.

evil genius skeptical arguments Descartes imagined an evil genius who exerts all his powers to deceive me: there is really no material world, but the genius makes me have just the kinds of experience I actually have, so all my beliefs are false, though I have no way of discovering this. Descartes took this scenario to suggest that I actually lack knowledge, since I can't exclude it.

exemplify abstract artifacts *exemplify* the properties they actually have, like being abstract and being artifacts. They do not exemplify (but rather encode) properties that no abstract object could have, like smoking a pipe.

exotic object one that is either nonexistent, nonactual, or nonconcrete.

exportation inference an inference in which a phrase is given wider scope, for example, the inference from "John thinks that some pigs fly" to "There are some pigs that, John thinks, fly." As in this example, such inferences are often invalid. However, when a fiction concerns a real person, X, one can validly move from "According to the fiction, X is such-and-such" to "X is, according to the fiction, such-and-such."

expressivism in moral theory, the view that sentences like "Stealing is wrong" merely express attitudes, feelings, or emotions, and have no "factual" content.

extensional one mark of an extensional relation, like *being to the left of*, is that if sentences ascribing the relation are true, there must be things appropriately related by it. The contrast is with intensional (or nonextensional) verbs: John may long to ride Pegasus, even though there is no such thing as Pegasus. One can't happily think of this as reporting a relation between John and Pegasus; by the definition, it's certainly not an extensional relation if there is no Pegasus.

fiction operator an expression like "According to such-and-such a fiction". It's called an operator because it operates on a sentence like "Holmes drew deeply on his pipe" to make a new sentence, "According to *A Study in Scarlet*, Holmes drew deeply on his pipe." The sentence prefixed by the fiction operator can be literally, and nonfictionally true, even if the sentence it prefixes is not.

fidelity to a story being right about what the story says.

grue word invented by Nelson Goodman to reveal a problem with naïve conceptions of inductive projection. Something is grue just on condition that it's green and has been examined, or else hasn't been examined and is blue (see Goodman 1955: 74). If all emeralds are grue, the unexamined ones are blue.

hermeneutic fictionalism fictionalism attributed to ordinary thinkers (as opposed to theorists). Contrasted with revolutionary fictionalism, which claims that although ordinary thinkers do not in fact adopt fictionalist attitudes, they should do.

Holmes-surrogate possible object having all the properties explicitly ascribed to Holmes in the stories.

iff abbreviates "if, and only if".

illocutionary act an act involving the use of words, such as making a statement or making a promise.

inductive projection an argument which projects what has been experienced onto unobserved parts of reality. Example: we inductively project our past experience of a daily sunrise onto the future, believing that the sun will rise tomorrow.

instrumentalism the doctrine that scientific theories apparently about unobservables must be regarded as really only about observable things.

This involves reinterpretation. By contrast, fictionalists don't reinterpret. They say the problematic claims are simply false, but are useful fictions.

intensionality a feature of language, exemplified by "thinks about". Intensional expressions are particularly apt for expressing intentionality.

intentionality a feature of the mind, exemplified by *thinking about*. The distinctive feature is that one can think about things that do not exist.

intersective adjective one, say A, which combines with the noun that it modifies, say N, in such a way that "is an A N" is true of an object iff both A and N are true of it. For example, "red" is generally taken to be intersective, since something of which "red ball" is true is something of which both "red" and "ball" are true. But "toy", for example, is not intersective: "gun" does not have to be true of something of which "toy gun" is true.

irrealism the denial of realism (q.v.).

isomorphic sets are isomorphic iff there is a one–one mapping from the members of the one to the members of the other which preserves structure.

literalist one who believes that some purely fictional sentences, like "Holmes lived on Baker Street", are literally true.

logical construction technical expression in Russell's philosophy. If Xs are logical constructions out of Ys we don't need to be ontologically committed to Xs.

logical form in the context of the present discussion, the logical form of a sentence is supposed to reveal its ontological commitments and semantic workings. This book does not rely on the notion.

make-believe although this notion plays an important role, there's no neat definition of it that I am aware of. It's discussed and elaborated in chapter 1, especially sections 2–4.

maximal spatiotemporal region a spatiotemporal region is maximal iff it contains every point in space or time that stands in some spatial or temporal relation to any point in the region.

Meinongian views The central claim is that some things don't exist. See chapter 3.

Millian view of names the meaning of a name is simply its bearer. Names without bearers are meaningless (and so cannot be used to say anything intelligible). Sometimes "direct reference theory" of names is used interchangeably with "Millian theory", though some authors, like Salmon, make a distinction: see **direct reference theories of names**.

modal related to necessity, possibility, and essence.

modal realism the view (propounded by David Lewis) that nonactual things (worlds and their occupants) are as real as actual ones.

Müller–Lyer illusion The horizontal line in the figure on the left looks shorter than the horizontal line in the figure on the right, though they are in fact the same length:

negative free logic this logic allows for bearerless proper names, while requiring that every simple sentence in which such a name occurs be false. For further details, see Sainsbury (2005).

nominalism the doctrine that there are no abstract entities. Contrasted with Platonism.

nuclear versus extranuclear properties a problematic distinction within Meinongian views. Nuclear properties are those, like being a detective, which are attributed to nonexistent things. Extranuclear properties, like existence, concern metaphysical status, and cannot be possessed merely by being attributed.

object-dependence "John thinks about Pegasus" is object-dependent iff its truth requires there to be an object, Pegasus.

ontological commitment a philosophically disputed notion, much influenced by Quine. One usage is this: a sentence is ontologically committed to Xs if Xs must exist if the sentence is true.

ontology (i) theory of what there is. (ii) The ontology of a sentence consists in the things that must exist for the sentence to be true.

opacity word used by Quine to express failure of substitution of identicals.

paraconsistent logic a logic in which contradictions do not entail everything. Classical logic (and many other familiar logics) is not paraconsistent.

Platonism the doctrine that there are many abstract entities, lying outside space and time.

polysemy a polysemous word has more than one meaning, but the different meanings are systematically related. Thus "bottle" can mean a container or its contents.

possibile an object that is possible but nonactual (plural: possibilia).

prop technical term used by Walton for something playing a distinctive role in enabling a game of make-believe: props are generators of fictional truths. See section 1.4.

quantified modal logic the language of quantified modal logic (QML) is that of first-order logic plus boxes and diamonds, thought of as operators expressing necessity and possibility.

quantifiers expressions like "all", "some", and "none", that can be used to say how many things have a certain property.

quasi-fear technical term introduced by Walton for the kind of physiological events that normally accompany fear. See section 1.4.

realism concerning fictional characters, it's the view that they belong to our reality, not just to the world of the fiction.

reflexive relation one that everything bears to itself (e.g. being the same height as).

robust fictional character fictional character who belongs to our reality, and not just to the world of his or her fiction.

RWR reference without referents. This view has been defended by Sainsbury (2005) and is here sketched as an appendix to section 2.4. The main claim is that there can be intelligible nondescriptive empty names.

selection problem the problem that confronts Meinongians of explaining how authors manage to select the right nonexistent objects to tell their stories about.

sense data mental entities which are supposed by some theorists to be the immediate objects of perception.

set-theoretic union x is a member of the union of two sets, A and B, iff either x is a member of A or x is a member of B. In symbols: $(x \in A \cup B)$ iff $(x \in A \lor x \in B)$.

singular thoughts thoughts that purport to be about individual objects.

substitution of identicals the principle that coreferring expressions can be substituted for one another without affecting the truth or falsehood of the whole sentence. This is a linguistic principle, which clearly does not always hold, and is to be contrasted with the following exceptionless metaphysical principle (sometimes known as Leibniz's Law): if $x = y$ then x and y have all and only the same properties.

supervaluations in supervaluational semantics, the informal notion of truth is defined as supertruth, where a sentence is supertrue iff true for every admissible valuation and superfalse iff false for every admissible valuation. This allows for intermediate cases. In the case of fiction, the intermediate cases will mark the incompleteness of fictional objects: since the stories don't say how many hairs Holmes had when he first met Watson, "The number of his hairs was even" will come out true on some admissible valuations and false on others, and so will neither be (super)true nor (super)false. An admissible valuation, in the context of nonactualist semantics for fiction, is the assignment of a truth value to a pair consisting of a (fictional) sentence and a possible world in a way that respects the content of the fiction in question.

tautology a formula that takes the truth value *true* for every assignment of values to its propositional letters

transitive relation a relation, R, is transitive iff, for all x, y, z, if x has R to y and y has R to z then x has R to z. Being greater than is transitive, but being similar to is not. The blue cube is similar to the blue sphere (both are blue) and the blue sphere to the red sphere (both are spheres), but the blue cube is not similar to the red sphere.

ur-element member of a class that is not itself a class.

valid argument one in which the premises, if true, would guarantee the truth of the conclusion. An argument that is not valid is called invalid.

NOTES

Introduction

1 "[I]n pretend play, evolution has produced a suite of cognitive adaptations designed to make use of surplus resources in a safe environment to train strategies for dealing with dangerous or expensive situations that have not yet occurred" (Steen and Owens 2001: 292).
2 The explanation of this differential salience is quite complicated. Literary fiction is more closely bound to representation than is painting or sculpture: (a) the intrinsic features of a physical book (paper quality, ink color, font, etc.), unlike the intrinsic features of a sculpture or painting, have little or no relevance to its literary value; (b) a painting or sculpture may be nonrepresentational, in which case the notions of truth and falsehood are not literally applicable; (c) some representational paintings may be likened to documentaries, which makes them unlike literary fiction.

1 What is fiction

1 Suppose everyone mistook what was produced as a factual narrative for fiction. Should it then count as fiction? Possibly so; though I prefer to say it's a case of everyone mistaking fact for fiction. In any case, the authorial intentions will normally play the crucial role.
2 In historical novels, it's the other way round: it's not the historical events, but the little fictitious details (of meals, conversations, inner thoughts) that are intended to add realism, to make the story "come to life." In Solzhenitsyn's *The First Circle*,

Stalin is portrayed as wondering whether the time had come to liquidate his powerful minister Abakumov. A biographer of Stalin would be rash to attribute this thought to his subject on the basis of this passage, despite Solzhenitsyn's undoubted integrity.

3 So many oversimplifications have to be made. Here's a small one: an author includes in a novel the sentence, not in inverted commas, "Everybody just walks away" (Cormac McCarthy, *No Country for Old Men*). The reader does not have to make-believe this, but only that a character (Carson Wells) said this. In fact, Wells's suggestion was a feeble pipe-dream. A more interesting one: The Coen brothers' movie *Fargo* starts with the claim that what follows is based entirely on real events. This is not so. Are we supposed to believe the claim or make-believe it? Hard to say. If the former, then the movie must count as fiction thanks to the many fictional scenes it contains.

4 This characterizes typical cases. Atypically, someone might write a novel to see if they could do it, not intending that there be readers. (Though possibly this author sees herself as a reader.) In a more extreme case, as Alex Grzankowski suggested, someone might write what we intuitively count as a novel as a kind of therapy, firmly intending that there will be no readers.

5 Though not necessarily identical: even if historical information were always passed on by assertion, it would be one thing to pretend to pass on historical information and another to pretend to assert.

6 Currie accepts that his view is consistent with one reading of Lewis's: 1990: 50.

7 As Tim Button pointed out, pretense does not always involve deception (as in "Let's pretend ..."). Maybe there's no significant difference between the nondeceptive pretence of theism and make-believing in it.

8 The account of make-believe cannot be simply inserted in the specification of the intention. Even if knowledge is, as a matter of analysis, justified true belief, one who intends to acquire knowledge may not intend to acquire (mere!) justified true belief. This is consistent with regarding an account of what it is to X as helping understand what it is to intend to X.

9 That's not to say children don't hunger for better (and more expensive) props: they certainly do. The claim is only that better props often don't make for better games; the more expensive props often disappoint. I can agree with Barry Lee that some folk tales owe their power more to their content than to their mode of expression. It remains that quality of mode of expression is typically more significant than prop quality.

10 The puzzle (or, perhaps one should say, the family of puzzles) goes back at least to Radford (1975) and is still discussed, e.g. by Kim (2005b). Aidan McGlynn has suggested, I think correctly, that in a fuller discussion one would consider a weaker variant of (1), which is closer to what Radford actually wrote: if a person Vs an F (for some verb of emotion, V) then the person must believe in the existence of a relevant F. Here I'll assume that the belief required by (1) involves believing in the existence of the supposed object of the emotion, though it typically goes beyond this.

11 In later work, Walton (1997: 2) says that he never denied that consumers of fiction have genuine emotions. Rather, the claim was that one cannot rightly describe these emotions as directed on fictional characters. Charles is afraid, but does not fear the

slime. It's not certain that this accords with his earlier view, as in the text to which this note attaches.

12 "To the left of" is called extensional in that: (i) x can be to the left of y only if there are such things as x and as y; (ii) if $z = x$ and x is to the left of y, then z is to the left of y, and if $z = y$ and x is to the left of y then x is to the left of z. If one can be afraid of dragons even though there are no such things, then "is afraid of" does not meet the test for being extensional. "Intensional" is sometimes used for such verb phrases; one can treat this as meaning simply "not extensional". In the terminology used in chapter 6, the suggestion of the paragraph above is that "is afraid of" is an intensional verb phrase.

13 There is some affinity between this view and that argued for by Roberts (1988).

2 Realism about fictional objects

1 Although these authors give no evidence for their claim, it's supported by a survey conducted in the UK (thanks to Aidan McGlynn for drawing this to my attention):
Sherlock Holmes, the famous fictional detective, was so convincingly brought to life in Sir Arthur Conan Doyle's novels of the late 1880s that over half of us (58%) believe that the sleuth really lived and worked with his sidekick Watson at 221B Baker Street, North London. (http://uktv.co.uk/gold/stepbystep/aid/598605)
Depressing times for educators.

2 The multiple-choice part of the Texas driving test at one time had some alternative answers for candidates to choose from, including "I step on the gas and see if I can beat the train to the crossing" and "I make a U-turn and hightail it to the next crossing to get there before the train."

3 There is a subtlety (perhaps a defect) in the set-up of this example. The more natural form of the question is "What do you do?", so the answer will begin "I apply ...." It's hard so much as to understand what it would be for this simple present-tense sentence to be true absolutely. The only interpretation I can think of makes the present tense the habitual present, which is probably not what is intended in the context. The continuous present ("I am applying ...") makes the case one of narration, and so not as different from fiction as would be ideal.

4 Literalists Martinich and Stroll (2007: 27) would accept premise (2) (though I would not wish to accuse them of advancing the argument presented here): they say that truth in fiction is truth, but truth in which fiction-specific criteria are applicable; they insist that this difference of criteria does not involve a different truth property.

5 Parsons (1980: 177–8) gives a nice example of a deeply concealed contradiction.

6 This needs two qualifications. (1) "Character" may, perhaps like some uses of "personage", have as part of its meaning that anything of which the word is true is fictitious. Most ordinary novels, like the Holmes stories, do not say that there are characters in this sense: they say there are real people, detectives, doctors, and so on. If that's right, then the platitude is that there are stories according to which there are certain people and places, even though in fact there are no such people and places. (2) Although this is platitudinous, it does not add up to the content of the original "There are fictional characters", for the latter, though not the platitude, ensures that there are particular fictional characters. (The platitude might be made

true by fictions which made merely general claims: there are some detectives, and some doctors.) This defect, drawn to my attention by Marcus Glodek, is remedied in chapter 6 below.
7 In chapter 5 I discuss another rapid argument for fictional characters: "[F]ictional entities are created in a straightforward and unproblematic way by the pretending use of names: the fictional entity Jonathan Pine was quite literally and straightforwardly created by John le Carré's use of 'Jonathan Pine' in order to pretend, in the way definitive of fiction, to refer to a real person" (Schiffer 1996: 157).
8 She holds that fictional characters are abstract, and so cannot have human properties like being a detective. See chapter 5 below.
9 The view goes back at least to Mill (1843), and after some time in the doldrums enjoyed renewed popularity thanks to the work of Kripke (1972) – though Kripke is careful not to commit himself to this approach. The view has been defended by e.g. Salmon (1981) and Soames (2002). Some philosophers, like Salmon himself, treat the thesis of direct reference as purely negative: names cannot be analyzed as definite descriptions. In this terminology, the positive view, that a name owes its meaning to its bearer and nothing else, is the one deserving the title "Millian".
10 This receives support in Oliver and Smiley (2006: 322–3) under the label of the "Alibi Principle".
11 Extensional embeddings, like those produced by negation, can convert falsehood to truth. In these cases, the conversion is mandated: if s is false, then not-s is true, whatever s may be. By contrast, if John believes that s, for some false s, it does not follow that he believes every falsehood. The extension of a sentence is its truth or falsehood (as the case may be) and extensional operators like negation have outputs wholly determined by the extensions of their inputs. This does not hold for fiction operators: they are nonextensional.
12 In the interests of full disclosure, the word which occupies the last ellipsis in this quotation is "unreal". Both terminology and doctrine on this matter are murky. For more on the issue, see chapter 4 below.
13 Or so we shall pretend. In fact in one of the later stories Holmes is represented as a person of wide repute: "Europe was ringing with his name and ... his room was literally ankle-deep with congratulatory telegrams" (from the opening of *The Reigate Puzzle*).

3 Fictional objects are nonexistents

1 Though not Meinong himself. He thought that some beings exist (things like Mount Everest) and some merely subsist (like the number 9). Members of both categories have some kind of being (or as I will say: they have some kind of existence). Meinong could not have used MO to express his belief that there are things which neither exist nor subsist. He used the turn of phrase, which he admitted smacks of paradox, "There are objects of which it is true that there are no such objects." I hope the less paradoxical formulation given here will be easier to digest. There are many myths about what Meinong himself really thought: see Oliver 1999: §6.
2 There are indeed examples of things that don't exist (unicorns, etc.). It doesn't follow that there are such things as unicorns. Compare the quotation from Parsons at the head of this section.

3 This view is defended by Sainsbury (2005), and the general approach is described in more detail in the appendix to section 2.4, above.
4 Van Inwagen does not use this example to support Meinongianism. Rather, he holds that fictional characters exist, but are abstract things. He offers an independent consideration against Meinongianism, namely that he cannot understand it.
5 The Meinongian will probably wish to draw on something like the distinction between nuclear and extranuclear properties in discussing this example; the distinction is introduced in the section that follows this. In the sense in which the sentence is true, an extranuclear property is ascribed; in the sense in which it is false (Holmes is portrayed as retiring), it ascribes a nuclear property,
6 The interest of this version of Meinongianism was impressed on me by Markus Glodek.
7 We'll see in chapter 5 that nonliteralist Meinongianism may have some trouble distinguishing itself from abstractism.
8 On standard Meinongian views, such objects of thought will typically be very incomplete. The round square, for example, will have no properties other than being round and square (and perhaps being thought about). It will have no size or color properties. Ensuring this incompleteness would require versions of the M principles according to which an object of thought has all and only the relevant properties. This aspect is discussed in the next section, when we turn to the question of what nonexistents are available to be fictional characters.
9 In classical logic "$\exists x(Fx \,\&\, \neg Fx)$" entails an arbitrary sentence "p" (which could itself be "$A \,\&\, \neg A$"). In a natural deduction system, one could assume "$Fa \,\&\, \neg Fa$", simplify out each conjunct, derive "$Fa \vee p$", and then apply "$\neg Fa$" to the disjunction to yield "p". A step of existential quantifier elimination would then make the arbitrary p rest on the original, existentially quantified, premise.
10 There is room for scholarly debate about exactly which argument Russell intended (on some readings it might just be the one that involves the move from "something is F and not-F" to the conclusion that there must be contradictory singular truths "this is F" and "this is not-F"). Likewise, it's debatable whether Priest's argument presented two paragraphs further on in the text above is properly described as a generalization of Russell's.
11 Follows even in a suitable logic for Meinongian views? I think so. A Meinongian will say that the classical rule of existential quantifier elimination is valid only when the "arbitrary object" used in the proof (denoted by "a" in the proof sketched in note 9 above) exists. The Meinongian will of course think that something self-identical exists, so this problem for a proof of "A" from "there is an x such that $(x = x \,\&\, A)$" does not arise.
12 Priest (2005) also offers a form of Meinongianism not requiring the distinction between nuclear and extranuclear properties.
13 These questions are not intended as refutations of nonliteralist Meinongianism. The last question might be answered by analyzing creativity as bringing it about that nonexistents possess representational properties.
14 The nonliteralist option is that he will come to be invested with the property of being represented to live in Baker Street. I won't make this option explicit in the remainder of the section, though I think it shares the problems I attribute to literalist Meinongianism.

15 "As we intuitively say" because the intuitive saying seems to be uncritically making use of Holmes's identity, even as we try to specify the properties which individuate him. Parsons is strangely calm about this apparent circularity: he says he is not trying to provide a definition, but only to link ordinary English to a theoretical specification (1980: 55).
16 Zalta calls himself a Meinongian, but for reasons to be discussed later I classify him as an abstractist, and so his overall position is discussed in chapter 5. His view has relevant similarities to the Meinongian one discussed here.
17 Maybe by "having completely in mind" Zalta means bringing to mind the character and all his properties. No doubt that makes having completely in mind a practical impossibility, but it loses track of any special connection between an object's individuating properties and our capacity to think of it.
18 We don't even need the first sentence. Both a factual and a fictional narrative could simply begin: "He looked at his watch."
19 It's plausible to suggest that understanding a name with a referent, as opposed to understanding these other locutions, does require a relation to that referent. For an irrealist about fiction, fictional names can be understood even though they don't have referents (see section 2.5), and so, on their view, this relation never obtains.
20 Philosophers are fond of what one might call fictional fictions. "Suppose there were a fiction with just the following content: ....." The Meinongian has to allow that a nonexistent fiction can introduce us to nonexistent fictional characters. But nonexistents were supposed to be causally inert, and so not capable of introducing anything to anything.
21 Nonliteralist Meinongians will have a hierarchy of representational properties (Gonzago is represented [in *Hamlet*] as being represented [in the play-within-the-play] as murdered), and can do justice to the distinction between existents and nonexistents by saying that only the former have nonrepresentational properties.
22 What makes this second point so is worthy of attention. It's not the case that the novel says there's a brother. There is no general rule allowing us to import the negation (and so move to: the novel says there's no brother). We can make the inference in the particular case because the presence of a brother would have made so much difference to the story that we take it we are supposed to infer that there is no brother.
23 Or perhaps there is just one such sloop: the existentially generic sloop (see Lewis 1970).

4 Worlds and truth

1 A reflexive relation is one that everything bears to itself.
2 A relation, R, is transitive iff, for all x, y, z, if x has R to y and y has R to z then x has R to z. Being greater than is transitive, but being similar to is not. The blue cube is similar to the blue sphere (both are blue) and the blue sphere to the red sphere (both are spheres), but the blue cube is not similar to the red sphere.
3 Standard modal semantics can be reworked in terms of possibilities rather than worlds, where a possibility is something which is like a possible world, but which may or may not be complete. See Forbes 1985: 18f. and 43f. The notion of completeness is not absent, re-emerging (under the label of refinement) in the semantics for negation.

4 Standard models for propositional modal languages are set-theoretic structures based on worlds. The nature of the worlds themselves, however, is irrelevant to the models. I've been told that Saul Kripke regretted having used the phrase "possible worlds" in his "Semantical Considerations on Modal Logic" (1963), wishing he had instead used a neutral term like "indices".

5 In later work, Lewis did not offer arguments like this. For one thing, he required possible worlds to be complete, whereas the belief that things could have been otherwise contains no such notion.

6 Perhaps Parsons's doorway exists in infinitely many distinct nonactual worlds, with a different man in it at each world. If that's what he has in mind in the quotation above (which in fact seems rather unlikely), the present point is irrelevant to his position.

7 The reference is to Jorge Luis Borges, "Pierre Menard, Author of the Quixote" (*Ficciones*, Buenos Aires, 1944; English translation, New York: Grove, 1962).

8 They can't be what Lewis (1986) calls modal ersatzists, treating possible worlds as, for example, actual sets of consistent sentences. For then the true metaphysical nature of a supposedly nonactual fictional character is actual. This view, on my taxonomy, is an abstractist view of fictional characters, discussed in the next chapter.

9 As far as I can see, one could give a possible worlds account of fiction operators while remaining irrealist about possible worlds (and so not being a nonactualist about fictional characters). This is not a view I will discuss.

10 Maybe he envisages a response to the battle of Hastings objection along the following lines: relevant gratuitous changes are those which directly affect the story. Since the battle does not, there will be relevant worlds in which it occurs, worlds in which it does not, and worlds in which it occurs but in a slightly different way. It may be that this response is circular, and it may fail to allow for Lewis's preferred kinds of importation from the actual (e.g. the topography of London, many aspects of which are of no direct relevance to the story).

11 Perhaps (as Alex Grzankowski suggested) people could believe that Hamlet suffered an Oedipus complex without bringing the Oedipus concept to bear (they believe that Hamlet unconsciously desired to kill his father and marry his mother). The point in the text requires only that this belief was not common in Shakespeare's day, which seems likely.

12 Those who worry that the example is not really a tautology, on the grounds that it would not be true if the name had no referent, could replace "George Bush" by a fictional name from the story (bearing in mind that realists are the target here). More serious opposition comes from those who regard it as acceptable that every tautology is true in every story. Two relevant observations: first, it may be that there is more than one kind of fiction operator. Let T be a classical tautology, whose subject matter is quite unrelated to fiction F. "According to F, T" sounds worse to my ear than "In F, T". We'll find other evidence for such a contrast later. Second, a fiction in which classical tautologies are not tautologies seems a possibility. This fiction insists, perhaps absurdly, that T is not a tautology, and indeed is false. It seems strikingly misguided to say that, according to it, T.

13 Heintz (1979: 93) cites Ray Bradbury's "A Sound of Thunder" as having more or less this structure. Aidan McGlynn tells me that similar contradictions arise in the *Back to the Future* movies.

14 One could add many other examples, like Howard Crick in *Stranger than Fiction*, who (according to the movie) is both purely fictional and also real.
15 Pirsig says in the Introduction: "it should in no way be associated with that great body of factual information relating to orthodox Zen Buddhist practice. It's not very factual on motorcycles, either."
16 The argument does not depend on the falsehood that, according to the stories, Holmes is neither under 6 foot 2 nor 6 foot 2 or more. We have more information about Holmes's height than some readers might recall (thanks once again to Aidan McGlynn's expertise). In *A Study in Scarlet* Watson describes him thus: "In height he was rather over six feet, and so excessively lean that he seemed to be considerably taller."
17 Kripke also argues that unicorns are an impossible species of beast. His reasoning is structurally similar: creatures of very different species (he measures this in terms of genetic composition; it might have been better to have used cladistic considerations) have equally good claims to be unicorns. If a creature of any one species counts as a unicorn, all the other candidate species would also be the unicorn species. That shows that no species could be the unicorn species; so there could be no unicorns.
18 (*)   Holmes has F at a world at which he exists iff, according to the stories, Holmes has F.
   i.e. (1) For all properties F and worlds w, (Holmes has F at w) iff (according to the stories Holmes has F).
       (2) There is some property ø such that:
           (a) not (according to the stories Holmes has ø) and
           (b) not (according to the stories Holmes does not have ø). (Incompleteness).
       (3) Not (Holmes has π at Ω) (from (1) and (2a), instantiating on w and F).
       (4) Not (Holmes does not have π at Ω) (from (1) and (2b)).
       (5) (3) and (4) are contradictory, so Ω is not a possible world.
       (6) Since Ω was arbitrary, Holmes does not exist at any possible world and so is not a possible object.
19 There is a further reason for doing this. Fictional characters, if there are such things, have modal properties. Holmes smoked a pipe, but might not have done so – this contingency is an implicit part of the story. If we are going to represent these modal properties in terms of possible worlds, we need a second dimension of world variation, one not given in (*).
20 This is Priest's approach. Although, as we'll see in the next section, his *Towards Non-Being* (2005) is the locus classicus of an impossibility version of nonactualism, he says that this is not needed to accommodate incompleteness, but only to make room for those fictional characters that are ascribed inconsistent properties (2005: 123).
21 Although Lewis (1978) is not entirely explicit, an account of this form would be entirely in keeping with his approach in that paper. We saw above that he uses just this strategy in the case of the outback; and he offers a similar application to the problem of the many (Lewis 1993).
22 All Holmes-surrogates lived in Baker Street; hence, by the account, Holmes lived in Baker Street, an unwanted result. A theorist would no doubt wish to permit only

world-relativized truth conditions, though as the surrogates belong to different worlds it's not entirely straightforward to do this.
23 The theory can assign truth to "There is just one Holmes." In this respect, the situation is parallel to the (downward) Löwenheim–Skolem theorem: even a theory that has a sentence we are inclined to interpret as saying that there are non-denumerably many things has a denumerable model. We need the metaphysics of the metatheory which assigns truth to "There is just one Holmes" to harmonize with the intuitive interpretation of that sentence, and it does not.
24 Although Priest's inconsistent story was specially designed to make a philosophical point, overt inconsistency has become a common fictional device. For example, in the novel *Fight Club* (Chuck Palahniuk, 1996) the narrator is asleep while Tyler is active, but the narrator is Tyler. We have already noted several other examples (science fiction, the movie *Stranger than Fiction*, and so on).
25 A closed world is one closed under some consequence relation R (a relation holding between sets of sentences and sentences). A world is closed under R iff, if there is a subset of the sentences true in the world that is R-related to a sentence s, s is also true in the world.
26 Literalist Meinongians generally stress the incompleteness of nonexistent objects, regarded as denizens of our world. The features we've mentioned are said not to lead to contradictions, but only to be manifestations of incompleteness. A Meinongian incomplete object can supposedly have a determinate height without there being a determinate height it has. Such surprises will be a feature of the most humdrum fictions, not just weird ones.

5 Fictional entities are abstract artifacts

1 Some might prefer to say that being outside of time and outside the causal nexus are essential to being abstract. Such readers should treat subsequent occurrences of the word "abstract" as an abbreviation for "abstract*", where this means, simply, nonspatial and nonmental.
2 There's also a version of the abstract artifact view according to which fictional characters are created not by authors but by critics and other consumers of the fiction (van Inwagen 1977; Schiffer 1996 [in some but not all passages]). The version mostly discussed in this chapter, which attributes the creation to authors, seems to me clearly superior, for reasons discussed in section 5.2 below. The version in which creation is attributed to critics avoids none of the objections I bring to bear on the authorial creation version.
3 The expression of the distinction by the words "exemplifies" and "encodes" comes from Zalta (1983; see also Zalta 1988: 14ff.). Essentially the same distinction has been presented by van Inwagen (1977, 2003) under the heading (in the later work): having versus holding. It may be related in interesting ways to the Meinongian distinction between extranuclear and nuclear properties. Could an abstract artifact theorist do without it? Possibly so. One way to avoid the distinction is to say that purely fictional names, in their uses to narrate and retell a tale, have no semantic referent (as irrealists insist), but do have a referent in critical contexts, for example "Holmes was created by Conan Doyle." I briefly discuss this kind of approach below.

Although Zalta (in particular) has developed a rich logical theory of encoding, less has been done to address the philosophical question: how does an abstract object encode, and does encoding make that which encodes like an element of a language? Some of the options considered by Lewis (1986) in his development of different versions of ersatzism could usefully be applied to the notion of encoding.

4 A recherché problem, posed by Shalom Lappin: Suppose a biography is widely but erroneously taken to be a novel, and generates many sequels and spin-offs. These become so fantastic that we eventually have to regard them as pure fictions, rather than as fictions about the perfectly real person who features in the original biography. Yet there was no moment of creation, no specific event which brought this fictional entity into existence.

5 It's also hard to distinguish structurally from Meinongian views: all names are names of something, existent or nonexistent.

6 In more recent work, Thomasson seems to prefer the view that there is this kind of ambiguity, for while she stoutly affirms that fictional names refer to abstract entities in extrafictional discourse, she is tempted by the view that they don't refer at all as used within fiction: "perhaps one should accept that fictional names do not refer to fictional characters in fictionalizing discourse" (2003: 214).

7 "Why posit a semantic ambiguity when it is both insufficient in general and superfluous for the special case it seeks to explain?" (Kripke 1977: 401).

8 Van Inwagen only uses the word "abstract" once in the paper (speaking of theoretical entities as abstract (1977: 304)). But he's emphatic that fictional characters don't occupy space (306).

9 Van Inwagen throughout regards "There are fictional characters" as intertranslatable with "$\exists x$ (x is a fictional character)" (2003: 137, 143, 145). The presence of the "$\exists$" in the second sentence suggests it is first order (or readily first-order formalizable), whereas an irrealist will see the English sentence as expressing something nonextensional, which eludes first-order formalization.

10 Thanks to Markus Glodek and Bryan Pickel, who drew my attention to distinct inadequacies.

11 The adequacy of this paraphrase is supported by the distinction between relational and specific occurrences in sentences built from intensional verbs: see section 6.3 below. The issue of specificity in connection with exportation inferences was discussed earlier in section 3.5.

12 "x is represented as y" is unusual in that it seems it can be true even though neither variable is replaced by an expression for an ordinary object, e.g. "Pegasus is represented as a flying horse."

13 Probably my "According to fiction F" corresponds to the phrase "In fiction F" in other mouths (e.g. Lewis's). I suspect there are other distinctions to be made here, with no pre-existing terminology that reliably expresses them.

14 For details, see section 6.5 below.

15 "[A]ny adequate theory must be able to explain ... the sense in which 'Emma Woodhouse doesn't exist' is true" (Thomasson 2003: 214).

16 The proposal presumably involves backtracking on the way the problem was set up, which involved accepting that, on abstract artifact theory, Sherlock Holmes neither encodes nor exemplifies the (nonmetalinguistic) property of existing.

17 Tim Button, in discussion, made this suggestion on behalf of the abstract artifact realist.
18 Gabriel Segal, in discussion, urged this position on behalf of the abstract artifact theorist.

6 Irrealism: fiction and intentionality

1 Those who believe, as I do, that it can be true that unicorns are rather like horses, even if there are no unicorns, will see this account of intensionality as somewhat too restrictive. Treating the more restrictive notion, however, is quite enough of a task for one chapter.
2 Completing the argument requires the claim that this cannot be quantification over properties, for then the witness should be a noun-phrase expression that refers to a property, for example "the property of being friendly", whereas what's needed is an adjective ("friendly").
3 In cases of this kind, we are close to a conditional. With some redundancy, I could as well have replied: If it's fine tomorrow, I'll go for a walk. It's a delicate question (that I will not address) whether we should use conditionality to explain presupposition, or presupposition to explain conditionality.
4 Quine is a famous proponent of paraphrase, and seems to understand it as replacement: "The relation [of a paraphrase S'] to S is just that the particular business that the speaker was on that occasion trying to get on with, with help of S among other things, can be managed well enough to suit him by using S' instead of S" (Quine 1960: 160).
5 There may be limitations to the principle. Perhaps it would be silly to agglomerate fictions of very different genres. And some agglomerations will embed an inconsistency under the agglomerated operator.
6 The example is owed to Mark Kalderon, in discussion.
7 Might it still not be that many sloops would satisfy Jack's desire? Suppose the construction company decided to build two identical ships, one to fulfill Jack's commission and one for speculative sale. The company has not fixed on which of the boats is to serve which purpose. Would not either satisfy Jack's desire? If so, his desire does not have the specificity of a relational one. The point is not decisive. There's no doubt that my desire to spend time with my wife is entirely wife-specific. That's consistent with my being no less happy spending time with an indistinguishable duplicate of my wife (assuming I am ignorant, I am as happy as I would have been with the real thing). But that's beside the point: only my wife can satisfy a wife-specific desire, in the sense of making it true, even if I can be "satisfied", in the nonphilosophical use of that expression, when that desire is not made true.
8 A more demanding conception of failures of specificity and relationality can be effected by adding the negation of any earlier entry on the list. These semantic conditions commit (at least on the face of it) to exotic nonactuals, so they will not be the irrealist's ultimate way of expressing the distinctions.
9 The y-position in "x worships y" arguably supports SI (in which case it would not be an example of the failure of the inference under discussion), for reasons of essentially the kind shortly to be discussed for desire and fear.

10 Detailed above in the appendix to section 2.4.
11 Quine first offers as an "expansion": "The commissioner is endeavoring that the commissioner finds the chairman of the hospital board" (1960: 152). He becomes dissatisfied with this (1960: 153). The sentence to which this note attaches is not Quine's, but it retains the operator + sentence form (endeavors that p) as opposed to Quine's operator + infinitive (endeavors to cause himself to find) in his sentence (5) (1960: 154). "Find" is still an intensional verb, but since it occurs in the scope of an intensional operator, the whole sentence can be true regardless of whether or not there's a chairman of the board. Later in the discussion (154) Quine refers to an "expansion" as a "paraphrase", but, in conformity with his overall skepticism about meaning, he does not take synonymy to be a requirement on paraphrase (159).
12 I again depart in minor detail from Quine's formulations. If Ernest does not know that he is Ernest, there might be something wrong with the sentence to which this note attaches, even though a sentence closer to Quine's final formulation is true: For some lion, Ernest is endeavoring to shoot it. This problem is orthogonal to that under discussion.
13 "The paraphrases were such as to meet most or all the likely purposes for which the originals might be used, except insofar as such needs include brevity or familiarity" (Quine: 1960: 191).
14 My view on this issue has been substantially improved by discussion with Tim Crane, though he does not accept it.
15 Other notions of ontological commitment are appropriate for other purposes. For example, one might say that Fs belong to the ontology of a theory (a set of sentences closed under a relation of consequence) iff there's a theorem of the theory which says that there are Fs; or one might say that Fs belong to the ontology of a person iff that person can know a priori that it would be inconsistent to combine what she believes with the claim that there are no Fs. The various notions are very far from co-extensive. Expressions of the form "x is ontologically committed to y" themselves involve intensional verbs, as Church (1958) says. The explication in the text is one way to offer an operator reduction, the operator in this case being modal rather than one used to attribute a propositional attitude.
16 This is not quite right. (i) It has the unwanted result that an impossible sentence includes everything in its ontology. By contrast, it seems intuitive to say that unicorns must exist for "Unicorns exist" to be true, but centaurs don't need to. (ii) If there are necessary connections between distinct existences (for example, if I could not have existed if my father had not) a sentence about one of the two will, unintuitively, have the other in its ontology (e.g "I am hungry" will have my father in its ontology). I believe these problems (impressed on me by Bryan Pickel) do not need to be resolved for the purposes of the present discussion, important as they are in other contexts.
17 Tim Button issued this challenge in discussion.
18 The standard view can be doubted (the counterexample is owed to Tim Button): suppose a tribe that stressed the importance of monotheism came to believe that they had been confused, and they had been in reality worshipping two gods. Perhaps we can describe their pre-enlightenment state as one in which they worshipped a god even though they worshipped no god in particular.
19 Richard (2001) offers this argument and rejects the inference from (2) to (3).

20 Timothy Williamson and Ralph Wedgwood encouraged me to explore this option.
21 "Dotty Otley, the actress who is playing the part of Mrs Clackett, comes out of character to comment on the move" (stage direction in Michael Frayn's *Noises Off* [1977]: 366). This passage also makes use of the notion of a part. The part of Mrs. Clackett is quite different from Mrs. Clackett herself (it can be played by Dotty Otley whereas Mrs. Clackett herself cannot literally be played), and is a candidate for being an abstract entity.

7 Some fictionalists

1 For a useful historical survey, from which many points in this section are drawn, see Rosen (2005); for a more contemporary survey, consult Eklund (2007). Any attempt completely to delineate the history of fictionalism should mention Vaihinger: "The principle of Fictionalism ... or rather the outcome of Fictionalism, is as follows: 'An idea whose theoretical untruth or incorrectness, and therewith its falsity, is admitted, is not for that reason practically valueless and useless; for such an idea, in spite of its theoretical nullity may have great practical importance'" (1925: viii [preface to the English edition]).
2 Galileo did not take Cardinal Bellarmine's advice to present his opinion "as a hypothesis and not as an absolute truth" (quoted by Rosen 2005: 39).
3 The original Latin is "Hypotheses non fingo", and it has been suggested that "feign" might be better than "frame" as a translation of "fingo" (Cohen 1962). Elsewhere Newton says one should not feign hypotheses: "the main Business of natural Philosophy is to argue from Phaenomena without feigning Hypotheses" (*Optiks*, Bk. 3, query 28). This supports the link between fictionalism and this usage of "hypotheses", and helps explain how Newton's famous phrase comports with his actual practice, in which, while steering clear of fictionalist feignings, he framed many a hypothesis (as we would express it).
4 Hume is not the only philosopher to confuse the nature of a representation with the nature of what it represents.
5 It is not quite obvious what "All those statements" refers to. Perhaps it is to the sentence I have elided: "If you say 'There is a universe' that meaning of 'there is' will be quite different from the meaning in which you say 'There is a particular', which means that 'the propositional function "x is a particular" is sometimes true'."
6 Very compressed. For example, "Hadrons are composed of quarks" cannot be interpreted as saying that the devices which detect hadrons are composed of devices which detect quarks, so there's no simple rule of replacing an expression that apparently refers to an unobservable by one that refers to instruments.
7 Something is grue just on condition that it's green and has been examined, or else hasn't been examined and is blue (see Goodman 1955: 74). If all emeralds are grue, the unexamined ones are blue.
8 At least, that's how van Fraassen interprets the passage containing the famous "hypotheses non fingo" from the General Scholium to Bk III, *Mathematical Principles of Natural Philosophy*: "[we] have not yet assigned a cause to this power [sc. gravity] ... to us it is enough, that gravity does really exist, and act according to the laws we have explained" (quoted by van Fraassen 1980: 94).

9   A fully exact statement of the position is quite tricky. Presumably a nominalist, who thinks there are no numbers, and so no prime numbers, should think that it's not the case that 4 is a prime number and that there's no prime number greater than 3 and less than 5.
10 x is a member of the union of two sets, A and B, iff either x is a member of A or x is a member of B. In symbols: $(x \in A \cup B)$ iff $(x \in A \vee x \in B)$.
11 And Lewis would be the last to suggest it can. Lewis himself, despite his modesty towards mathematicians, is ready to tell cosmologists that there are a plurality of other worlds which have generally escaped their notice (along with many unrecognized heavenly bodies, Big Bangs, and so on). For Lewis is a "modal realist": he believes that there really are worlds or universes other than our own, causally isolated from us, with their own space–time and with plenty of bulky objects. They are, of course, nonactual; but he says they are real.
12 This skates over some tricky issues. For a more detailed account, see Shapiro 2000. Field, in later work, allows that there's a sense in which there are many mathematical truths: "the sense in which '2 + 2 = 4' is true is pretty much the same as the sense in which 'Oliver Twist lived in London' is true: the latter is true only in the sense that it is true according to a certain well-known story, and the former is true only in that it is true according to standard mathematics" (1989: 3). He soon adds that standard mathematics had better be a "good story" (1989: 3).

8 Fictionalism about possible words

1 Fictionalism is usually defined as a doctrine about sentences rather than thoughts. It seems to me thoughts matter more; those who disagree will not find that much goes wrong if they replace "thought" by "sentence".
2 David Lewis (1986) uses the expression "modal realism" not for the view that there are real modal facts (e.g. the modal fact that there could have been talking donkeys) but for realism about possible worlds (the view that there really are many nonactual possible worlds). "Modal fictionalism" was presumably fashioned after this usage.
3 This might mislead. Lewis takes the idiom of possible worlds to be basic, and explanatory of ordinary modal talk. It's not that (officially, at least) he tailors the possible worlds talk to reflect features of a more primitive modal idiom.
4 If we wish to be properly faithful to Lewis (1986) the quantification in a case like this would not be overtly over worlds but over counterparts: some counterpart of Socrates is snub-nosed. This reflects Lewis's belief that objects do not inhabit more than one world, so that possibilities for an object at our world are represented by various properties possessed by that object's counterparts at other worlds. "Counterpart theory", as Lewis calls it, is an essential element in his own version of the view that there are a plurality of worlds.
5 A language could contain both quantification over worlds, in the style of PW, and also ordinary modal idioms, like *must* and *can*. Lewis aspires to reduce the latter to the former, so for his purposes it is essential that the language of PW should not contain modal idioms, as opposed to quantification over worlds.
6 Lewis's modal realism also aspires to a reductive analysis. With some caveats, Lewis says that a possible world is a maximal spatiotemporal entity, and this specification

is apparently not modal. The relevant notion of maximality is given thus: if x is in w and y stands in any spatiotemporal relation to x then y is in w.
7. Entailment is usually understood as a modal notion: A entails B iff necessarily, if A, then B.
8. Lewis's claim has been disputed, e.g. by Sainsbury (2001).
9. This is explicit in Lewis (1986). As far as the axioms of the 1968 paper go, worlds within worlds are not excluded. But if we add that the relation that expresses what it is for something to be in a world ("I") is transitive, which seems wholly consonant with Lewis's intentions, even the 1968 paper would rule out worlds within worlds.
10. For a diagnosis of the underlying cause of the problems, see Nolan and Hawthorne (1996).
11. The language of quantified modal logic (QML) is that of first-order logic plus boxes and diamonds, thought of as operators expressing necessity and possibility.
12. "Translation into counterpart theory can settle disputed questions in quantified modal logic" (Lewis 1968: 123).

9 Moral fictionalism

1. The other argument is based on "perspective shift" (Kalderon 2005a: 43–50). I'll not be discussing it.
2. This should lead to a qualification of the following claim on behalf of fictionalism: "The semantics offered for moral language, after all, is the same semantics as that which the realist offers" (Nolan *et al.* 2005: 28).
3. For RWR semantics see section 2.4 (appendix) above and Sainsbury 2005. To give an idea of the RWR approach in a way which fits the present issue: "Vulcan" is described in RWR semantics by an axiom on the lines: for all x, "Vulcan" refers to x iff x = Vulcan. An analogous clause for "evil" (as a noun) would be: for all x, "evil" refers to x iff x = evil. As the first is neutral on whether there is any such thing as Vulcan, the second is neutral as to whether there is any such thing as evil. (This neutrality presupposes negative free logic.)
4. A wrinkle: since on this view no moral properties are instantiated, claims like "Kindness is good" are false, so presumably their negations are true, so "It's not the case that kindness is good" is true, strictly and literally. As we've noted before, all the fictionalisms we've discussed require careful formulation to avoid this problem.

BIBLIOGRAPHY

Adams, Fred, Gary Fuller, and Robert Stecker (1997). "The Semantics of Fictional Names." *Pacific Philosophical Quarterly* 78: 128–48.
Balaguer, Mark (2008). "Fictionalism in the Philosophy of Mathematics." *Stanford Encyclopedia of Philosophy*. Online at http://plato.stanford.edu/entries/fictionalism-mathematics
Benacerraf, Paul (1973). "Mathematical Truth." *Journal of Philosophy* 70: 661–80.
Bentham, Jeremy (1822). *First Principles Preparatory to Constitutional Code*, ed. P. Schofield. Oxford: Clarendon Press 1989.
Bentham, Jeremy (1843). The Works of Jeremy Bentham. Edinburgh: William Tate. Available in a range of electronic formats at: http://oll.libertyfund.org/index.php?option=com_staticxt&staticfile=show.php%3Ftitle=1996&Itemid=99999999
Berkeley, George (1710). *A Treatise Concerning the Principles of Human Knowledge*.
Berkeley, George (1713). *Three Dialogues between Hylas and Philonous*.
Burgess, John and Gideon Rosen (1997). *A Subject with No Object*. Oxford: Oxford University Press.
Carroll, Noel (1991). "On Kendall Walton's *Mimesis as Make-Believe*." *Philosophy and Phenomenological Research* 51: 383–7.
Church, Alonzo (1958). "Ontological Commitment." *Journal of Philosophy* 55 (23): 1008–14.

Cohen, Bernard (1962). "The First English Version of Newton's Hypotheses Non Fingo." *Isis* 53: 379–88.
Crane, Timothy. (2001). "Intentional Objects." *Ratio* 14: 336–49.
Currie, Greg (1990). *The Nature of Fiction*. Cambridge: Cambridge University Press.
Deutsch, Harry (1991). "The Creation Problem." *Topoi* 10: 209–25.
Donnellan, Keith (1974). "Speaking of Nothing." *Philosophical Review* 83 (1): 3–31.
Doyle, Arthur Conan (1930). *The Casebook of Sherlock Holmes*. Online at http://infomotions.com/etexts/literature/english/1800-1899/doyle-case-381.htm
Eklund, Matti (2007). "Fictionalism." *Stanford Encyclopedia of Philosophy*. Online at http://plato.stanford.edu/entries/fictionalism/
Evans, Gareth (1982). *The Varieties of Reference*. Oxford: Clarendon Press.
Field, Hartry (1980). *Science without Numbers: A Defence of Nominalism*. Oxford: Basil Blackwell.
Field, Hartry (1989). *Realism, Mathematics and Modality*. Oxford: Basil Blackwell.
Field, Hartry (1991). "Metalogic and Modality." *Philosophical Studies* 62: 1–22.
Field, Hartry (1992). "A Nominalistic Proof of the Conservativeness of Set Theory." *Journal of Philosophical Logic* 21 (2): 111–23.
Findlay, J. N. (1935). "Emotional Presentation". *Australasian Journal of Philosophy* 13: 111–21.
Fine, Kit (1982). "The Problem of Non-Existence: 1. Internalism." *Topoi* 1: 97–140.
Forbes, Graeme (1985). *The Metaphysics of Modality*. Oxford: Clarendon Press.
Forbes, Graeme (2006). *Attitude Problems*. Oxford: Clarendon Press.
Frege, Gottlob (1984). "On Sense and Meaning." In *Collected Papers on Mathematics, Logic and Philosophy*, ed. Brian McGuinness. Oxford: Basil Blackwell, 157–77 (originally published 1892).
Friend, S. (2007). "Fictional Characters." *Philosophy Compass* 2: 141–56.
Godfrey-Smith, P. (2003). *Theory and Reality: An Introduction to the Philosophy of Science*. Chicago: University of Chicago Press.
Goodman, Nelson (1955). *Fact, Fiction and Forecast*. Cambridge, Mass.: Harvard University Press; 4th edn., 1983.
Grice, H. P. (1975). "Logic and Conversation." In *Syntax and Sematics*, vol. 3, *Speech Acts*, ed. P. Cole and J. L. Morgan. New York: Academic Press, 41–58.
Heintz, John (1979). "Reference and Inference in Fiction." *Poetics* 8: 85–99.
Hume, David (1739–40). *A Treatise of Human Nature*.
Jacquette, D. (1996). *Meinongian Logic. The Semantics of Existence and Nonexistence*. Berlin: de Gruyter.

Jardine, Nicholas (1984). *The Birth of History and Philosophy of Science. Kepler's 'A Defence of Tycho against Ursus' with Essays on Its Provenance and Significance.* Cambridge: Cambridge University Press.
Johnson, Samuel (1765). "Preface to *Shakespeare*."
Joyce, Richard (2005). "Moral Fictionalism." In *Fictionalism in Metaphysics*, ed. Mark Kalderon. Oxford: Clarendon Press, 287–313.
Kalderon, Mark (2005a). *Moral Fictionalism*. Oxford: Clarendon Press.
Kalderon, Mark (ed.) (2005b). *Fictionalism in Metaphysics*. Oxford: Oxford University Press.
Kim, Seahwa (2005a). "Modal Fictionalism and Analysis." In Kalderon (2005b): 116–33.
Kim, Seahwa (2005b). "The Real Puzzle from Radford." *Erkenntnis* 62: 29–46.
Kripke, Saul (1963). "Semantical Considerations on Modal Logic." *Acta Philosophica Fennica* 16: 83–94.
Kripke, Saul (1972). *Naming and Necessity*. Oxford: Basil Blackwell (2nd edn. 1980).
Kripke, Saul (1977). "Speaker's Reference and Semantic Reference." In *Contemporary Perspectives in the Philosophy of Language*, ed. Peter A. French, Theodore E. Uehling, Jr., and Howard K. Wettstein. Minneapolis: University of Minnesota Press, 6–27. Reprinted in Peter Ludlow (ed.) (1997), *Readings in the Philosophy of Language*, Cambridge, Mass.: The MIT Press, 383–414.
Larson, Richard (2002). "The Grammar of Intensionality." In *Logical Form and Language*, ed. G. Preyer and G. Peter. Oxford: Clarendon Press, 228–62.
Leibniz, Gottfried (1686). *De Veritatibus Primis*.
Leslie, Alan (1987). "Pretence and Representation: The Origin of 'Theory of Mind'." *Psychological Review* 94: 412–26.
Lewis, David (1968). "Counterpart Theory and Quantified Modal Logic." *Journal of Philosophy* 65: 113–26.
Lewis, David (1970). "General Semantics." *Synthese* 22: 18–67.
Lewis, David (1973). *Counterfactuals*. Oxford: Basil Blackwell.
Lewis, David (1978). "Truth in Fiction." *American Philosophical Quarterly* 15: 37–46.
Lewis, David (1986). *On the Plurality of Worlds*. Oxford: Basil Blackwell.
Lewis, David (1991). *Parts of Classes*. Oxford: Basil Blackwell.
Lewis, David (1993). "Many, But Almost One". In *Ontology, Causality, and Mind: Essays on the Philosophy of D. M. Armstrong*, ed. Keith Campbell, John Bacon, and Lloyd Reinhardt. Cambridge: Cambridge University Press, 23–42.
Liston, Michael (1993). "Taking Mathematical Fictions Seriously." *Synthese* 95: 433–58.
MacBride, F. (1999). "Listening to Fictions: A Study of Fieldian Nominalism." *British Journal for Philosophy of Science* 50: 431–55.

Mackie, John L. (1977). *Ethics: Inventing Right and Wrong.* Harmondsworth: Penguin Books.

Martin, Robert M. and Peter K. Schotch (1974). "The Meaning of Fictional Names." *Philosophical Studies* 26: 377–88.

Martinich, A. P. and Avrum Stroll (2007). *Much Ado about Nonexistence.* Lanham: Rowman and Littlefield.

Meinong, Alexius (1983). *On Assumptions,* trans. James Heanue, 2nd edn. Berkeley: University of California Press (originally published 1910).

Mill, J. S. (1843). *System of Logic,* 3rd edn. London: Parker.

Miller, Barry (2002). "Existence." *Stanford Encyclopedia of Philosophy.* Online at http://plato.stanford.edu/entries/existence/

Nolan, Daniel (2007). "Modal Fictionalism." *Stanford Encyclopedia of Philosophy.* Online at http://plato.stanford.edu/entries/fictionalism-modal/

Nolan, D. and J. O'Leary-Hawthorne (1996). "Reflexive Fictionalisms." *Analysis* 56: 23–32.

Nolan, Daniel, Greg Restall, and Caroline West (2005). "Moral Fictionalism versus the Rest." *Australasian Journal of Philosophy* 83: 307–30.

Noonan, Harold (1994). "In Defence of the Letter of Fictionalism." *Analysis* 54 (3): 133–9.

Oliver, A. (1999). "A Few More Remarks on Logical Form." *Proceedings of the Aristotelian Society* 99: 247–72.

Oliver, A. and Timothy Smiley (2006). "A Modest Logic of Plurals." *Journal of Philosophical Logic* 35: 317–48.

Parsons, Terence (1980). *Nonexistent Objects.* New Haven: Yale University Press.

Parsons, Terence (1982). "Fregean Theories of Fictional Objects." *Topoi* 1: 81–7.

Perszyk, K. J. (1993). *Nonexistent Objects: Meinong and Contemporary Philosophy.* Dordrecht: Kluwer Academic Publishers.

Priest, Graham (2005). *Towards Non-Being. The Logic and Metaphysics of Intentionality.* Oxford: Clarendon Press.

Prior, Arthur (1971). *Objects of Thought.* Oxford: Clarendon Press.

Proudfoot, Diane (2006). "Possible Worlds Semantics and Fiction." *Journal of Philosophical Logic* 35: 9–40.

Quine, Willard van O. (1948). "On What There Is." *Review of Metaphysics* 2: 21–36.

Quine, Willard van O. (1956). "Quantifiers and Propositional Attitudes." *Journal of Philosophy* 53: 177–87.

Quine, Willard van O. (1960). *Word and Object.* New York: Technology Press of MIT and John Wiley and Sons Inc.

Quine, Willard van O. (1969). *Ontological Relativity.* Cambridge, Mass.: Harvard University Press. This reprints the essay "Existence and Quantification" (1968), from which the quotation at the start of chapter 6 is taken.

Radford, Colin (1975). "How Can We Be Moved by the Fate of Anna Karenina?" *Proceedings of the Aristotelian Society* 69: 67–80.
Richard, Mark (2001). "Seeking a Centaur, Adoring Adonis: Intensional Transitives and Empty Terms." *Midwest Studies in Philosophy* 25: 103–27.
Roberts, Robert C. (1988). "What an Emotion Is: A Sketch." *The Philosophical Review* 97: 183–209.
Rosen, Gideon (1990). "Modal Fictionalism." *Mind* 99 (395): 327–54.
Rosen, Gideon (1993). "A Problem for Fictionalism about Possible Worlds." *Analysis* 53 (2): 71–81.
Rosen, Gideon (1995). "Modal Fictionalism Fixed." *Analysis* 55 (2): 67–73.
Rosen, Gideon (2005). "Problems in the History of Fictionalism." In *Fictionalism in Metaphysics*, ed. Mark Kalderon. Oxford: Oxford University Press, 14–64.
Rosenkranz, Sven (2007). *The Agnostic Stance*. Paderborn: Mentis-Verlag.
Routley, Richard (1980). *Exploring Meinong's Jungle and Beyond*. Canberra: RSSS Monograph no. 3.
Russell, Bertrand (1903). *The Principles of Mathematics*. Cambridge: Cambridge University Press.
Russell, Bertrand (1905a). "On Denoting." *Mind* 14: 479–93.
Russell, Bertrand (1905b). Critical notice of Meinong's *Untersuchungen zur Gegenstandstheorie und Psychologie*. *Mind* 14: 530–8.
Russell, Bertrand (1908). "Mathematical Logic as Based on the Theory of Types." *American Journal of Mathematics* 30: 222–62.
Russell, Bertrand (1918–19). "Lectures on the Philosophy of Logical Atomism." *Monist* 28 (1918): 495–524; 29 (1919): 32–64, 190–222, 345–80. Reprinted in R. C. Marsh (ed.) (1956), *Bertrand Russell: Logic and Knowledge. Essays 1902–1950*. London: George Allen and Unwin, London, 177–281.
Russell, Bertrand (1925). "Mind and Matter." In *Portraits from Memory*. London: George Allen and Unwin, 1956; pp. 140–60 in the Readers Union edn., London, 1958.
Russell, Bertand (1940). *An Inquiry into Meaning and Truth*. London: George Allen and Unwin.
Russell, Bertrand and Alfred North Whitehead (1910–13). *Principia Mathematica*, 3 vols. Cambridge: Cambridge University Press.
Russell, Bruce (2007). "A Priori Justification and Knowledge." *Stanford Encyclopedia of Philosophy*. Online at http://plato.stanford.edu/entries/apriori/
Sainsbury, R. M. (2001). *Logical Forms: An Introduction to Philosophical Logic*, 2nd edn. Oxford and Cambridge, Mass.: Blackwell Publishers.
Sainsbury, R. M. (2005). *Reference without Referents*. Oxford: Clarendon Press.
Salmon, Nathan (1981). *Reference and Essence*. Princeton: Princeton University Press.

Salmon, Nathan (1998). "Nonexistence." *Noûs* 32 (3): 277–319.
Sawyer, S. (2002). "Abstract Artifacts in Pretence." *Philosophical Papers* 31: 183–98.
Schiffer, Stephen (1996). "Language-Created Language-Independent Entities." *Philosophical Topics* 24 (1): 149–67.
Searle, John R. (1975). "The Logical Status of Fictional Discourse." *New Literary History* 6 (2): 319–32.
Shapiro, Stewart (2000). *Thinking about Mathematics*. Oxford: Oxford University Press.
Smiley, T. (2004). "The Theory of Descriptions." In *Studies in the Philosophy of Logic and Knowledge*, ed. T. R. Baldwin and T. J. Smiley. Oxford: Oxford University Press, 131–61.
Soames, Scott (2002). *Beyond Rigidity*. Oxford: Oxford University Press.
Stalnaker, Robert (1973). "Presuppositions." *Journal of Philosophical Logic* 2 (4): 447–56.
Stanley, Jason (2001). "Hermeneutic Fictionalism." *Midwest Studies in Philosophy* 25: 36–71.
Steen, Francis and Stephanie Owens (2001). "Evolution's Pedagogy: An Adaptationist Model of Pretense and Entertainment." *Journal of Cognition and Culture* 1: 289–321.
Strawson, P. F. (1950). "On Referring." *Mind* 59: 269–86.
Strawson, P. F. (1967). "Is Existence Never a Predicate?" *Critica* 1: 5–15.
Thomasson, Amie L. (1999). *Fiction and Metaphysics*. Cambridge: Cambridge University Press.
Thomasson, Amie L. (2003). "Speaking of Fictional Characters." *Dialectica* 57 (2): 207–26.
Vaihinger, Hans (1925). *The Philosophy of "As If". A System of the Theoretical, Practical and Religious Fictions of Mankind*. New York: Harcourt, Brace & Co.
van Fraassen, B. (1980). *The Scientific Image*. Oxford: Clarendon Press.
van Inwagen, Peter (1977). "Creatures of Fiction." *American Philosophical Quarterly* 14: 299–308.
van Inwagen, Peter (2003). "Existence, Ontological Commitment and Fictional Entities." In *The Oxford Handbook of Metaphysics*, ed. Michael J. Loux and Dean W. Zimmerman. Oxford: Oxford University Press, 131–57.
Voltolini, A. (2006). *How Ficta Follow Fiction*. Dordrecht: Springer.
Walton, Kendall L. (1990). *Mimesis as Make-Believe: On the Foundations of the Representational Arts*. Cambridge, Mass.: Harvard University Press.
Walton, Kendall L. (1997). "Spelunking, Simulation, and Slime: On Being Moved by Fiction." Online at http://www.communicatio.hu/kurzusok/2004052/walton/spelunkingsimulation.htm
Wolterstorff, N. (1980). *Works and Worlds of Art*. New York: Oxford University Press.

Wood, James (2008). *How Fiction Works*. New York: Farrar, Straus, and Giroux.
Woods, John (1974). *The Logic of Fiction: A Philosophical Sounding of Deviant Logic*. The Hague: Mouton.
Yablo, S. (2005). "The Myth of the Seven." In Kalderon (2005b): 88–115.
Zalta, E. N. (1983). *Abstract Objects: An Introduction to Axiomatic Metaphysics*. Dordrecht: Reidel.
Zalta, E. N. (1988). *Intensional Logic and the Metaphysics of Intentionality*. Cambridge: Mass.: The MIT Press.
Zalta, E. N. (2003). "Referring to Fictional Characters." *Dialectica* 57: 243–54.

INDEX

abstract things and nominalism, 2, 3, 168–74, 177, 184, 205, 206, 209, 213; abstract artifacts, xi, 3, 22–3, 33, 41, 42, 63, 73, ch. 5, 120, 121, 210, 224n1,2,3, 225n6,8,16, 228n21; *see also* nonconcrete
acceptance (contrasted with belief), 2, 143–7, 153ff, 157, 162, 200–1, 207, 208, 209,
accessibility, 69–70, 190, 191, 204
actualism, 100, 184–8, 193, 205, 206, 209
Adams, F., 36, 122
assertion, 8–10, 27, 59, 107, 119, 121, 125, 201
Austen, J., 7

Balaguer, M., 174
Ballard, J. G., 200
Barnes, J., 22
Benacerraf, P., 172
Bentham, J., xiii, 152, 158, 174

Berkeley, G., xiii, 24, 154–7, 174
Bermúdez, J. L., xix
Borges, J. L., 222n7
Bradbury, R., 79, 222n13
Burgess, J., 174, 176
Button, T., xix, 217n7, 226n17, 227n17,18

Caddick, E., xix, 147
Carroll, N., 14
Cervantes, 74, 76, 94
Chekhov, A., 19, 148
Church, A., 227n15
cognitivism: *see* noncognitivism
Cohen, B., 228n3
Coleridge, S.T., 8
Conservative extension, 169, 171–2, 292
constructive empiricism, xiii, xix, 152, 154, 157, 161–8, 174, 191–2, 204, 209
consumers of fiction, 5–6, 11, 14, 97, 98, 111, 113, 217n11, 224n2

Copernicus, N., xiii, 153
counterpart theory, 85, 186, 188, 190–1, 210, 229n4, 230n12
Crane, T., xix, 151, 227n14
Currie, G., vi, 6–7, 9, 10, 13, 21, 217n6

Darwin, C., 17, 84, 164
David, J.-L., 9, 20
de re/de dicto, 96–7, 124, 149, 210
Deutsch, H., 91
Dickens, C., 22, 57, 100, 104, 105
Doyle, C., vii, 1, 31, 53, 57–8, 59, 60–2, 76, 80, 84, 93, 96, 98, 99, 111-3, 139, 142, 218n1, 224n3

Eco, U., 5
Eklund, M., 174, 228n1
eliminativism, xiv, 153, 160, 161, 174, 178–9, 185–6, 194, 207
empirical adequacy, 2, 210
encoding, xi, 93-5, 97-9, 108, 111–3, 205, 210, 224-5n3, 225n16
ersatzism, 72, 186, 207, 222n8, 225n3
Evans, G., 36, 43
evil genius, 25, 210
exemplifying: 210; *see* encoding
existence, puzzle of, ix, 40, 47–50, 67, 108–11
exotic objects, 23, 26, 32, 35, 36, 37, 41, 104, 115, 116, 119, 122, 126, 127, 130, 132, 133, 136, 137, 138, 139, 141, 143, 210, 226n8
exportation inferences, 34, 51, 65–6, 210–1, 225n11
extranuclear properties: *see* nuclear properties
Ezcurdia, M., xix

fear: and fiction, vi, 15–20
fiction operators, x, xii, 2, 3, 29, 42, 64, 68, 74, 75–82, 101, 102, 105, 107, 111, 123, 124, 177, 180, 181, 182, 184, 202, 211, 219n11, 222n9,12
fictional meaning, 5
fictionalism, xiii–xvii, 2, 173–4, 175–7, 204, 205–8; hermeneutic versus revolutionary: 176, 183, 200, 202; about mathematics, xiv, xix, 168–73, 191–2, 204, 205; modal, 179; about modality, 181–3; about morality, xv–xvi, ch. 9; about possible worlds, xiv–xv, 3, ch. 8, 204; strong versus timid, 183–4; about unobservables: *see* constructive empiricism
fictive intentions, vi, vii, 4, 6–8, 21
fidelity (to a fiction), vii, 2, 26–31, 41, 74–82, 105, 112, 122, 123, 125, 137, 147, 211
Field, H., xiii, xiv, 2, 152, 168–73, 174, 176, 177, 178, 204, 205 208, 229n12
Findlay, J. N., 13
Fine, K., 26, 94
Flaubert, G., 81, 122, 123, 124
Forbes, G., 127, 151, 221n3
Frayn, M., 228n21
free logic, 40, 213, 230n3
Frege, G., xvii, 36–7, 40
Friend, S., 114

Galileo, 154, 228n2
Glodek, M., xix, 219n6, 220n6, 225n10
Godfrey-Smith, P., 174
Goodman, N., 163, 211, 228n7
Goodman, V., xix
gorgons, 127–9
Grice, H. P., 165, 210
Grzankowski, A., xix, 217, 222n11

Harman, G., 164
Hawthorne, J., 230n10
Heintz, J., 222n13

240 INDEX

Hempel, C., 164
Hill, D., xix
Hume, D., xiii, 12, 157, 228n4

imagining, vi, 10–2, 14, 17, 20, 185
instrumentalism, 162, 209, 211
intensionality, ix, xiii, 103–7, 116–7, 126–46, 149; operator versus predicate: xii–xiii, 130, 131–43, 212, 226n1; intensional verbs (transitives) characterized, 103–4, 116, ch. 6.3
intentionality, ix, xii, 35, 42, 50, 65, 67, ch. 6, 212, 226; marks of, 126–7
intersective adjective, 35, 212
irrealism: see realism

Jacquette, D., 67
James, H., 148
Jardine, N., 154
Jeshion, R., xix
Johnson, S., 13
Joyce, J., 148
Joyce, R., xvi, 201–4

Kafka, F., 124
Kalderon, M., xv–xvi, 174, 193–202, 204, 207, 208, 209, 226n6, 230n1
Kim, S., 21, 217n10
Kripke, S., x, xvii, 38, 69, 84, 88, 90, 98, 184, 185, 189, 219n9, 222n4, 223n17, 225n7

Lappin, S., 225n4
Larson, R., 132, 134
lax obligation, xv, 194, 196–8
Lee, B., xix, 217n9
Leibniz, G. W., 69, 214
Leslie, A., 1
Lewis, David, x, xiv, xv, 10, 26, 65–6, 71, 72, 73, 74, 75–83, 85, 89–90, 170, 179, 180–2, 183, 184, 185–8, 190–2, 207, 212, 217n6, 221n23, 222n5,8,10, 223n21, 225n3,13, 229n11,2,3,4,5,6, 230n8,9,12
Liston, M., 171, 172
literalism, vii, 26–31, 37, 52, 53, 63, 83, 84, 86, 112, 119, 125, 146, 212, 218n4

MacBride, F., 174
Mackie, J., 193, 194, 199, 202, 204, 207
make-believe, vi–vii, 7–14, 16–7, 19–20, 95–6, 106, 113, 212, 213, 217n3,8
Manning, S. B., 100
Martin, R. M., 26
Martinich, A., 14, 24, 26, 218n4
McCarthy, C., 217n3
McGlynn, A., xix, 217n10, 218n1, 222n13, 223n16
Meinong, A., viii, 46, 55, 67, 219n1
Meinongianism, viii–x, ch. 3, 212; defined: 45–6; literalist Meinongianism: 52–5, 63, 89, 113, 224n26; nonliteralist Meinongianism: ix, 53, 56–7, 64, 220n7,13,14, 221n21
Menard, P., 74, 76, 94, 222n7
Messud, C., 81–2
Mill, J.S., xvii, xviii, 96, 219n9
Miller, B., 67
modal logic, x, xv, 68, 69–72, 189, 191, 213, 222n4, 230n11,12
modality, fictionalism about: see fictionalism about possible worlds
Müller-Lyer illusion, 18, 213
myth, vii, xix, 7, 21, 32, 41–2, 44, 51, 116, 126, 141, 150, 177, 206

Newton, I., 154, 164, 165–6, 228n3,8

Nolan, D., 174, 192, 230n10,2
nominalism, 168–9, 170, 171, 172, 173, 174, 176, 177, 184, 185, 193, 205–6, 213, 229n9
nonactual objects, viii, x, 22, 32, 63, ch. 4, 93
noncognitivism, xv, 193–201, 209
nonconcrete objects, viii, xi, xviii, 23, 26, 32, 35, 42, 63, 73, 84, ch. 5, 115, 130, 141, 205, 207, 210
nonexistent objects, viii, ix, xviii, xix, 23, 26, 32, 35, 41, 42, 43, ch. 3, 73, 84, 93, 104, 115, 130, 141, 205, 206, 207, 210, 213, 214, 219, 220n8, 221n20,21, 224n26, 225n5
nonextensional, 38, 41, 211, 218n12, 219n11, 225n9
nonliteralism: see literalism, *also* Meinongianism, literalist
Nozick, R. 196, 197, 198
nuclear (extranuclear) properties, ix, 56, 57, 59, 67, 213, 220n5,12, 224n3

Oliver, A., xix, 219n10,1
ontological commitment, 107, 117–8, 140–1, 212, 213, 227n15
Osiander, A., xiii, 153, 174
Ovid, 5
Owens, S., 216n1

Palahniuk, C., 224n24
Papineau, D., xix
paraphrase, xii, 42, 73, 101–2, 115, 117–8, 120, 121, 124, 132, 134, 135, 150, 180, 181, 182, 225n11, 226n4, 227n11,13
Parsons, T., 41, 44, 45, 46, 56, 57, 59, 66, 67, 72, 74, 151, 218n5, 219n2, 221n15, 222n6
Pérez-Reverte, A., 143
Perszyk, K. J., 67

Pickel, B., xix, 225n10, 227n16
Pirsig, R. M., 223n15
Platonism, 168, 194, 213
polysemy, 98, 138–9, 213
possible (impossible) objects, ix, x, 46, 74, 82–7, 88, 211, 213, 223n18
possible words: see worlds, possible
pretense, vi–vii, 1, 8–12, 13, 27–8, 36, 43, 95, 97, 106–7, 121–2, 124–5, 201, 216n1, 217n5,7, 219n7
Priest, G., 45, 56, 67, 72, 74, 80, 87, 88, 90, 130, 135, 220n10,12, 223n20, 224n24
Prior, A., 138
prop, 13, 14, 16, 19, 213, 217n9
proper names, xvii–xviii, 36–39, 45, 49, 52, 54, 101, 108, 113, 122, 138, 146, 199, 213, 221n19
Proudfoot, D., 79, 80, 87, 88
Proust, M., 4–5, 22
Putnam, H., 196, 197, 198
pyrrhonism, 153

QML, 189, 190, 191, 213, 230n11
Quine, W., 46, 65, 67, 68, 72, 74, 115, 127 132–4, 140, 144, 168–9, 213, 226n4, 227n11,12,13

Radford, C., 21, 217n10
realism (and irrealism), vii– viii, ix, x, xi, xii, xiii, xiv, ch.2, 46–7, 51, 73, 90, 91, 99, 100–1, 103, 104, 107, ch. 6, 162, 163, 164, 184–6, 192, 199, 205–6, 207, 212, 213, 214, 216n2, 226; modal, x, 71, 73, 74, 83, 179, 180, 192, 212, 229n2,6
reductionism, xii, xiii, xiv, 69, 132–8, 140, 142, 143, 160–2, 174, 185–6, 194, 227n15
Renoir, A., 9, 20
replacement (versus paraphrase), 24,

101–2, 118–21, 123, 124, 134, 135, 143, 226n4
Richard, M., 151, 227n19
Roberts, R. C., 218n13
robust fictional characters, viii, xii, 32–6, 41, 42, 72, 73, 101, 104, 115, 121, 147, 214
Rosen, G., 3, 174, 176, 177, 179, 180–90, 192, 228n1,2
Rosenkranz, S., 23
Routley, R., 72, 74
Russell, Bertrand, xiii, xvii, 24, 25, 40, 44, 47–8, 52, 55, 56, 120, 158–61, 168, 174, 212, 220n10
Russell, Bruce, 173
RWR (Reference Without Referents), viii, xii, xiii, xvi, xvii, xviii, 37–40, 43, 132, 138–9, 141, 142, 199, 200, 210, 214, 230n3

Sainsbury, R. M., 37, 43, 213, 220, 230n8,3
Salmon, N., 97, 98, 212, 219
Sawyer, S., 114
Schiffer, S., 95, 125, 219, 224n2
Schotch, P. K., 26
Searle, J., 8, 10, 95, 125
Segal, G., xix, 226n18
selection problem, ix, 58, 60–3, 67, 93, 214
semantics, viii, xvi, xvii, 3, 29, 36, 39, 69, 71, 72, 74, 83, 86, 98, 106, 121, 122, 128, 130, 133–4, 137, 165, 168, 185, 189, 190, 198–200, 214, 221n3, 230n2,3
Shakespeare, W., 12, 32, 78, 109, 110, 222n11
Shapiro, S., 229n12
Smiley, T., 55, 219n10
Soames, S., 219n9
Solzhenitsyn, A., 216n2

Spurling, H. 22
Stalnaker, R., 146, 209
Stanley, J., 44
Steen, F., 216n1
Strawson, P., 23, 41–2, 51, 118
Stroll, A., 14, 24, 26, 218n4
supervaluations, x, 83, 86, 88, 214

Thomasson, A., xi, xix, 33–5, 43, 64–5, 91, 107, 108–10, 114, 225n6,15
time travel, 30, 79, 94
Tolstoy, L., 122, 123, 124
transitive relation, 71, 190–1, 204, 214, 221n2, 230n9; *see also* intensionality, operator versus predicate
Trevor, W., 81
truth: fictional (or in fiction), vii, x, 7, 14, 26–31, ch. 4, 213, 218n4; under a presupposition, vii, xii, xiii, 27–30, 118–9, 125, 143–8; *see also* acceptance

unicorns, 21, 32, 35, 44, 45, 46, 47, 66, 103–5, 128, 134, 135, 151, 219n1, 223n17, 226n1, 227n16
Ursus, N., 154

Vaihinger, H., 228n1
van Fraassen, B., xiii, 2, 152, 154, 157, 161–8, 174, 176, 208, 209, 210, 228n8
van Inwagen, P., xi, 42, 43, 52, 57, 96, 98, 99–107, 114, 149, 220, 224n2,3, 225n8,9
Voltolini, A., 43, 114

Walton, K., vi, 8, 9, 10, 12–20, 21, 26, 36, 43, 106, 122, 125, 213, 214, 217n11
Wedgwood, R., 228n20

Whitehead, A. N., 159, 161
Williamson, T., 228n20
Wolterstorff, N., 21
Wood, J., 4, 148
Woods, J., 26, 27, 28, 31
worlds: closed, 79, 86, 88, 209, 224n25; fictional, x, xiv, xv, 26, 32, 45, ch. 4, 179; impossible, x–xi, 86–90; possible, x, xiv–xv, 3, ch. 4, 158, ch. 8, 204, 205, 206, 221n3, 222n4,5,8,9, 223n18,19, 229n2,3,6; fictionalism concerning, xiv–xv, 3, 158, ch. 8, 193, 204, 205, 206, 207; realism concerning: x, 72–4, 229n2,6

Zalta, E. N., 36, 59, 60, 67, 221n16,17, 224n3

eBooks – at www.eBookstore.tandf.co.uk

A library at your fingertips!

eBooks are electronic versions of printed books. You can store them on your PC/laptop or browse them online.

They have advantages for anyone needing rapid access to a wide variety of published, copyright information.

eBooks can help your research by enabling you to bookmark chapters, annotate text and use instant searches to find specific words or phrases. Several eBook files would fit on even a small laptop or PDA.

NEW: Save money by eSubscribing: cheap, online access to any eBook for as long as you need it.

Annual subscription packages

We now offer special low-cost bulk subscriptions to packages of eBooks in certain subject areas. These are available to libraries or to individuals.

For more information please contact webmaster.ebooks@tandf.co.uk

We're continually developing the eBook concept, so keep up to date by visiting the website.

www.eBookstore.tandf.co.uk